SIMPLIFIED CLASSIFIEDS

1001

Real Estate Ads
That *Sell*

William H. Pivar
Bradley A. Pivar

Real Estate Education Company
a division of Dearborn Financial Publishing, Inc.

McKay

While a great deal of care has been taken to provide accurate and current information, the ideas, suggestions, general principles and conclusions presented in this book are subject to local, state and federal laws and regulations, court cases and any revisions of same. The reader is thus urged to consult legal counsel regarding any points of law—this publication should not be used as a substitute for competent legal advice.

Publisher: Kathleen A. Welton
Associate Editor: Karen A. Christensen
Senior Project Editor: Jack L. Kiburz

Published by Real Estate Education Company a division of Dearborn Financial Publishing, Inc.

Printed in the United States of America

10 9 8 7 6 5 4 3

Library of Congress Cataloging-in-Publication Data
Pivar, William H.
  Simplified classifieds: 1,001 real estate ads that sell / William
H. Pivar, Bradley A. Pivar.
    p. cm.
  Includes index.
  ISBN 0-7931-0086-0 (pbk.)
  1. Advertising—Real estate business. 2. Advertising, Classified.
3. Advertising, Newspaper. 4. Real estate listings. I. Pivar,
Bradley A. II. Title.
HF6161.R3P587 1990
659.1′933333—dc20   90-39299
                                                  CIP

Table of Contents

Foreword

I was delighted when I discovered *Classified Secrets: Writing Real Estate Ads That Work.* The authors did a superb job of providing real estate professionals with a formula to write real estate ads with maximum effectiveness. I was working half a world away in Australia on a parallel course in writing (*The Supergreat Guide to Successful Real Estate Advertising* and *The Australian Real Estate Advertising Handbook*), producing videos and conducting workshops in real estate advertising when I discovered that Bill and Brad Pivar were kindred spirits. By telephone and with dozens of letters we freely shared our ideas. I was excited with the concept of *Simplified Classifieds,* because it fulfills a real need.

I have said many times that good classified ads take time and sweat to produce, even with a superior guide such as *Classified Secrets.* Nevertheless, this is an age of instant pudding and microwave cooking; people want results fast. The 1,001 ads of *Simplified Classifieds* can be adapted readily to produce dozens of quality ads for any property. There are ads to fit every temperament from the practically ribald to those dripping with nostalgia. The common thread running through these ads is that they are all written to make your phone jump off the hook.

A famous advertising man said every good copywriter is a good thief. Real estate people have long copied ads that I have written and those written by Bill and Brad Pivar with staggering results. This book should not only help you make the phone ring, but more importantly make sales.

Incidentally, you will note my contributions with some supergreat ads from Down Under.

Ian Price
Surfer's Paradise, Australia

Preface

Classified Secrets was our first book to guide real estate brokers in writing effective classified ads. We received critical acclaim as well as comments from many brokers that they just could not take the time to develop their ads from scratch. In addition to *Classified Secrets,* they wanted a book of "super" ads that were original but could be modified readily for other homes. They wanted ads divided into property categories or features, and they wanted an index so they could quickly locate appropriate ads.

This book, *Simplified Classifieds,* is the result of our efforts to meet those needs. We feel it is a tool that, along with *Classified Secrets,* will enable you to increase the effectivenss of your advertising. You will note that ads are written in a number of styles so that you can choose ads with which you are comfortable. And if you have written an ad you feel is outstanding, we would like to hear from you so that we may include it, with appropriate credit, in a later edition of this book.

William H. Pivar
Bradley A. Pivar
75-496 Desert Park Drive
Indian Wells, CA 92210-8356

Acreage Ads

Undeveloped acreage parcels appeal to many buyers, including those looking for larger homesites or vacation homesites, those who want campsites or places to hunt, investors, developers and builders. Homes with acreage are found in a separate category.

The price is not given in this case, but readers will realize it is probably priced just under $100,000.

The question and answer ad technique was developed by Gordon Wearing-Smith of Barry Plant Real Estate in Doncaster, Australia.

While parcel price is not given, it really isn't needed. Buyers will understand that the price is slightly under $620,000. Note "development ready" doesn't necessarily mean plans or permits have been obtained. If this were the case, it should be spelled out in the ad. Available utilities doesn't mean utilities are to the property, only that they can be brought to the property.

3
10 Acres Builder Ready

Zoned for homes or mobile homes, over 40 lots are possible from this gently rolling parcel. Gas, water, electricity and sewer are available. Development ready and yours at less than $2,000 per lot.

Clyde Realty   476-8200

The price is probably slightly under $80,000, but as a price per lot it seems a bargain.

4
200 Acres

You will be excited when you see what is happening in this area. Unusual circumstances have forced the owner to sell what is destined to become a major development for only $1,000,000. Terms are available.

Clyde Realty   476-8200

5
10 Acres
40 to 50 Lots Possible

This desirable West Side parcel directly in the path of progress can be yours for only $75,000. Call today, as opportunity seldom knocks twice.

Clyde Realty   476-8200

6
Arrowheads and
Pottery Shards

have been reported found on this 10-acre, mostly wooded site, which is only 45 minutes from the civic center. While the Indians who lived here didn't commute, they must have enjoyed the clean, crisp air; the chatter of squirrels in the hickory trees; magnificent vistas; and cold, clean water flowing year-round from a natural spring. The old ways are surely the good ways, and they can be yours at $79,900.

Clyde Realty   476-8200

This ad appeals to people looking for a homesite. Indian artifacts are a very positive feature for many buyers.

Acreage parcels often have buildings other than homes on them. If a parcel might sell as a homesite, a desirable use for such a structure should be considered.

The words used in this ad paint a desirable picture.

11
Roam for Miles

on the quiet roads and trails from your own 2½ acres in the woods. There's a perfect spot to build a home or cabin in a clearing next to a huge boulder. Your chance for tranquility at $19,500.

Clyde Realty   **476-8200**

12
East of the Sun, West of the Moon

This wooded, 5-acre site is really secluded. Your in-laws will never find you unless you draw them a map, yet it's less than 50 minutes from the civic center. This is a great spot for weekends or for the rest of your life. While it's heavenly, the price is down to earth at $47,500.

Clyde Realty   **476-8200**

13
Loon Magic

Have you ever been enthralled by the haunting call of a loon over the water? It's the sound that makes you happy there's still a wilderness. This 2½-acre parcel has frontage on a 100+-acre lake where loons and deer are the only residents and eagles still soar. It's an idyllic spot for your vacation home or year-round living. Available at $19,000 with 20 percent down.

Clyde Realty   **476-8200**

14
5 Acres Hidden Pond

Giant bass are just waiting for you. While secluded off a quiet country lane, you will delight in the tranquil meadow carpeted with wild flowers and the ancient oak and hickory grove that is home to squirrels, raccoons, opossum and at least one curious fox. It's a site for future happiness at $39,500.

Clyde Realty   **476-8200**

Note that the following ad for the same parcel of land uses a slightly different approach.

15

5-Pound Bass

swim in the natural pond on this retirement-perfect, 5-acre wooded parcel. There's a sunlit meadow that is perfect for your homesite and garden. An opportunity unlikely to be repeated at $39,500.

Clyde Realty   **476-8200**

This kind of ad can be easily tailored for any property near water. For example:

10-Pound Trout

have been caught from the dock of this . . .

16

Thoreau Lovers

These 5 acres are presently home to deer, raccoons and other 4-footed creatures. Several excellent homesites will appeal to artists, writers and naturalists. Your own nature preserve for less than the cost of a city lot at $39,500.

Clyde Realty   **476-8200**

If the property has a pond, some variations of the ad title might be "Walden's Pond," "The Forest Primeval" or "Ah! Wilderness."

17

Feed the Deer

on your own 5 acres of woods and meadows just 50 minutes from the city. This unsurpassed natural beauty with several great homesites can be yours for only $27,500.

Clyde Realty   **476-8200**

18

Land — Lots of Land

on 10 acres sprinkled with beech and oak trees less than 1 hour from the civic center on an all-weather road. This is the perfect site for your commuter, vacation or retirement home, or you can hold it as an investment likely to increase dramatically in value. We won't see an opportunity like this again at $69,500. Owner financing available.

Clyde Realty   **476-8200**

An "all-weather" road is usually a gravel road. If the road is paved, however, it should be stated in the ad.

19

To the Woods

A 20-acre wilderness parcel fronting on an all-weather road can be your escape from the city. There is a year-round flowing spring, a sun-drenched meadow carpeted with wild flowers and marketable hard-woods and pine. It's the perfect setting for your future at $36,500. Ask us about the great terms.

Clyde Realty   **476-8200**

20

20 Acres
No Signs

Mrs. Higgins from our office couldn't find this wilderness parcel reputed to be on an all-weather road with a year-round flowing stream. If you are adventuresome, we will grab the maps and compass and lead you on a search party. Incidentally, it can be purchased with $4,000 down. Full price $19,500.

Clyde Realty   **476-8200**

21

10 Acres
Mountain Domain

This is a magnificent wooded site with year-round access and an in-comparable view. It's the ideal place for a very special home and can be yours for only $10,000.

Clyde Realty   **476-8200**

22

You Will Be
Intoxicated

with the natural beauty of this 5-acre site less than 1 hour from the city. It has incomparable views of nature's changing seasons, magnificent trees and distant hills. After only one look, you'll want this for your very own. Priced to sell quickly at $34,500.

Clyde Realty   **476-8200**

23

Peace and Pines—5 Acres

With end-of-the-road seclusion and incomparable views, this perfect homesite is less than 1½ hours from Chicago. Once you see it, you will want to stay. Take advantage of a unique opportunity at $32,500.

Clyde Realty   **476-8200**

This heading shows the parcel's size and that it is wooded and secluded. Possible variations are as follows: "Amid the Pines—5 Acres," "Woodland Odyssey—5 Acres."

24

Nature Boy

You will love this 40 acres of wilderness offering boulders, trees and lots of furry animals. It's about 10 miles to nowhere and is a great place for a hermit with $17,000.

Clyde Realty   **476-8200**

25

Creatures Cavort on 10 Acres

Deer and bear have reportedly been sighted on this scenic woodland setting less than 1 hour from the city. It's a great place for camping, a vacation cabin or retirement home. You must see the beauty of this parcel! For a small price at $29,500.

Clyde Realty   **476-8200**

26

An Hour to Nothing

These 20 acres are so remote that even Rand McNally can't locate them. While situated on an all-weather road, it will take our map and a scout troop to find this spot. There is a year-round flowing creek, and several great homesites are available. Find seclusion from the world at $29,500.

Clyde Realty   **476-8200**

The word "seclusion" is attractive to naturalists, survivalists and would-be hermits.

27

Happy Camper— 5 Acres

Your own woods and even a hill make this a delightful spot to build your hideaway. It certainly is a site for your future happiness at $29,500.

Clyde Realty   **476-8200**

28

The Bandit Black Bart

is reputed to have hidden out amidst a group of giant rocks on this 10-acre, wooded parcel that has remained unchanged for centuries. Bart probably reveled in the magnificent view of the setting sun over the distant hills and drank from the crystal-clear spring bubbling from the rocks. This is the perfect site for your future at an affordable $29,500.

Clyde Realty   **476-8200**

Stories about well-known local outlaws or pioneers add romance and desirability to a parcel of land. The following ads add romance to property by utilizing probable or actual facts.

29

The Blue and the Gray

Civil War troops once bivouacked in the quiet meadow on this 20-acre, mostly wooded site. They are long gone, but on a quiet summer night it is said you can still hear young voices raised in song by ancient campfires. This is a very special place for a special buyer. Offered at $49,500. Terms available.

Clyde Realty   **476-8200**

This type of description can be applied to many areas in our country. Point out that troops passed through the land by using a phrase such as "Jeb Stuart's cavalry galloped through this quiet meadow on the way to . . ." or indicate that troops camped on the land. (Do not say that troops died there.)

30

Wild Flowers

provide a blanket of color over these 10 hillside acres. There also are several majestic oaks and so many great spots that you won't know which one to choose for your dream home. Construction priced at only $69,500.

Clyde Realty   **476-8200**

31

Fur Traders and Indians

probably camped along the shore of the meandering, fish-filled river bordering this 10-acre, highly wooded site. You can build your dream home with your own timber. Power and phone are available, and it's priced to sell at $19,500.

Clyde Realty   **476-8200**

32

Cowboys and Desperados

probably camped under the cotton-wood tree by the bank of the quiet river that crosses this very special 10 acres. There is a great swimming hole that is currently home to at least one fat trout. This is a site for your future at a very affordable $39,500.

Clyde Realty   **476-8200**

33

A Treasure Site— $49,500

Rumor has it that Silas Jones, a local miser, buried his entire collection of collar buttons beneath one of the 20 giant oak trees on this magnificent 2-acre site that overlooks the entire valley. Even if you fail to find the treasure, we think you will be amply rewarded.

Clyde Realty   **476-8200**

The treasure, of course, is a spoof, but the ad will appeal to those looking for a homesite. Its positive features are the view and trees.

2

Architectural Style

Architectural style is an important selling point for a home. By mentioning a home's architectural style or the name of its architect, you add an element of prestige. Architectural style is emphasized in many of this book's ads appearing under other categories such as Older Homes (Chapter 21) and Luxury Homes (Chapter 17). The following ads, however, use architectural style as their focal point.

35

Rhett Butler Colonial

Five soaring columns support the portico of this Virginia-inspired mansion. Set on 9 lush acres, it looks like it's right out of the pages of *Gone with the Wind*. There are 4 master suites plus 2 guest or servant suites, a greenhouse, stables, tennis court, pool and every other amenity you desire. The home for those who have earned the very best is proudly offered at $3,500,000.

Clyde Realty   476-8200

34

Shutters and Clapboard

This much sought-after New England Colonial has 3BR, 2 baths and a double garage and is located on a large lot sprinkled with mature hardwoods in Weston Hills. It's the answer to your dreams and has everything you want including a family room and screened-in summer porch. Yours for the taking at $175,000.

Clyde Realty   476-8200

If you're dealing with an older home, use language such as "historical mansion," "preserved from yesterday and updated with the conveniences of tomorrow" or "Registry eligible."

36

Scarlett and Rhett

would feel right at home in this Virginia Colonial with its soaring white columns and covered portico. There are 3BR, 2 baths, a very private den, a glassed conservatory, full basement and a three-car garage. In impeccable condition, this fine residence is impressive but not expensive at $249,500.

Clyde Realty　　　**476-8200**

37

Federal Colonial—4BR

Painstakingly authentic with fine detailing and classic lines set amidst ancient hardwoods, this home exemplifies all that is great in American architecture. The copper, brick and pine kitchen; dual stone fireplaces; and random-plank maple flooring show that nothing was spared to make this one-of-a-kind residence a home even the most meticulous buyer can be proud of. Unpretentious luxury at $339,500.

Clyde Realty　　　**476-8200**

Because "4BR" is an important feature, it was included in the heading of the ad.

38

Crown Moldings

and exquisite detailing make this the most authentic 3-bedroom, 2½-bath New England Colonial we have seen. While almost new, this home looks like it has been around since the Revolution. Its modern systems don't detract from the elegance of its design. Special features include a 2-car carriage house; full basement; pegged hardwood floors; a tile, brick and copper kitchen to delight any chef; two fireplaces; central air; and several ancient oak trees on an estate-sized setting in the most sought-after area of Westport. This is the place for your future at $219,500.

Clyde Realty　　　**476-8200**

39

Williamsburg Colonial

You will be proud to be the owner of this picturesque residence that combines the charm of a bygone era with today's conveniences. This home features 3BR, 2½ baths, a bright family room opening onto a picnic-perfect patio, a fully fenced yard, a separate workroom in the huge garage and two fireplaces for those cold, wintry nights. It's set on nearly an acre, including a perfect garden spot. Everything about this home is impressive, except the price. $219,500.

Clyde Realty　　　**476-8200**

40

Williamsburg Revisited

The most authentic Virginia Colonial we have ever seen, this 3-bedroom and den, 2-bath home is resplendent in magnificent detailing from the high ceilings, crown moldings, ancient timber fireplace mantle and impeccable wall coverings. Set on an estate-sized lot in Bellwood, this family home offers all the amenities one could wish for carefully integrated into the design so as not to break the mood of a happy, gentler time. Available for your future at $269,500.

Clyde Realty   **476-8200**

41

Nantucket Colonial—4BR

This distinctive clapboard design skillfully incorporates the warmth of an earlier era with all the conveniences of tomorrow. You will love its gleaming hardwood floors; huge, bright country kitchen; stunningly conceived master suite; and ancient wood mantle over the rose brick fireplace. There are 2 baths and a 2++-car garage. This home will definitely return your love at $197,500.

Clyde Realty   **476-8200**

42

Proper English Brick

A fine Edwardian residence for the family who appreciates gracious living. The 12-foot ceilings, crown moldings, carved mantles and leaded glass will transport you to an England of a far gentler time. The manor features 3BR, 2 full baths, formal drawing room and richly paneled library. The commodious garage has a small upstairs apartment for guests or live-ins. A proper residence at $345,000.

Clyde Realty   **476-8200**

This ad is appropriate for a large, older brick home.

43

Smashing!

A proper English manor house for the buyer with civilized taste. The leaded glass, fine woodwork and brick and stone construction blend together to give this 3-bedroom, 2½-bath residence an ambiance of understated elegance. Discerningly priced at $225,000.

Clyde Realty   **476-8200**

44

Edwardian Gentility

This 3-bedroom, redbrick English Traditional was built for gracious living with its large bright rooms that include a richly paneled den, high ceilings and fine wood detailing. There is a full basement, a 2-car brick garage and the ideal spot for a patio and garden in the walled yard. Close to everything, you won't believe the price at $79,500.

Clyde Realty   **476-8200**

This is obviously an older brick home with one bath that is located close to the city center. There has been an increased interest in many of these fine homes.

45

Proper English

You must see this ivy-covered, 3-bedroom, 2½-bath brick Tudor residence with leaded glass, impressive woodwork, a walnut-paneled study, rooms of baronial proportion and all the accouterments of a truly fine home. Set on an estate lot in Weston Hills, it is designed for those interested in quality and dignity rather than fad and flash. Proudly offered at $435,000.

Clyde Realty   **476-8200**

46

Country English— 5 Bedrooms

plus the 2-bedroom carriage house of this proper English manor that can be used for guests, staff or as a separate rental unit. The main house has 12 rooms and features an estate office with its own entrance, a paneled music room, intricate woodwork seldom seen in this country and a general ambiance of quality. There is a pool, formal rose garden and a greenhouse. For one who refuses to compromise on quality, this civilized residence is available at $695,000.

Clyde Realty   **476-8200**

Both size and architectural style are combined in the preceding heading. Note that a den can be described as an "estate office."

47

The British Are Coming

At last a proper British Town House! This redbrick, 3-bedroom, 2-bath residence reflects the subdued quality of fine craftsmanship. The proper English garden is enclosed by a high wall, and there's a garage for 2 motor cars. Offered to you at $93,500, it's strongly recommended you contact the estate agent at once.

Clyde Realty   **476-8200**

48

To the Manor Born

Charles Dickens would have loved this English Manor House situated among the rolling hills of Middlebury. Architecturally perfect on almost an acre of impeccably maintained grounds and with amenities to please even the most fastidious, this 9-room, 3-bedroom estate comes complete with its own rose garden and English hedge. It's the ultimate in civilized living at $279,500.

Clyde Realty   **476-8200**

An alternate heading might be "Charles Dickens Would Have Loved This."

49

"I Say, Old Chap"

Would you like a frightfully civilized, 9-room, 3-bedroom, 2-bath residence with every conceivable option an anglophile could possibly want? Patterned after the fine estates in York, this English brick masterpiece was built not for the years but for the centuries. It's your opportunity to be lord of the manor at $219,500.

Clyde Realty   **476-8200**

50

Irish Manor House

No blarney. This handsome 3-bedroom, 2-bath estate appears to have been transported from County Cork. Old-world craftsmanship is evident in the intricate detailing and exceptional woodwork. On almost 2 rolling acres, this is a heritage for your family that we proudly present at $379,500.

Clyde Realty   **476-8200**

51

Sassy French Provincial—4BR

reminiscent of the country homes near Lyon, where entertaining and hospitality were inseparable from gracious living. You will appreciate the stone construction and slate roof that endures for centuries. There is a garden to delight you, a separate guest house and over an acre of resplendent grounds. An investment in fine living at $850,000.

Clyde Realty   **476-8200**

52 Norman Farmhouse

Mansard roof, cathedral ceilings, flagstone entry, leaded glass, carved French doors and copper-hooded fireplace are just a few of the features of this architecturally perfect masterpiece designed by one of our greatest living architects, Henry LaPage. Set on almost a full acre, there are 3 baronial-sized bedrooms, 3½ baths, a unique family room and an enclosed porch. In better-than-new condition, you will want it as your own for $850,000.

Clyde Realty　　　**476-8200**

53 Spanish Eyes

Tons of tile, delicate arches, massive beams, white stucco and a myriad of colorful flowers and plants give this 3-bedroom, 2-bath hacienda a very special charm. There's a 2-car garage and a huge family room. Situated on an oversized lot in a premier West Side location, it's priced no more than an ordinary home at $249,500.

Clyde Realty　　　**476-8200**

54 Spanish Omelet

Arches, tile and huge beams combine to make this 3-bedroom, 2-bath, West Side masterpiece a very tasty dish at

$179,500

Special features include family room, 3-car garage, central air, delightful fenced yard and giant Norway pine. One look and we will put up the "sold" sign.

Clyde Realty　　　**476-8200**

55 Your Own Mariachi Band

would have the perfect place to practice next to the bubbling fountain in the red-tiled courtyard of this arched and beamed Spanish Colonial. The authentic design of this 3-bedroom, 2½ bath masterpiece has a warmth seldom achieved in a home. This home offers generously proportioned rooms, a richly paneled den or quiet place, soaring ceilings, massive beams, delicate balconies with intricate ironwork, tons of tile and everything a fine hacienda should have. Bring your castanets, and a fiesta lifestyle can be yours at $349,500.

Clyde Realty　　　**476-8200**

56

Stone and Glass

Form and function blend together in this stunningly conceived New Mexico Contemporary to achieve a unique union of comfort for family living and graciousness for entertaining on a grand scale. The free-flowing floor plan features 3 master suites, a very private study and a kitchen right out of *House and Garden*. The walls of glass and soaring ceilings make this home seem as one with the natural surroundings. With every imaginable luxury appointment, this is an unparalleled residence at $695,000.

Clyde Realty   **476-8200**

The above heading can be modified for any type of architectural style.

57

Frank Lloyd Wright

inspired this Prairie Style, 3-bedroom, 2-bath home that seems as one with the environment. There is a 2-car garage, family room, 2 fireplaces and lavish use of stone and glass. A one-of-a-kind masterpiece at $179,500.

Clyde Realty   **476-8200**

58

Frank Lloyd Wright Inspired

Hillside and home merge in natural harmony in this brick, stone and glass Prairie Style Contemporary. Stunningly conceived and excitingly different, this home is sophisticated yet it captures the casual flavor of the Southwest. The home offers a dramatically proportioned living room with soaring ceilings and walls of glass, 3 master suites and a separate studio to appeal to artist or writer. This bold statement requires your action today at $387,500.

Clyde Realty   **476-8200**

59

Captain Kirk

would love to explore the vast space of this 9-room, 3-bedroom and den Contemporary with its soaring ceilings. The views through the walls of glass stretch to the very edge of eternity. Truly a spectacular residence at $450,000.

Clyde Realty   **476-8200**

60

Dramatic—Yes Expensive—No

This 3BR, 2-bath Colorado Contemporary with its huge beams, native stone and glass offers a refreshing change from the ordinary. An outstanding design blends home and surroundings to make magnificent vistas seem part of the living area. This is an opportunity for the family secure enough to depart from the ordinary at $289,500.

Clyde Realty   **476-8200**

61

Not Ordinary

This 3BR, 2½-bath Colorado Contemporary is a one-of-a-kind masterpiece designed by Ernst Schmidt. You'll love the way the house blends into the wooded hillside. Amenities include 3-car garage, state-of-the-art kitchen, huge family room, soaring ceilings, walls of glass, a million-dollar view and a party-sized deck. Over 3,000 sq. ft. of luxury living can be yours at $379,500.

Clyde Realty   **476-8200**

Mentioning the name of the designer, even when not well known, adds prestige and desirability. When a home has more square footage than the average home, this should be included in the ad.

62

Not a Tract Home

This 3-bedroom, 2½-bath, one-of-a-kind Contemporary in a wooded hillside setting does not resemble any of the homes your friends live in. A conformist would hate the cantilevered view decks, 16-foot ceilings, music loft, Scandinavian fireplace, enormous living area, Eurostyle kitchen and flowing floor plan. This home will scare followers but is bound to delight leaders. Priced for those very few at $247,500.

Clyde Realty   **476-8200**

This ad presents an unusual treatment for a Contemporary home.

63

Escape the Subdivision

This 3-bedroom, 2-bath, architect-designed American Bungalow set in a neighborhood of quality homes clearly expresses your individuality. It is designed for comfortable family living with a full-length covered veranda, high ceilings with a feeling of spaciousness, a 2+-car garage and a very private music room for your quiet place. Offering far more than any tract home at an affordable $189,500.

Clyde Realty   **476-8200**

This ad emphasizes that the home was specifically designed and is not a "cookie cutter" tract home.

64

Architectural Digest

did not feature this Carolina Colonial embraced by a columned portico, but they should have. This fine 3BR, 2½-bath, triple-garage residence is a striking statement of design with its authentic detailing and multipaneled windows that begin at the knee and seem to go on forever. There's a feeling of happy spaciousness making this the perfect home for family living or entertaining on a grand scale. Set on dream landscaping in a Brentwood estate setting, this home features baths sheathed in marble and a private cherry-paneled den. Elegance beyond words can be yours for $385,000.

Clyde Realty   **476-8200**

3

Astrological Signs

There are many people who read astrological daily forecasts in the newspapers. While all are not believers, most are interested in what the daily or weekly forecast predicts for them. These types of readers will be attracted to any astrological reference, even if it pertains to a different sign, and will tell others what they read about the various astrological signs.

Astrological signs can be effectively used in ad headings to force such a person to read an entire ad. Even those with no interest in astrology will be attracted to an ad out of curiosity, especially if their own sign is referenced. The ads that follow are based on the general characteristics attributed to astrological signs. For additional ideas, we recommend Linda Goodman's best-seller *Sun Signs,* available through Bantam Books.

65
Are You an Aries?

If so, you get what you want, and you want to be indulged by the best. This 3-bedroom, 2½-bath Colonial on the most desirable street in Westlake will please even the most fastidious Aries with its 2++-car garage, majestic maple trees, native stone fireplace, richly paneled den and a country-sized kitchen that will delight any chef. For $179,500, it can be your sign for the future.

Clyde Realty   **476-8200**

66

Aries

You are far above the ordinary, so this 3BR, 2½-bath American Colonial in prestigious Westlake Village is perfect for you and your family. There is a 2++-car garage (with room for an RV), 10-foot ceilings, slate foyer, gracefully curved staircase, hardwood floors, family room, central air and every conceivable built-in on an impeccably landscaped site. Any Aries will appreciate the value at $219,500.

Clyde Realty   **476-8200**

67

For the Friendly Aries

As an Aries, you are an unusually friendly person, ideal for this 3BR, 1¾-bath American Traditional on a tree-canopied street in the friendliest of neighborhoods where neighbors greet each other by name and everyone knows how the little league team is doing. The home has a 2-car garage with space for a workbench, a full basement, rocking-chair-ready front porch, wood-burning fireplace, hardwood floors that reflect loving care, an apple tree and beautiful flowering shrubs. Even the price is friendly at $89,500.

Clyde Realty   **476-8200**

68

Taurus

You want your own space, and we have it for you—a 3-bedroom, picture-perfect Cape Cod set on almost an acre of privacy amidst giant oak and hickory nut trees. There is a long paved circle drive, family-sized garden, double garage plus a separate storage building that would make an ideal studio or private place. The home has a full basement, fireplace, gleaming woodwork and a delightful glassed conservatory off the family-sized kitchen. A private world for you at $214,500.

Clyde Realty   **476-8200**

A sun room or glass-enclosed porch can be referred to as a "conservatory."

69

Taurus?

If so, you savor a quiet, comfortable life. We have just the home for the lifestyle you crave. This 3BR, 2-bath, brick and cedar Cape Cod on a wooded estate-sized lot in East Hampton offers a large living room with river-rock fireplace; quiet, paneled den; double garage with workbench; full basement; central air; and 3 apple trees in a private but friendly neighborhood. All this at a price that won't upset you—$117,500.

Clyde Realty   **476-8200**

70

Attention Taurus

You're steady and tranquil, and we have just the home to match. A 3-bedroom, white clapboard American Traditional with a huge rocking-chair front porch, hardwood floors, a glorious glassed and screened sun room, country-sized kitchen and 2++-car garage on a huge lot with a delightful garden in an established neighborhood of fine homes and immaculate lawns. A home for today and many tomorrows. At $93,500, hurry or some Gemini will be there first.

Clyde Realty   **476-8200**

71

Gemini!

You want a home that reflects your individuality, not a cookie-cutter version of your neighbor's home. This exceptional 3BR, 2-bath Colorado Contemporary in Westwood melds wooded hillside and striking residence together, much in the style of Frank Lloyd Wright. With sweeping decks, soaring ceilings, massive native stone fireplace, family room and a spacious flowing floor plan, this home was designed for gracious living. At $319,500, you should expect to double your pleasure.

Clyde Realty   **476-8200**

72

Attention Gemini

You'll double your pleasure with this 3BR, 2½-bath Colonial on its almost 1-acre, wooded site in Weston Hills. This is a home designed for comfortable family living with a private, richly paneled den; open family room; delightful dining patio; screened and glassed, 3-season porch; and a huge double garage with room for bikes, trikes and workshop. It's twice as nice as anything you have seen at $249,500.

Clyde Realty   **476-8200**

73

Are You a Gemini?

If so, you savor your privacy, but there are times when you want to entertain with many friends around you. We have just the home to meet your diverse needs. This 3-bedroom, 2½-bath Colorado Contemporary with its sweeping decks, soaring ceilings, flowing floor plan and magnificent vistas is the perfect home to enjoy the closeness of your family, intimate entertaining or entertaining on a grand scale. As a Gemini, it will take only one look to see that this is the home the stars ordained for you at $269,500.

Clyde Realty   **476-8200**

74

If You're a Gemini

it will take only a quick glance to know this is the home for your future. This 3-bedroom, 2-bath Vermont-style Colonial on a large site down a quiet, tree-lined street in Westhaven is perfect in every detail. You will love the huge hardwood trees, including several maples for your own syrup. The home features large, sun-filled rooms; extensive wood trim; gleaming oak floors; a kitchen delightful to behold; a double garage; and an intimate dining patio. One look and it will be yours at $189,500.

Clyde Realty   **476-8200**

75

Are you a Cancer?

If so, you're a couch potato who enjoys home. Well, we have the home you will love to enjoy—a 3BR, 2-bath California-style ranch with a double garage on an estate-sized lot in West Highlands. There is a great family room, lovely fireplace, hardwood floors and a fenced yard with a delightful covered patio. All this at $214,500. Enjoy! Enjoy!

Clyde Realty   **476-8200**

76

If You're a Cancer

you are not superficial. Glitter and plastic doesn't impress you. You want a substantial home. This red-brick, 3-bedroom, 1¾-bath Georgian Colonial surrounded by ancient beech and oak on a quiet tree-lined street in Westhaven will, however, impress you. It was built to last for many tomorrows with its hardwood trim and floors, triple-glazed windows, full-poured basement and super insulation. Special features include a spectacular fireplace, oversized living room, family room, country-sized kitchen, 2+++-car garage, a perfect spot for your garden and an ambiance of quality living. It's priced no more than an ordinary home at $169,500.

Clyde Realty   **476-8200**

77

If Cancer Is Your Sign

you love cooking, and you will love the tile, copper and brick fantasy kitchen in this 3BR, 2-bath, native stone and glass Arizona Contemporary. This home features sweeping decks, woodland views, soaring ceilings, a 2+++-car garage and the finest hillside location in all of Westwood. It fits your image at $219,500.

Clyde Realty   **476-8200**

78

Cancer

This is the home to match your changing moods—from quiet contemplation to joyful entertaining on a grand scale. This 3-bedroom, 2-bath English-style brick Traditional on a large lot in desirable Westhaven offers privacy, yet space. The huge manicured yard is just the place for puttering or for a garden party. The paneled den will be your private quiet place, and the huge great room has space for a dozen friends plus a grand piano. The home features a state-of-the-art tiled kitchen, full basement, central air and a 2++-car garage. At $189,500, it is bound to attract a Gemini, so you better hurry and call.

Clyde Realty   **476-8200**

79

Leo

You love people, and you will love this 3BR American Traditional in the friendliest Westside neighborhood, where neighbors greet each other by name and stop to talk on their evening strolls. The home has rose bushes that are a neighborhood landmark, a rocking-chair front porch, 3 apple trees, a large garage, full basement and spacious rooms that are decorator-perfect. We can show you a delightful future at $89,500.

Clyde Realty   **476-8200**

80

Are You a Leo?

If so, you are bored with the commonplace. At last we have a home as individual as you are, one that stands out from the sameness of tract homes. Designed by Royal Wilson in the Prairie style of Frank Lloyd Wright, this 3-bedroom, 2½-bath masterpiece offers a private den with its own entrance, a kitchen that puts those in *House and Garden* to shame, a 3-car garage and by far the finest estate site you can find, with massive oaks and stately maples. We are not "lion" when we say, "This is as good as it gets at $398,500."

Clyde Realty   **476-8200**

81

A Leo Rules

and you will, too, from this 3BR, 2-bath, hilltop masterpiece with its wide decks and incomparable view. With soaring ceilings and walls of glass, you will feel like a master of those below. You will love the castle-sized fireplace, lion-sized den and the feeling of spaciousness in this one-of-a-kind architectural masterpiece. There is a 3-car garage and some of the largest pine trees you have ever seen. It's the place a Leo deserves at $298,500.

Clyde Realty   **476-8200**

82

If You're a Virgo

you're perfect and want a house to match. This 3-bedroom, 2-bath Westwood Colonial fills the bill to perfection with its 2++-car garage, wood-burning fireplace, family room, huge oak trees and financing to fit your needs. Priced for a Virgo at $169,500.

Clyde Realty   **476-8200**

83

For the Perfect Virgo

every detail is important. You will appreciate this brick and stone 3BR, 2-bath English Manor House constructed with the care reminiscent of old-world craftsmanship. The intricate, perfectly matched woodwork; gleaming oak floors; cut stone fireplace; huge hewn beams; and fine Venetian tile all show pride of workmanship. Set on a choice, impeccably landscaped estate lot in Southport, this home features a richly paneled den; 2++-car garage; full basement that would make a perfect hobby room; and zoned-controlled heating and cooling. A home as perfect as you are at $239,500.

Clyde Realty   **476-8200**

84

Virgo

You will be in control of your future as the owner of this 3-bedroom Cape Cod in Westhaven with its fenced yard, huge garden and apple tree. The home has an attached garage, full basement that can be finished for living space, and it is decorated in soft neutral tones. Amazingly affordable at $92,500, with great terms.

Clyde Realty   **476-8200**

85

A Virgo?

If so, you will appreciate the architectural purity of this 3BR, 2-bath Williamsburg Colonial with its intricate moldings and careful melding of form and function. The smallest detail has been considered. Features include a private den for reading or contemplation; oversized, sun-filled rooms; matched hardwood floors; baths sheathed in tile; and the loveliest wooded lot and garden in all of Westhaven. Priced perfectly at $219,500.

Clyde Realty   **476-8200**

The symbol of Libra is the balance scale.

90
If You're a Scorpio

you are one tough customer. Any home you buy will have to be near perfect, as you won't accept less than you want. This 3BR, 2-bath, cedar-shake Cape Cod is as close to perfection as you get. It has everything, including a double garage, family garden, fireplace, family room, delightful patio and the best location in Westport. The price is less than you'd expect at $319,500.

Clyde Realty   **476-8200**

Many people like the image of the tough customer who can't be convinced to buy what he or she doesn't want.

91
Scorpio

You are a competitive person, so don't let someone else snap up this 3BR, 2-bath, West Side American Traditional on its huge corner lot with twin oak trees in the front yard. This home has been impeccably maintained and features a double garage, huge kitchen with all the built-ins, a full basement and beautiful hardwood floors and trim. At only $89,500, you're going to beat the rest to this excellent buy.

Clyde Realty   **476-8200**

92
Sagittarius

You recognize a good deal when you see it and can act decisively. This 3BR, 2-bath, California-style ranch home in prestigious Westwood Heights with its double garage, family room, central air and huge oak trees will have you reaching for your checkbook when you realize it is priced at only $189,500.

Clyde Realty   **476-8200**

93
If You're a Sagittarius

you will love the exhilaration of living on top of the world. The cantilevered deck of this 3-bedroom, 2½-bath, New Mexico Contemporary seems suspended in space. At night, you can almost touch the stars. The family room is practically big enough for an archery range, and the soaring ceilings and glass walls make this architectural masterpiece seem part of the outdoors. Incidentally, there is a 3-car garage and a kitchen better than great. A definite bull's-eye at $289,500.

Clyde Realty   **476-8200**

98

Aquarius

A new age is dawning for you in delightful Holmby Hills. Set on the highest site overlooking the rest is this 3-bedroom, 2½-bath, stone and glass Arizona Contemporary with its sweeping decks, unmatched vistas, 3-car garage and over 3,000 sq. ft. of flowing floor space for the ultimate in fine living. It's your future at $249,500.

Clyde Realty   **476-8200**

99

Aquarius = Water Person

Any Aquarius will go wild with the 3 full baths and bubbling fountain that come with this 3-bedroom Spanish Renaissance home in prestigious Westhaven. With tons of tile, graceful arches, massive beams, 3-car garage, huge family room and lush landscaping that reflects loving care, this is a very special home for the water person at $219,500.

Clyde Realty   **476-8200**

A home with a pool is also ideal to target at an Aquarius.

100

If You're an Aquarius

you are a dreamer, and you dream of the perfect cottage set amidst tall trees and flowering shrubs. We can fulfill your dreams with this 2BR plus den American Bungalow in a fairy-tale setting. There is a cozy fireplace, hardwood floors, country-sized kitchen, a rocking-chair front porch and even the perfect family garden. It's waiting for you at $89,500.

Clyde Realty   **476-8200**

101

Pisces

You want things to be perfect. Well, we have a 3-bedroom, 2-bath ranch with a shake roof in the best Westside neighborhood that will please any Pisces. Better than new, there is a family room with a rose brick fireplace, a fully poured basement ready for finishing, a patio with a woodland view, a giant chestnut tree in the fenced yard and a 2++-car garage. This home is decorator-perfect with the tasteful neutral tones of the desert Southwest. No need to look further, as they don't get any better at $137,500.

Clyde Realty   **476-8200**

102

A Pisces Will

love the charm of this 3-bedroom, brick Traditional set among towering trees on a quiet Westside street where the neighbors take pride in their homes and lawns. Nooks and crannies abound to hold all those treasures accumulated at swap meets and garage sales. You will love the matched hardwood trim and paneling, gleaming oak floors, high ceilings and even the attic big enough for an artist's studio. Best of all, it's priced for a Pisces at $99,500.

Clyde Realty   **476-8200**

103

Attention Pisces

You're a creative person who will love the skylighted studio—perfect for the artist or writer—that comes with this 3BR, 2-bath American Traditional. On almost half an acre in Westport, you will go wild over the huge trees and flowering shrubs. This home also features a full basement with the perfect spot for a photographer's darkroom, 2-car garage and even a garden shed. Watch out, or some Gemini will try to get there first when he or she finds it's priced at only $119,500.

Clyde Realty   **476-8200**

You can also say, "the guest room, alcove or garden shed is a perfect studio for the creative Pisces artist or writer."

4

Bargain Homes

A bargain is a purchase that can be made for less than what is considered the value of a particular property. Some ads claim to be bargains, while others hint or imply that a bargain is possible. For example, an ad that states that a seller is highly motivated implies that the owner will accept less than what he or she would ordinarily accept in the absence of such motivation. Other ads give the impression that there is a bargain where one may not exist (e.g., an ad that indicates that a price has been drastically reduced).

Since everyone loves a bargain, bargain ads bring in calls even from people whose needs are significantly different from the features advertised for the bargain property.

Before you advertise a property as a bargain, obtain the owner's permission, since a bargain ad implies that the owner is not asking enough for the property. Never reveal an owner's motivation to sell without his or her permission, as this really invites offers lower than the asking price and reduces the owner's power in negotiations. In the same vein, never indicate that a price quoted is not firm without the owner's express consent.

104

It's Not for Sale

Miss Jones from our office says the 3-bedroom Cape Cod in Westport with the double garage, fireplace, hardwood floors and full basement isn't really for sale. She says it's a steal at $79,500.

Clyde Realty   476-8200

105

Serious Seller

has priced this 3BR, 2-bath French Provincial on an estate-sized lot in Rolling Estates thousands below the competition for an immediate sale. The home literally has everything. We welcome comparison shoppers, but at $239,500, you will find it stands alone.

Clyde Realty   476-8200

No reason for the sale is given in this ad, but it clearly indicates that the house is priced as a bargain. Bargains don't have to be low-priced homes.

106
$10,000/Room

That's right, but you must take all 9 rooms of this 3-bedroom, 2-bath, West Side American Traditional that includes a paneled den, delightful family room and double garage. You might qualify for a special low-interest loan. To find out, call us.

Clyde Realty   **476-8200**

The "low-interest loan" here can refer to an assumable loan, owner financing, FHA, VA or special state financing.

107
Giveaway—Almost

This 3-bedroom, Traditional ranch home with its full basement, hardwood floors, garage and garden is available for only $69,500.

Clyde Realty   **476-8200**

Ads like this are short and effective.

108
Sacrifice—$139,500

While no one really wants to profit from the problems of another, that is exactly what is about to happen. Because of unusual circumstances, the owner of this 3-bedroom, 2-bath American Traditional in Holiday Hills has set a price significantly below the appraised value that is bound to be accepted by the first buyer. If you want to be the one to make money the day you make your purchase, hurry or you will likely be too late.

Clyde Realty   **476-8200**

The above bargain ad is not subtle. This type of ad effectively motivates buyers to call and can result in a sale even when a house fails to meet the buyer's needs fully. No one likes someone else to get a bargain when they were there first.

109
Below Cost

Save thousands off the original cost of this 3-bedroom, 2-bath Cape Cod in the nicest West Side neighborhood. Great landscaping, a 2-car garage, hardwood floors and many builder upgrades make this our buy of the week at $89,500.

Clyde Realty   **476-8200**

This is not necessarily a new property. It is being offered for less than it originally sold for or cost to build.

110
The Price Is Right

Imagine a 3BR, 2-bath, West Side Colonial on a huge wooded lot with a double garage and a full basement for only $99,500.

Clyde Realty   **476-8200**

This short ad says it all and will bring in calls.

111
We Won't Tell

that you purchased this 3BR, 2-bath, West Side Colonial with family room, central air and an estate-sized wooded lot for only

$89,500

Your friends are bound to think you paid far more, so let them.

Clyde Realty   **476-8200**

The split or double-heading ad helps to grab the reader's attention. While this ad doesn't say the house is a bargain, it indicates that others will think so.

112
Jump!

on this 3-bedroom, 2-bath, executive ranch with double garage in Longview Heights, or you will be too late. You're not going to find a comparable home at $139,500.

Clyde Realty   **476-8200**

113
Guilty

If you can't take the guilt trip, then don't buy this 3BR, 2-bath Rancho Heights Colonial. It's certainly a great home. That's the problem—it's too nice for the price. You'll be stealing the property at only $114,500.

Clyde Realty   **476-8200**

Very little is said about the house, but this ad will attract a great many inquiries.

114

Pssst!
Want a Steal?

This 3BR, 2-bath West Side Colonial is priced so low that you will feel guilty about what you paid the poor seller. With its huge family room, cut stone fireplace, separate music room and superb overall condition, you know $197,500 is too low a price to pay for your family's happiness.

Clyde Realty   **476-8200**

Before advertising a home at a price below market price, compare the price to recent sales, so you can justify your claim.

115

Hysterical Owner

Sale fell through and owner now has 2 homes. This 3-bedroom, 2½-bath French Regency, set on an emerald lawn accented by flowering shrubs and roses, must sell *immediately* and is priced to move at $219,500.

Clyde Realty   **476-8200**

116

The Owners Must
Bite the Bullet

They put far too much money into this 3BR, 3-bath Nantucket Colonial that is within the sound of the surf. They tried to get it back but now it is

Desperation Time

In order to sell, they have disregarded our advice and lowered the price to $179,500. We will, therefore, entertain **full price offers** only.

Clyde Realty   **476-8200**

"Full price offers only" lets readers know the price has been lowered as far as possible. It is an effective advertising method.

This ad was inspired by Gordon Wearing-Smith, advertising manager for Barry Plant Real Estate Pty., Ltd., Doncaster, Australia.

117

Wife Walked Out!

and put a deposit on a new home. Now owners must unload this 3BR, 2-bath brick ranch in fashionable Clydesdale Estates. They priced it to sell quickly at $129,500, so to delay is to be sorry.

Clyde Realty   **476-8200**

This heading is an attention getter. The ad continues with the real reason for the sale—a motivated seller.

118

It's Desperation Time

Over 3 months on the market and no offers, so the owners have slashed the price on this 3BR, 2-bath West-lake Colonial on an estate-sized lot with professional landscaping, 2++-car garage, full finished basement (ideal for entertaining, home gym, hobbies or rainy-day playroom), massive stone fireplace, family room and a patio perfect for relaxation. You will "save big" at $164,500.

Clyde Realty   476-8200

If the amount of money cut off the price was substantial, you can end an ad with "You will save over $30,000 at $164,500."

119

Sell—Trade or?

Desperate owner told us to do what-ever we can to move this 3BR, 2-bath West Side French Provincial that is less than 5 years old. It has all the amenities, including built-in everything, double garage and su-perb landscaping. We priced it not just to move but to gallop off at $149,500.

Clyde Realty   476-8200

120

Estate Sale

The heirs want cash fast and have directed us to sell this 3-bedroom Cape Cod on a lovely tree-canopied lane in Westport as quickly as possible. This home shows loving care and features a full base-ment, double garage, magnificent plantings and a delightful dining patio. Priced to blow away the com-petition at $119,500.

Clyde Realty   476-8200

121

Absentee Owner Says, "Sell!"

This 3BR, 2-bath Arizona Contempo-rary located in a highly desirable subdivision of fine homes is priced below appraisal to sell quickly at $92,500.

Clyde Realty   476-8200

While no reason is given for the sale, po-tential buyers will feel there is a greater possibil-ity for a bargain when the seller is an absentee owner.

122

Owner Needs Cash

Must sell this 3BR, 2-bath ranch in a choice West Side neighborhood. Home features a full basement, family room, central air and new, neutral carpeting. Appraised at $180,000 but priced to sell at $169,000.

Clyde Realty   **476-8200**

123

Divorce Forces Sale

This is a unique opportunity to purchase a 3BR, 2-bath Colonial on an estate-sized lot in Applewood with all the amenities you desire for only $149,500. To delay means you'll be sorry.

Clyde Realty   **476-8200**

This basic ad can be used with other headings such as "Probate Sale," "Partnership Dissolution," "Bankruptcy Sale," "Owner Needs Cash" or "Desperate Owner."

124

Overbuilt, Underpriced

The builder insisted on every conceivable amenity in this 3BR, 2½-bath French Regency in the most fashionable area of Hillside Heights. In fact, he got carried away and built too fine a home. That is why it is available to you now at only $149,500, which is considerably less than its replacement cost. If bargains are your thing, call.

Clyde Realty   **476-8200**

This home is not necessarily new. If you are advertising a new home, insert "brand new" before "3BR."

125

A Dumb Owner

The owner of this 3-bedroom, 2-bath West Side stone and cedar Cape Cod isn't very bright. We told him we could get a lot more than he wants for his home because of its immaculate condition, new neutral Berber carpeting, child-safe fenced yard and finished basement. As agents, however, we must follow the owner's decision. All he wants is $149,500.

Clyde Realty   **476-8200**

Be certain to have the owner's permission before printing an ad like this. The next ad has a similar message.

126

The Owner Is Crazy

to sell this 3BR, brick ranch on its oversized lot in Hacienda Highlands for only $79,500. Grab your checkbook and rush to

Clyde Realty   **476-8200**

Get the owner's permission before using an ad that questions his or her mental state or indicates that a price is too low.

127

It's a Secret

Don't tell a soul that this newer, 3BR, 2-bath Cape Cod in enchanting Willow Creek can be purchased for only $125,000. Instead, grab your checkbook and rush to

Clyde Realty   **476-8200**

Alternative headings might be "Sh! It's a Secret" or "Shush! It's a Secret."

128

Why Would They Sell

a 3BR, 2-bath, West Side ranch home with a double garage in almost model-home condition for thousands less than its replacement value? Frankly, we don't know the owner's motivation. The owner knows what we think it's worth but has, nevertheless, set the price at $129,500.

Clyde Realty   **476-8200**

129

Last Chance—Auction

It's your opportunity to buy this 3BR, 1½-bath Cape Cod with double garage in a premier Lincoln Park location before foreclosure auction at only $79,500.

Clyde Realty   **476-8200**

130

To Be Auctioned

It's your chance to purchase a 3BR, 2-bath Clayton Hills Colonial with 2++-car garage and full basement at a price you set. One look and you will be as excited as we are. This house has it all—location, condition, floor plan, landscaping and everything on your wish list.

Saturday, Nov. 1—10 A.M. 1270 N. 132nd St.

For previewing and bidder qualification, call

Clyde Realty   **476-8200**

While display ads and handbills are ordinarily used for auctions, many buyers fail to read the larger display ads. Therefore, consider classified ads in conjunction with display ads.

131

Auction

On April 5th, this 3BR, 1½-bath Cape Cod with double garage in a premier Lincoln Park location will be sold to the highest bidder at a foreclosure sale. You can buy it this week without competition at $79,500.

Clyde Realty   **476-8200**

132

Best Offer Takes It

That's right. The owners say they want this 3BR, 2-bath, double-garage, California-style ranch in Westhaven, with family room and in-ground pool, sold *fast*. We have set a minimum price at the ridiculously low figure of $98,500. This is one opportunity you don't want to miss.

Clyde Realty   **476-8200**

This is not an offer to sell at $98,500. It is an auction sale, in which the owner asks for bids over $98,500.

133

Rare Circumstances

force the immediate sale of this 3BR, 1¾-bath Fox Point Cape Cod at a price that will delight you. Special features include breathtaking landscaping; an attached double garage; and a 3-season, screened and glassed porch. You would have expected to pay far more than the $159,000 price.

Clyde Realty   **476-8200**

You can see that it isn't necessary to give the reason for a sale to indicate sales motivation.

134

Can You Move Fast?

This 3BR, 2-bath, newer West side ranch with double garage, family room and full basement must be sold within 48 hours. It's a very special opportunity for the swift at $149,500.

Clyde Realty   **476-8200**

While it isn't stated that this house is a bargain, it is strongly implied. No reason is given as to why the house must be sold fast so that the reader will imagine reasons for an immediate sale.

135

72 Hours To Sell

Because of unusual circumstances, this 3BR, 2-bath, brick and cedar Cape Cod on the most desirable street in Westport must be sold this weekend. It's your chance to take advantage of a rare opportunity at $219,500.

Clyde Realty   **476-8200**

136

Builder in Trouble

Too many houses and too little cash. This is a once-in-a-lifetime opportunity to beat the bankruptcy court and get a brand new 3BR, 2½-bath Mediterranean Colonial in a premier location. It has amenities you dream about for only $219,500.

Clyde Realty   **476-8200**

New homes can be bargains, too.

137

The Fat Lady

is about to sing, and it will be all over for the owner of this 3-bedroom Cape Cod on a quiet, tree-lined street in Westbrook. After the foreclosure you'll have to pay much more due to foreclosure costs, but right now, you can buy this home with its lovely hardwood floors, central air and double garage for only $78,500.

Clyde Realty   **476-8200**

138

Panic-Priced

The owners have a choice: sell quickly or lose it all in foreclosure. While they love this 3BR, 2-bath home with over 2,000 sq. ft. of luxury appointments plus a 3-car garage in prestigious Truesdale Estates, they just can't make the payments. This presents you with a rare opportunity at $198,500.

Clyde Realty   **476-8200**

Another possible heading is, "Foreclosure Imminent." Again, don't reveal an owner's personal motivation without permission.

139

Foreclosure Imminent

You have a rare opportunity to purchase a Hillside Estates home at yesterday's price. This 3-bedroom, 2-bath sprawling ranch features a circle drive, 3-car garage and a kitchen right out of *Better Homes and Gardens*. Call today, because at $198,500, it won't be available tomorrow.

Clyde Realty   **476-8200**

An alternate heading is "Stop Foreclosure."

140

Stop Foreclosure

Owner can't make payments so must sell this 3BR, 1½-bath Traditional bungalow in a premier West Side location. This home features a garage, formal dining room, central air and two apple trees. Panic-priced at $79,000.

Clyde Realty   **476-8200**

141

Repossession

Lender must sell this 3BR, 2-bath California ranch in desirable Williamson Heights at a price you won't believe possible. An opportunity unlikely to be repeated at $169,000.

Clyde Realty   **476-8200**

Just enough about the house is given to make the reader want to know more and call.

142

Repo—4BR

2 baths, a double garage and a quiet family neighborhood make this split-level Colonial definitely our best buy at $144,500.

Clyde Realty   **476-8200**

Because "repossession" and "4BR" are both strong motivators, they were combined in the ad heading.

People assume a foreclosure means a bargain.

143

Government Foreclosure

Three-bedroom, 2-bath, West Side split-level ranch for only $89,500. We have other FHA and VA foreclosures as well.

Clyde Realty   **476-8200**

This is a short, effective ad. The last sentence serves as a "carrot" to bring calls on other types of property.

144

By Virtue of Default

on a security agreement, this 3BR, brick, American Traditional with a huge lot and double garage must be sold by the lender. This is your opportunity for an exceptional purchase at only $97,500.

Clyde Realty   **476-8200**

This is simply another way to show foreclosure.

If more than 1 bath exists, it should be noted.

If location is not mentioned in the newspaper category and the location is desirable, mention it in the ad.

145

Repossession Bargain

The seller took back this 3-bedroom, West Side split ranch. It includes double garage, central air, magnificent oak tree and a delightful garden spot. Priced below appraisal for immediate sale at $69,500.

Clyde Realty   **476-8200**

146

Ordered Sale

You can own a 3BR, 2½-bath, executive ranch with a 3-car garage on a choice wooded site on the most prestigious street. It features a huge family room, baths sheathed in marble, cathedral ceilings, central air and every built-in imaginable. Auction-priced at only $179,500.

Clyde Realty   **476-8200**

Note: The ad does not indicate that this is a court-ordered sale but gives that impression. It could have simply been ordered sold by the owners, in which case it would be an ordinary listing. "Auction-priced" gives the very strong impression of a bargain.

147

Notice

We have been ordered to sell a 2-year-old, 3BR, 2-bath, double-garage Nantucket Colonial, having approximately 2,000 sq. ft., on a wooded acre in Westwood for the price of $149,500. Interested parties should contact the agent.

Clyde Realty   **476-8200**

This bargain ad is similar to the previous ad. However, it does not use adjectives (more in the style of an official notice).

148

Official Sale

Pursuant to a resolution of the board of directors of Acme Industries, the following property is ordered sold: Westwood—3BR, 2½-bath, Colonial, single-family residence with double garage and family room. It has approximately 2,200 sq. ft. of living area. The price is set by the corporation at $149,500. Contact corporate agent.

Clyde Realty   **476-8200**

This ad format gives the impression that it is a public sale (which to many people means a bargain), although the corporation owner has simply asked the agent to sell the property.

149

Excess Property

This 3BR, 2-bath, Westwood Colonial has been ordered sold by the corporate board of directors. Features include a double garage; full basement; central air; and an oversized, wooded site. Liquidation-priced at $149,500.

Clyde Realty   **476-8200**

150
Court-Ordered Sale

By order of the Superior Court for the county of Riverside, this 3BR, 2-bath Colonial in Westhaven must be sold. The home has approximately 2,000 sq. ft. and features a family room, natural stone fireplace, covered terrace and professional landscaping. Full price, clear of all encumbrances, has been set at $189,500.

Clyde Realty   **476-8200**

An ad such as this is appropriate when the court has ordered the sale for partnership dissolution, divorce settlement or probate sale. The fact that the court is ordering the sale will give the impression of a bargain to many readers.

151
Accountant Says, "Sell!"

Corporation must dispose of 3BR, 3½-bath, Tennessee Stone Colonial on the most prestigious street in Ridgecrest. Offering over 3,000 sq. ft. of luxury living, this home makes what you have been working for worthwhile. Priced to sell quickly at $295,000.

Clyde Realty   **476-8200**

A bargain need not be low-priced.

152
Public Announcement

By order of the Circuit Court of Hilton County, this 3BR, 2-bath Contemporary residence **must be sold!** Cedar and stone, it offers magnificent vistas through expansive walls of glass and amenities too numerous to mention. Priced for immediate sale at $219,500.

Clyde Realty   **476-8200**

This announcement ad includes adjectives.

153
A New Ball Game

The price of this 3BR, 2-bath, double-garage American Traditional in the Clayton School District has been drastically reduced. Call now, as it won't last at $89,500.

Clyde Realty   **476-8200**

A price reduction doesn't necessarily indicate a bargain, but it gives the impression of one.

154

Too Good To Be True?

Most really fantastic bargains turn out sour, so why should you believe the owner of this quality 3BR, 2-bath ranch home with a 3-car garage and full basement in Eagle Heights would sell it for only $169,500 (which is thousands less than what is being asked for similar property)? Something must obviously be wrong, but we don't know what it is. See if you can figure out what the catch is. Call.

Clyde Realty   **476-8200**

This is an extremely effective ad to intrigue the reader without giving much information about the property. (See the following ad for a similar treatment.)

155

Catch a Falling Price Tag

We are embarrassed at how low the owners have reduced the price on this 3BR, 2-bath Wyoming Contemporary set on a knoll overlooking almost an acre of lawn, woods and flowers. With its richly paneled den, huge fireplace, delightful patio and sun-filled family kitchen, we know we can sell it in a few more days for far more than the reduced price of $198,500.

Clyde Realty   **476-8200**

This ad uses more adjectives than the prior ad to sell an image as well as a bargain.

156

Price Slashed! $89,500

If you have looked at 3-bedroom Cape Cod homes in Newberry Park, you know the price is a bargain even if it doesn't include a double garage, central air and a finished basement ideal for a children's play center, home gym or hobby room. Call today, or you will surely be sorry tomorrow.

Clyde Realty   **476-8200**

Because the price has been cut, this ad also points to a bargain.

157

Fishy

It can't be true. No one would sell a 2-bedroom, expandable Cape Cod on a wooded half-acre on the North Side for only $137,500. Is there a catch? Call and find out.

Clyde Realty   **476-8200**

158

Free Home

The value of the lot under this 3-bedroom Traditional in a prime West Side location is about equal to the price for both house and lot at $89,500.

Clyde Realty   **476-8200**

Very little is said about the house. The ad is designed to get inquiries for further details. It is likely that many of the inquires will have to be switched to other properties for sale. This ad is appropriate when zoning makes a lot more valuable for another use, or when a home is modest compared to other homes in a highly desirable area.

159

Live or Demolish

The price of this 3BR Morningside Heights home isn't much more than the value of the lot. You therefore can live in relative comfort until you can afford the best. Then, just tear it down and build your dream home. It's an unusual opportunity to live in one of the most prestigious communities for only $149,500.

Clyde Realty   **476-8200**

Like the previous ad, this one implies that the home is almost free when you consider lot value.

160

Professional Drinker

or retired bartender wanted, as this 3-bedroom American Traditional is right next to the corner tavern. While the tavern does cater to a family business and noise isn't really a problem, having a tavern next door has resulted in the almost give-away price of $69,500 with low-down, low-interest seller financing.

Clyde Realty   **476-8200**

This ad pushes the home's negative features and appeals to the bargain hunter.

161

Interest Rates High?

They sure are, and anyone is a fool to pay them unless they got a price so low it compensates for the high interest. Check out this Weston Hills, 3BR, 2½-bath California-style ranch in pristine condition. With a huge family room, 2+-car garage, fireplace, full basement, professional landscaping and screened lanai, you expect the price to be at least $200,000. You can take advantage of the market and become the owner for $164,500.

Clyde Realty   **476-8200**

This ad very simply tells how the real estate market works. When interest rates rise, demand drops. When demand is reduced, people who wish to sell must lower their prices.

5

Condominiums and Cooperatives

Condominiums, cooperatives, community apartment projects and planned unit developments are similar in that they are all governed by a board elected by individual shareholders or owners. They also are usually multi-unit structures. Condominium property offers an attractive alternative to renting because an owner is protected against rent increases, builds equity and obtains the tax deductions of home ownership. Condominium ownership appeals to retirees because the maintenance is taken care of by others, so the owners have greater freedom. Many also like the security offered by condominium projects. Because condominium housing generally sells for significantly less than similarly sized single-family residential property, the lower price appeals to many first-time home buyers. A number of condominium projects also have extensive recreational facilities. These units have special appeal both as vacation homes and for those wanting to live a certain type of lifestyle.

Ads can be tailored to specific types of buyers by stressing the features likely to appeal to them. Many ads in other sections of this book, particularly those for vacation homes, (chapter 30), can be readily tailored for condominiums. If a newspaper has the heading "Condominiums," it isn't necessary to repeat the word "condo" in the ad. If not, be clear as to what you are offering.

162

Forks and Salt Shakers

are about all you need with this decorator-furnished, 2BR, 2-bath end unit in prestigious Clydesdale Terrace. You will love the 10-foot ceilings, majestic views, state-of-the-art kitchen and subtle earth-tone decor of the Southwest. There is a 2-car garage and a very private patio plus all the amenities of a fine resort. A very special home at $149,500.

Clyde Realty   476-8200

A great many condominiums, especially those used as vacation homes, are sold fully furnished. An end unit (or corner unit) is desirable because of the extra privacy, and it generally has better light due to more windows.

163

In the Racquets

As the owner of this spacious, 2BR, 2-bath ground floor unit with a very private dining patio, you'll have the choice of 6 courts for tennis as well as pools, spas and clubhouse activity. The price a steal at $79,500.

Clyde Realty   **476-8200**

A ground floor unit is generally more attractive than the second floor in a walk-up building.

164

Into the Raquets?

If so, you will love this 2BR, 2-bath Embassy unit at Mission Hills. Decorated and furnished by Joshua Jones in a warm medley of muted tones, it is only a few steps from the courts and a 9-iron away from an 18-hole championship course. At $177,500, all you really need to bring is your toothbrush.

Clyde Realty   **476-8200**

While the heading is quite similar to the prior ad, its treatment differs greatly.

Mentioning a decorator's name lends desirability to a unit, even though the decorator might not be well known.

165

Tennis Anyone?

You can have a resort lifestyle and your very own courts. This 3BR, 2½ bath garden unit offers the privacy of your own home plus the amenities of a world-class resort. Decorated by Herman Fey, this home captures the essence of the Southwest with its soft earth-tone decor and brilliant accents. It's a home that definitely deserves your immediate attention at $398,500.

Clyde Realty   **476-8200**

A garden unit is a first floor unit.

166

Trees and Tees

This villa has 2 bedrooms, 2 baths and a den and is sheltered by giant beech and hickory nut trees on the 7th fairway at Callaway Hills Country Club. Other features include a garage big enough for 2 cars and golf cart, high ceilings, soft decorator colors, a delightful dining patio, and a great view from your living and family room. All this makes it a very special home at $189,500.

Clyde Realty   **476-8200**

A villa can refer to an attached home or a single-family home.

167

Golf Club Membership

included with this 2BR, 2-bath impressive end unit in prestigious Morningside. Eighteen marvelous holes, 6 courts, pools, spa and clubhouse can all be yours. Soaring ceilings, 2-car garage, views of the fairways, private patio and an intimate fireplace make this an exceptional offering at $179,500.

Clyde Realty   **476-8200**

A number of developments have club membership that passes with the units. There are, of course, fees.

168

A Silent World

High on the 23rd floor, this spacious 2BR, 2-bath corner unit with its 27-foot living room is in a private world above the sounds of the city. The delightful dining terrace offers a breathtaking view of the city lights beneath your feet. Far above the rest at a down-to-earth price of $249,000.

Clyde Realty   **476-8200**

Higher units offer a view, quietness and cleaner air.
Corner units mean more windows and are thus very desirable.

169

Batman

would love the view of the city from this 32nd-floor perch (2BR, 2-bath condominium). A delightful balcony for dining out, walls of glass, high ceilings and spacious rooms make this the residence above all others. Priced to excite at $289,500.

Clyde Realty   **476-8200**

170

Love in the Air

Twenty-two stories above the world is a 2BR, 2-bath private place made for you. There are two balconies—one ideal for dining and entertaining above the lights and the other for soaking in the sun. Rooms of generous proportions and amenities include a wood-burning fireplace, a state-of-the-art kitchen, jacuzzi baths sheathed in marble and an incomparable river view. An opportunity unlikely to be repeated at $389,500.

Clyde Realty   **476-8200**

This is a different treatment for a property similar to that in the previous ad.

171

Halfway to Heaven

in this spacious 22nd-floor, 2BR, 2-bath luxury condominium with its high ceilings, intimate balcony and incomparable view. In a full-security building with concierge services, this is truly the height of luxury at $349,500.

Clyde Realty   **476-8200**

The word "intimate" is used favorably to describe something small.

172

Junk the Car

This 10th-floor, 2-bedroom estate in a prestigious, electronic-security building is within walking distance from everything. There is a delightful deck; spacious, bright rooms; and high ceilings for only $139,500.

Clyde Realty   **476-8200**

173

Harried Executive

will love this 2BR, 2-bath, river-view unit with high ceilings, wood-burning fireplace and a lovely dining terrace because it's only a 5-minute walk from the civic center. Other features include underground parking, electronic security systems and baths sheathed in marble. A seldom available opportunity at $249,500.

Clyde Realty   **476-8200**

This ad is for a central-city condominium. It stresses location.

174

Cranston Towers— 1 Bedroom

Are you a private person? Would you like a sophisticated, adult unit in a fully soundproof building offering underground parking and state-of-the-art electronic security? Would you like a private terrace for sunbathing or intimate dining alfresco where you can look down on the world? If your answer is "yes," call at once for an unusual opportunity at $119,500.

Clyde Realty   **476-8200**

This ad is aimed at single people. Its readers will think it was written just for them.

175

Space Out

Tired of dwarf-sized rooms? Want your own space without having to leave the city? This 1-bedroom condominium offers a great room for a grand piano and a bedroom with space for a harem. Call today or at $89,500 you will be crowded out of this opportunity.

Clyde Realty   **476-8200**

176

Big City Blues

Doomed to another night in front of the TV? Would you like an exciting alternative to apartment living? This huge, 1-bedroom condominium only minutes from the heart of the city offers you the opportunity for the lifestyle you have dreamed about. Take the elevator to your own health club with its heated pool, relaxing spa and sauna, or relax with your friends on the roof garden. All the amenities of a fine resort can be yours. You won't believe the financing available, and the price is right at $159,500.

Clyde Realty   **476-8200**

This is a different way of treating a highrise condo. It's designed to appeal to single buyers.

177

Condo-Maximum

Nothing is mini about this Brentwood, 3BR, 2½-bath garden unit with its bright spacious rooms and soaring ceilings. There is an oversized 2-car garage, two separate patios and a huge fireplace. All the privacy of a single-family estate is available at a very affordable $189,500.

Clyde Realty   **476-8200**

178

Condomax

At last a condominium with all of the amenities and privacy of a single-family home! This 2BR and den, 2-bath, Barcelona end unit in Sunrise offers 2,000 sq. ft. of luxury, including an interior atrium, soaring ceilings, fireplace, private courtyard for dining or relaxation and incomparable views. In addition, you get all the benefits of a luxury resort such as pools, spas, health club and tennis. It's the ultimate in quality of life at $198,500.

Clyde Realty   **476-8200**

This ad is aimed at readers who prefer a single-family home.

179

Pick of the Litter

This is the best 2BR, 2-bath unit in all of Morningside. Decorated in neutral tones of the Southwest with incomparable views, this better-than-new home has a double garage, fireplace and Berber carpeting and is priced at no more than the ordinary at $129,500.

Clyde Realty   **476-8200**

This is an excellent example of an ad to use when several agents are advertising units within the same development.

180

Landlord Trouble

Is your rent going up each year and your landlord suddenly deaf when you ask for anything to be done? Why not own your own 2BR apartment with a great view in a friendly West Side elevator building. The apartment also has underground parking, an electronic security system and a price of only $279,500 and association fees of just $219/ month. This is the only unit available, so act fast.

Clyde Realty   **476-8200**

Many readers identify with escalating rents and unresponsive landlords. Since only one unit is available, you can use an urgency appeal. If the association fees are less than expected, they should be mentioned in the ad.

181

A Classic

High ceilings and gleaming hardwood detailing are reminiscent of a time of gracious living. This immense, sunbathed 2-bedroom estate in the sky offers view, location, lifestyle and an address to be envied. This is your chance for a home as individual as you are. Proudly offered at $695,000.

Clyde Realty   **476-8200**

This ad is for a unit in an older high-rise in a prestigious location.

182

Loft—Bicycle Factory

This 1,500-sq.-ft. loft with brick walls and huge wooden beams was part of one of the world's largest bicycle factories in the 1890s. Sixteen-foot ceilings and a wall of glass make it the perfect studio. Only 5 minutes from the Loop, with parking included, this loft deserves your investigation at $89,500.

Clyde Realty   **476-8200**

A loft that was formerly used for an unusual purpose can generate interest.

183

Loft—One Big Room

That's right, with approximately 1,000 sq. ft. in 1 room and a 14-foot ceiling, this loft is only minutes from Madison Avenue. Included is indoor parking and a key elevator. Oh, there's also a bath and the kitchen cabinets are in, but everything else is up to your imagination. Will sell fast at $194,500.

Clyde Realty   **476-8200**

Lofts are in demand in large cities.

184

Loft—2,000 Sq. Ft.

Fourteen-foot ceilings, soundproof concrete and brick construction, protected parking, and a key-operated elevator are some of the features of this recently transformed space just minutes from Times Square. You will love the Euro-style kitchen, the gleaming bath sheathed in tile and the general feeling of spaciousness and light with windows that start at the knees and don't stop until they reach the ceiling. Not to be duplicated at $319,000.

Clyde Realty   **476-8200**

Loft units are very desirable, so include the word "loft" in the heading.

185

The Last 6

Only 6 spacious, 2BR, 2-bath townhouses remain in Mariner's Walk, where the air is clear and the wind is calm. Vitality radiates from the fresh, sun-filled rooms. Community facilities include tennis, racquetball, a complete health club, pool, spas and sauna. Destined to sell out fast at $111,500–$119,000. When they do, only those who live here will be able to play here.

Clyde Realty   **476-8200**

A classified ad can be used for selling a number of units. This ad is for new units and can be modified for resale units with the heading "Only 6."

186

Only 1 Left

This is the last 2BR, 2-bath corner unit in Hillside Terrace. Bright, spacious rooms, marble-faced fireplace, baths sheathed in tile, Eurostyle kitchen and upgraded appliances make this a unit bound to appreciate. It is yours at $137,500.

Clyde Realty   **476-8200**

Classified ads can be used to sell new condos as well as resale units. The heading "Only 1 Left" can refer to the last condo available or to corner units, first floors units, or even floor plan.

187
Retire
Where the Action Is

Tired of sitting around watching your arteries harden? In friendly Victoria Highlands you can use community pools, steam rooms, spas, sauna, fitness center and craft shops. Join an aerobics class or even learn Kung Fu. We have community-organized events and tours just about every day. Prices for new 2-bedroom condominiums with garages start at only $69,500. Don't you think you deserve this lifestyle?

Clyde Realty   476-8200

This is an effective way of advertising new units in a condominium retirement community.

188
Nudists

A full body tan is possible on the very private deck of this spacious 2BR, 2-bath corner unit in one of the finest developments on the West Side. Gated security, soundproofing, recreational facilities that would shame most fine resorts and friendly neighbors can be yours at only $169,500.

Clyde Realty   476-8200

The above heading attracts attention and also implies that the unit offers privacy. The remainder of the ad promotes a very desirable unit.

189
Come Play with Us

at Breverton Villas, which offers tennis, swimming, a fitness center and much more. This desirable 2BR, 2-bath corner unit has been upgraded beyond belief and is only $89,500 with association fees far lower than you ever imagined. This is the only one available, so you better act fast.

Clyde Realty   476-8200

This is an attention-getting heading. The fact that the unit advertised is the only unit (or unit of its type) on the market makes it seem more desirable.

190
Fun Place

The pool and spa just outside your door, a 2-minute walk to courts and clubhouse and friendly neighbors make this 1-bedroom floor unit a great place to live. At only $69,500, the payments will seem like rent. The first happy camper with $5,000 down gets it.

Clyde Realty   476-8200

This ad appeals to younger singles and couples looking for vacation units.

191

Don't Worry— Be Happy

Everything is done for you as owner of this 2BR, 2-bath poolside garden unit in gate-guarded Hillside Terrace. A private patio; double garage; cozy fireplace; light, spacious rooms; and all the amenities of a fine resort, including tennis and health club membership, make living a delight at a very affordable $137,500.

Clyde Realty   **476-8200**

193

Not an Apartment

This 2BR, 2-bath garden condominium in Westport Hills is a whole new way of life. There are, of course, soaring ceilings; spacious, bright rooms; a huge fireplace; and a very private patio. Included is every amenity of a world-class resort with tennis, pool, spa and a super health club. It's an "investment of a lifestyle" at $129,500.

Clyde Realty   **476-8200**

192

Small and Dreary

and it doesn't even have a view. But this 1-bedroom, South Side unit has a great location and a price that is out of the past. A truly exceptional value at $69,900.

Clyde Realty   **476-8200**

194

OK! Don't Believe Me!

You know darn well it isn't possible to find a spacious 2BR, 2-bath unit in a quality building in a desirable West Side location for only $149,500. Check it out, but if you delay, I'll tell you it is sold and you'll never believe it actually existed.

Clyde Realty   **476-8200**

Even though this ad has a negative heading, it's an attention getter and will bring in the calls.

This is also an attention-getting, negative heading. It is an appropriate type of ad when the price seems low.

195

Never Be Lonely

in this 2BR, 2-bath garden home in Mariner's Walk. This is not a community where old people sit around and complain. It's one where vibrant people enjoy life. Just about every activity imaginable is here—pools, spas, steam rooms, courts and craft shops. We have even heard talk about a planned hang-gliding club. For only $79,500, you can be a part of a lifestyle you'll love.

Clyde Realty   **476-8200**

This heading has a strong appeal to many elderly people.

Since terms are not important to most elderly purchasers, they are not included (except on the bottom end of the housing market).

A hang-gliding statement will show those who fear retirement housing that the home is a fun place, not an "old folks home."

196

X-Rated

- Intimate hot spa with room for 2
- Private terrace for full-body tanning
- Mirrored master bedroom
- Sensuous double-sized shower
- Cuddle-up fireplace

This 2BR, 2-bath unit in a premier West Side location is definitely for sophisticated adults. Even the price will delight your senses at $189,500.

Clyde Realty   **476-8200**

This ad will get attention, but use it only in large cities.

197

Extra
Extra

Everything is upgraded in this 2BR, 2-bath, seldom-available Montecito garden unit in prestigious Rancho Park. You will love the large, sun-filled rooms that offer the privacy of a single-family home with none of the worry plus country club recreational facilities. To look is to own, at $97,500.

Clyde Realty   **476-8200**

198

Condominiums

Deepwell	1/1	$ 58,500
Mariner's Walk	2/2	$ 74,500
Ridgecrest	2/2	$ 89,500
Skyhaven	3/2	$ 94,800
Westview	2/2	$112,500
Mountainback	2/2	$129,900
The Lakes	3/2½	$139,500
Horizons	3/3	$164,500

Clyde Realty   **476-8200**

A simple listing of units, sizes, BR/bath and price indicates that you have many units available, and this will increase your calls.

199

Sell the Lawn Mower

The maintenance is provided for you when you live in this spacious 2BR, 2-bath garden unit in Ridgecrest. Designed with an emphasis on privacy, you will love your private garden patio and interior atrium. There is a fireplace for warming your toes and a kitchen you only dream about. Plus, you get all the amenities of a fine resort at a price of only $139,500.

Clyde Realty   **476-8200**

The above heading communicates the idea that the owners of this unit have someone else to do their yard work.

200

Victoria Estates— Resale

It's hard to believe, but you can get this 2BR, 2-bath large end unit with garage for only

$69,500.

You get more than a home. This is a lifestyle with community events, clubs, church groups, craft centers, sports and the finest keep-young fitness center you have ever seen with saunas, spas, pools, steam rooms and the latest exercise equipment. You can even join Jazzercize and Kung Fu classes. Don't miss this exceptional opportunity.

Clyde Realty   **476-8200**

This ad is designed for those who want to live in a retirement community.

201

Garden Unit—$59,500

This lovely 2-bedroom home in Claridge Estates features a private garage and delightful patio. It's just steps to the pool and clubhouse. This one will go fast.

Clyde Realty   **476-8200**

Note that the low price of this unit is mentioned in its heading. If a unit has more than 1 bath, it should be stated in the ad copy. Likewise, if the garage is more than a 1-car garage, it should also be stated.

202

For the Wild Life

You will enjoy the two-legged kind around the pool, spa, courts and health club of Brentwood Palms. You'll love this oversized unit with its king-size master suite and huge living area with a very cozy fireplace and soaring ceilings. Join the party for only $74,500.

Clyde Realty   **476-8200**

This ad is for a 1-bedroom unit.

203

Brown Thumb

Let someone else tend the lawn and exotic plantings as the owner of this 2BR, 2-bath, upgraded Barcelona unit in Sunrise. You will love the happy decor of tasteful neutral tones with colorful accents. It has all the seclusion of a private home— even your own double garage combined with all the amenities of a world-class resort. Look and you will own at $179,500.

Clyde Realty   **476-8200**

Almost every condominium is upgraded from the basic unit with at least 1 option.

204

Schlepp No More

A first-floor, 2-bedroom garden unit with attached garage means no elevator, no stairs, and no schlepping. This unit has spacious, bright rooms; a delightful patio; and a kitchen that's a dream at a price that won't mean bankruptcy—$129,500.

Clyde Realty   **476-8200**

"Schlepp" is a Yiddish word for drag or carry. The above ad is most effective in metropolitan areas, where its readers are apt to know common Yiddish expressions.

205

This Won't Last

As the only available 1-bedroom unit in Berkdale less than 15 minutes from the city's center, this extra-large unit has been updated beyond belief. You will love the plush (neutral) carpets and soft colors in the sun-drenched living areas. The gourmet kitchen includes everything on your wish list. You will have to act fast at $139,500.

Clyde Realty   **476-8200**

This ad is appropriate when similar units are currently unavailable in a development.

206

We Mow the Lawn

You just enjoy the lifestyle of this Mariner's Walk, 2BR, 2-bath, tastefully decorated town house that has been upgraded beyond belief. Close to pool and clubhouse, it offers a 2-car garage, family room and a delightful dining patio. All the privacy of a single-family home with none of the responsibilities can be yours at only $139,500.

Clyde Realty   **476-8200**

207
Corinthian Villas—$139,500

It's the home you always wanted, with none of the problems. This 2BR, 2½-bath corner unit with its own double garage offers all the privacy of single-family living with none of the responsibilities. When the grass grows, the leaves fall and snow piles up, you will appreciate the lifestyle you deserve. With exceptional financing, your immediate action is warranted.

Clyde Realty   **476-8200**

If the price is a strong feature, it should be added to the heading.

208
Mariner's Walk

At last a condominium offering the privacy of a single-family home. This sought-after Oxford model features double master suites, huge living area and 2½ baths. Much more than a place to live, it is your entry into the carefree world of fun and leisure. Available now at $243,500.

Clyde Realty   **476-8200**

Emphasize privacy when advertising soundproof buildings, end units, semidetached units and smaller developments. A lack of privacy is the reason many people don't like condominium living.

209
Champagne Condominium

Upgraded beyond belief, this 2BR, 2-bath garden unit in Ridgecrest has every built-in and option imaginable. There is even a lushly landscaped interior atrium, soaring entry, fireplace and secluded dining patio. For the buyer who will not compromise, it is priced at $149,500.

Clyde Realty   **476-8200**

This ad takes a luxury-home approach.

210
Guarded Gates

lighted parking areas and pathways plus the latest in electronic security are just a few of the features you'll like about this 2BR, 2-bath, poolside model in prestigious Flintridge Estates. All the amenities of a fine resort including a magnificent clubhouse and friendly neighbors can be yours. Priced to sell quickly at $112,500.

Clyde Realty   **476-8200**

Many people, particularly the elderly, are obsessed with security. It is, therefore, an important feature in ads. While you should mention the type of security, never represent a unit as being secure. This can be regarded as a warranty, which will make you liable for damages on losses suffered because of negligent security.

211

Ocean View Terrace

You deserve to be pampered with carefree living. No snow to shovel or grass to cut. This upgraded Shaughnessy model features an elegant master suite, separate den or music room and a view that is practically forever. You won't believe the low maintenance fees. Priced to sell this weekend at $129,900.

Clyde Realty   **476-8200**

The name of the development or area, if desirable, can be the heading. The price can also be added to the heading.

212

Broadcrest

Are you ready for a resort lifestyle with big-city sophistication? This 2BR, 2-bath corner unit offers the ultimate in luxurious appointments, country club amenities and an address to be envied. All at an affordable $139,500.

Clyde Realty   **476-8200**

The name of the development is indicated in the heading.

213

Lock the Doors

and travel the world knowing the maintenance will be taken care of when you live in Mariner's Walk. This lovely 2BR, 2-bath end unit with its private patio offers the seclusion and amenities of a fine single-family residence with none of the responsibilities. Tastefully decorated with just about every upgrade offered, this sought-after Barcelona model with a double garage is priced to sell quickly at $119,500.

Clyde Realty   **476-8200**

Different ad treatments can be used to appeal to different interests.

214

Mariner's Walk

is a planned, recreationally oriented community with a balanced environment where you and your family will enjoy the best life has to offer. This 3BR, 2½-bath garden unit exudes an aura of style, comfort and sophistication with a dazzling array of exquisite features to delight the senses. At $197,500, this is a unique opportunity deserving your immediate attention.

Clyde Realty   **476-8200**

This ad communicates a mood without giving many details.

215

Sell the Kids

and you can qualify as owner of this 2BR, 2-bath end unit in the mature adult community of Brentwood Pines. High ceilings, walls of glass, great views, fabulous built-ins, a natural fireplace, baths sheathed in marble and all the amenities of a fine resort make this the life you deserve. It won't last at $119,500.

Clyde Realty   **476-8200**

This ad is for a retirement community.

216

Join

the hundreds of families who have discovered Hillcrest. You will fall in love with this 2-bedroom Presidential model with its greenbelt views, soaring ceilings, central air, intimate patio and professional decorating with extras galore. With all the activities, you will find Hillcrest a whole new way of life at an affordable $89,500.

Clyde Realty   **476-8200**

217

Hedonist?

If you love wild parties and believe indulgence begins with oneself, then you'll truly love this 1-bedroom, 1½-bath unit with a view (of the pool and spa) in Hillside Terrace. The large, bright rooms have been decorated to excess with mirrors and bright hues. There is a private patio for dining alfresco and a party-sized room with a fireplace for cuddling up. Everything is wild except the price—$137,500.

Clyde Realty   **476-8200**

This ad is aimed at the single person who appreciates a humorous tone.

6

Family-Oriented Ads

Family issues provide the motivating factor for most working parents, as they want to do everything they can for their children. The choice of a home is influenced by the parents' perception of the benefits it offers their children.

Family love can thus be the focal point of effective advertising. While many ads contained elsewhere in this book also appeal to the needs and lifestyles of children, the ads in this chapter are specifically centered around the family.

218

Don't Like Kids?

Then you'll loathe this 3BR, 2-bath American Traditional in a family neighborhood of Westwood. The home is only 1 block from a park with ballfields and a playground. Trikes and skaters glide down the sidewalks, and bikes fill the streets. In the early evening, an army of little people plays kick the can in the alley. Worse yet, you can expect children to want to "snitch" the fruit from your 2 apple trees. The only thing you'll like about this home is the price—$89,500.

Clyde Realty   476-8200

This ad is, of course, aimed at families.

219

Happiness

is a yard with a swing and lots of kids your age in the neighborhood. This 3BR, 2-bath family home in a friendly West Side family community is the answer to happiness. There is even a 2-car garage and a full basement with separate workroom. Family priced at $79,500.

Clyde Realty   **476-8200**

Very little is mentioned about the house. The ad is short but sells an image.

220

Children Only

Little League, soccer, Pop Warner football, Junior ice hockey leagues, scouts and more are here for your children. If you're not willing to get involved, look elsewhere because here you'll be out of place. The 3BR, 2-bath, double-garage, Traditional brick ranch offers a family room big enough for a troop of Brownies, a fenced yard that will hold a gaggle of children and their dogs and it's only 3 quiet blocks to grade and middle schools. Low-down FHA financing is available, and it's priced at the FHA appraisal of $119,500.

Clyde Realty   **476-8200**

If the school or school district is especially desirable, mention names in the ad.

221

Bare Feet Wiggling

in the grass and almost a half-acre for your children to roam on this pleasant wooded site. Besides the large family room, the full, dry basement is a great place for a rainy-day playroom. Incidentally, the house has 3 bedrooms, 2 baths, a double garage and a lot more for optimum family living. $117,500.

Clyde Realty   **476-8200**

222

Cul-de-Sac Safe

Family home in the friendliest neighborhood offering 3 tribe-sized bedrooms and a fenced yard. Best of all, it is only 2 short blocks to Midvale School. An investment in your family at $139,500.

Clyde Realty   **476-8200**

A prime concern to parents is their children's safety. Here's a variation on this ad.

No Screeching Brakes

Located on a quiet cul-de-sac. . . .

223

Remember
Kick the Can?

There's still a place where children can run free and neighbors still sit on front porches on warm summer evenings. This 3-bedroom Nantucket Colonial offers more than just the charm of a gentler time. It also offers your family the way of life they deserve at an affordable $97,500.

Clyde Realty   **476-8200**

This ad sells nostalgia. It causes the reader to think back to the pleasant aspects of his or her childhood and makes an older home seem very desirable.

224

Kick the Can

and hide and seek are still played in this family neighborhood, where neighbors take pride in their homes and families. You can walk to schools and parks from this 3BR American Traditional with its full basement, garage and delightful garden. What better place for your family at $79,500?

Clyde Realty   **476-8200**

225

Hopscotch

is still played on the sidewalks of this quiet, tree-lined street. You will hear the sound of roller skates and carefree laughter. This 3BR, 1½-bath Cape Cod, set back from the street behind a white board fence and colorful plantings, offers a full basement, hardwood floors, formal dining room, country kitchen and a basketball hoop on the double garage. Waiting for your family's tomorrow at an old-fashioned price—$87,500.

Clyde Realty   **476-8200**

226

Kidding Around

You deserve a perfect branch to hang a swing; a huge, fenced, child-safe yard; and a quiet, tree-lined street with sidewalks just made for roller skates. Your children will love this 3BR, 1½-bath New England Cape Cod in a family neighborhood full of friends their own age. This home includes a huge double garage; country-sized kitchen; corn-popping fireplace; large, bright rooms; and a feeling of warmth and happiness. For your family at $79,500.

Clyde Realty   **476-8200**

227

We're Not Kidding

Your children will love this 3-bedroom West Side home. There is an old oak tree in the backyard waiting for a child's swing. A boy and his dog will love bunking in their own rugged, paneled bedroom. There's even a storybook nursery just waiting for you. At $98,500, this is your chance to create fond memories for your future.

Clyde Realty   **476-8200**

This ad was inspired by an ad written by Ian Price of Surfer's Paradise, Australia.

228

Friendly Dog

is not included with this 3-bedroom family home in the Hillside School District. With a short walk to schools and parks, this is the ideal home for a happy family. It features a fireplace to gather 'round on cold wintry nights and a tree-shaded, fenced yard children will love. The full, dry basement makes a perfect rainy-day playroom, and the double garage has room for cars, bikes, trikes and a red wagon. It's the perfect home for Fido and the rest of the family at $118,500.

Clyde Realty   **476-8200**

Adding the name of the school district tends to give an area more prestige, even though it might not really be that outstanding.

229

Ringo Starr

didn't stay here, but Beatle records were played constantly in the separate teen suite of this 3BR, 3-bath Colonial with 2½-car garage in the nicest area of Orchard Heights. The basement recreation room can hold more than 100 screaming teenagers. The owners maintained their sanity because of the split floor plan. They also used the backyard garden as their escape. Their children are now grown, so it's your turn at $179,500.

Clyde Realty   **476-8200**

230

Children Wanted

There's room for a cub scout pack in the family room of this 3-bedroom American Traditional located in an old-fashioned West Side community where life still centers around one's family and neighbors still lend a helping hand and watch over one another. This is truly a wonderful investment in your peace of mind at $89,500.

Clyde Realty   **476-8200**

This ad makes a virtue of the fact that it is an older home in a long-standing community.

231

A Hill for Sledding

sidewalks for skating, and a great field for playing—what more could a child hope for? This 3BR, 2-bath Spanish Colonial has a large fenced yard perfect for small children. You will love the distinctive architecture, the lush landscaping and the friendly neighborhood where people obviously care about their homes and each other. We consider this to be an exceptional opportunity at $149,500.

Clyde Realty   **476-8200**

232

Lots of Tots

can play in the fully fenced backyard of this 3-bedroom Colonial that is only a short walk from Hampton School. The large dry basement is perfect for a rainy-day playroom, and there's plenty of room for bikes and trikes in the oversized double garage. The best part is that it's family-priced at $89,500, with a low-low down payment. The worst part is that this is a one-of-a-kind situation, so be the first family to call.

Clyde Realty   **476-8200**

233

Go Where the Growing's Good

Set in a quiet family neighborhood of well-tended homes and lawns is this 3-bedroom, white clapboard Cape Cod with its shutters and multi-panel windows. There is a huge, fenced yard for children and puppies; a full basement ideal for a rainy-day playroom; corn-popping fireplace; and plenty of room for bikes and trikes in the oversized double garage. A very special family home at $97,500.

Clyde Realty   **476-8200**

234

Puppies and Children

will love the huge, fenced yard of this 3BR, 2-bath, double-garage American Traditional built for family living. Generously proportioned, sun-brightened rooms provide a happy feeling of freshness. Mrs. Burns, one of our sales associates, says she would love to start a family here. (Incidentally she's 67, but don't tell her we revealed her age.) Oh, there's low-down financing available, and at $117,500 we suggest you load up your station wagon and take a look right now.

Clyde Realty   **476-8200**

Little comments about sales associates have a humanizing effect that can distinguish your ads from those of others. This ad promotes a chatty, friendly reader/broker relationship.

235

Back to School

Unusual circumstances allow us to offer this 3-bedroom family home on a quiet tree-canopied street in the desirable Westlake School District for only $120,000.

Clyde Realty   **476-8200**

While the reason for the sale is not given, the ad hints at a possible bargain. Very little is said about the house. This ad is designed to make readers want to know more.

236

Once upon a Time

in a land not very far away, a family made a wish that their new home would endure for generations and bring joy to all who lived there. History has shown their wish has come true. This Arizona Traditional with its 3 bedrooms, paneled music room, front parlor and great room is magnificent in proportion and concept and awaits your family. Priced at $189,500, it's truly a home for joyous living.

Clyde Realty   **476-8200**

While not specifically aimed at children, this ad for an older home sells a family mood.

237

If You Didn't Care

you wouldn't be looking for a home for your family. This 3BR, 2-bath, double-garage Cape Cod charmer offers everything you can hope for. Located on a quiet tree-lined street in a West Side neighborhood dedicated to family values, it is within walking distance of parks and schools. With the unfinished attic bonus room, this home offers room to grow. The tribe-sized kitchen can seat the largest family, and there is a separate dining area as well. The best part is that you won't have to sell your soul to the devil to care for your family. It's affordably priced at $119,500.

Clyde Realty   **476-8200**

238

A Childhood Dream

Your children's memories will be of a quiet, tree-lined street; sidewalks for roller skating; a park just minutes away; lots of true friends; and a white-shuttered Colonial, 3-bedroom home set back from the street behind a white picket fence. Come and see the place where future memories will be made. Priced for you at $89,500.

Clyde Realty   **476-8200**

This ad appeals to those who love family life. As written, it could also apply to an older home in an established neighborhood.

If there is more than 1 bath, it should be noted.

While there's not much detail in this ad, its primary purpose is to bring in calls.

239

Special thanks to Gordon Wearing-Smith, Barry Plant Real Estate Pty. Ltd., Doncaster, Australia.

7

Fixer-Upper Ads

When you advertise a property as a fixer-upper, prepare for your phone to ring. As a general rule, this type of ad brings a greater response than any other ad.

Fixer-upper ads imply a bargain, and a property is considered a bargain if the purchaser is able and willing to renovate and make repairs. While ads normally use glowing adjectives, fixer-upper ads attract callers in direct relationship to the property problems. In fact, many advertisers overly denigrate property to attract more callers. By doing so, prospective buyers are often pleasantly surprised when they see the property.

The heading of a fixer-upper ad should clearly indicate that the property has problems. The simple heading "Fixer-Upper" is adequate and effective.

Never advertise a property as a fixer-upper without the owner's permission. You don't want an owner to be angry because his or her dream house is described as a dump.

240

The Bottom of the Barrel

We avoided advertising this one as long as possible, since it will take a miracle to sell it at any price. Sure it has 3 bedrooms, 2 baths and is in a desirable West Side neighborhood, but beyond this, there's nothing else that's positive. To say it has been neglected would be a compliment, as it needs just about everything. We know it's habitable because we found an old mattress and a pile of cigarette butts in a corner of the basement. The price is a low $59,000, but don't expect much.

Clyde Realty   476-8200

This ad will make the phones ring. It was inspired by a Roy Brooks ad (London, England).

241

Leaky-Roof Special

Besides the roof, things are not right inside this 3-bedroom, West Side, Cape Cod disaster. The plumbing leaks, the water heater is shot, the air conditioner spews out heated air and the place looks like it has never seen a paint brush or a vacuum cleaner. We would be ashamed to advertise it if it weren't for the price, $79,500.

Clyde Realty   **476-8200**

This ad literally shouts "bargain" for the fixer-upper buyer.

242

The Roof Leaks

the paint is peeling and the plumbing is not well in this 3-bedroom Cape Cod with double garage on a quiet, tree-lined, West Side street.

Fix It Up

and it can be the pride of the neighborhood instead of its shame. Priced to reflect problems at $79,500.

Clyde Realty   **476-8200**

A split heading is very effective. The positive features of this home are its basic structure (Cape Cod with double garage), location and price.

243

Old—Dingy—Cheap

Sure the neighborhood is great and this 3-bedroom Traditional may be structurally sound, but it all ends there. This is a fixer-upper that makes every other fixer-upper look like a palace. Don't take our word for it. Call and see what a mess $35,000 will get you.

Clyde Realty   **476-8200**

A true buyer of fixer-uppers will be captivated by this ad. The property has a low price, is in a good area and is structurally sound—the 3 features this type of buyer looks for.

While the word "cheap" shouldn't ordinarily be used in an ad, this is an exception.

244

Not a Model Home

In fact, it's going to take some work to make this 3-bedroom American Traditional the sort of place you want to live in.

It's a Fixer-Upper

Paint and plaster, nails, and even some strong glue will be needed to mend this neglected West Side home. The amazing thing is it doesn't look half bad from the outside, and the neighborhood is rather pleasant. The price is pleasant too at $89,500.

Clyde Realty   **476-8200**

245

A Turkey

This 3-bedroom West Side Traditional needs just about everything, but if you can

Fix It Up

you should be able to save in a big way. The neighborhood is great, and most of the problems appear to be cosmetic. At $87,500, it is an exceptional opportunity.

Clyde Realty   **476-8200**

246

Pygmalian

Under the grime there's a real gem awaiting your discovery.

Fix It Up

and this 3-bedroom American bungalow will be a home that elicits envy. The classic lines; beamed, wide overhangs; covered porch; formal brick fireplace; hardwood floors; and separate dining room are just a few of the features that will excite you. Make no mistake, while presently livable, this is a genuine fixer-upper. Priced accordingly at $69,500.

Clyde Realty   **476-8200**

If the area is desirable, a few words regarding the neighborhood should have been included in the above ad.

247

Henry Higgins

would have a hard time turning this older, 3BR American Traditional into anything close to *My Fair Lady*. The roof leaks (only when it rains), the plumbing clanks and gurgles, the decorating is medieval and whatever is breakable is broken. The area is rather nice, but the really redeeming feature is price, $69,500.

Clyde Realty   **476-8200**

This type of ad is better for a smaller newspaper with fewer ads, as it might otherwise be overlooked by some fixer-upper buyers who don't realize who Professor Higgins is.

248

Miserable

That's how Mrs. Hopkins of our office describes this 3BR, 2-bath newer Cape Cod in a rather fashionable West Side neighborhood. The decorating is early dungeon style (dark and dreary), the garden features weeds and thistles and the carpets are badly stained. There are some nice hardwood trees, a double garage and a rather nice family room with a fireplace, but frankly, right now the house does look depressing. The price is also depressed at $89,500.

Clyde Realty   **476-8200**

Note that the negative features of this home are really cosmetic in nature and are far outweighed by the positive features.

249

The Worst House

in the nicest West Side neighborhood of fine homes. This 3-bedroom brick ranch appears to be a senior citizen, but according to its birth certificate, it is still a teenager. This is undoubtedly the result of raucous living. It's a home not for the timid, but a rare opportunity at $137,500 if you're not afraid of getting your hands dirty.

Clyde Realty   **476-8200**

The above is an ad for a fairly new home in rough condition.

250

Don't
Be Deceived

by the rather pleasant appearance of this 3-bedroom Cape Cod in Ridgeline. The 3-foot weeds and cracked windows are the good points; inside it is a shambles. We think a former resident used the walls to release repressed aggression. The carpet has spots caused by something we certainly don't want to know about. It's the shame of an otherwise pleasant neighborhood and is priced accordingly at $79,500.

Clyde Realty   **476-8200**

If this kind of ad is to be used in a newspaper with many ads, consider the 2-line heading "Fixer-Upper. Don't Be Deceived." Otherwise, the ad probably will be overlooked by many potential fixer-upper buyers.

251

Fixer-Upper—
Country Acre

The skylight in this 3-bedroom country home is really a large hole in the roof. While there are no bats in the attic, at least one family of pigeons calls it home. A barn comes with it. Mrs. Higgins of our office says she would prefer living in the barn. On the positive side, the house looks good on the outside—one could even say picturesque. Definitely for the unusual buyer at $67,500.

Clyde Realty   **476-8200**

In this ad, the word "garage" could be substituted for "barn." Instead of a hole in the roof you could say, "Ventilation is great in this . . . at least until the broken windows are replaced."

252

Better Than a Cave

but not much better. This 3BR, West Side American Traditional is a certified

Fixer-Upper

While the roof doesn't appear to leak, this place needs a lot of hammering, painting and general fixing. The problems are reflected in the price of $79,500.

Clyde Realty   **476-8200**

253

Fix It Up

but the tough decision is should you start with a paint brush or a bulldozer? This 3BR bungalow was probably ugly when it was built, and it doesn't wear its age very well. The porch and steps are dilapidated, the siding isn't at all well, the lawn is non-existent, the roof definitely needs work and the garage seems to sag. The location is surprisingly great, and this is the only eyesore in a fine neighborhood of well-cared-for homes. While it isn't very much, it's a chance to get your children into the Midvale School District for only $47,500.

Clyde Realty   **476-8200**

The strong point in this ad is location. In addition, the ad has family appeal.

254

As Is

and it isn't very good. A rather nice West Side neighborhood is the site for this 3BR brick ranch with double garage in deplorable condition. It has been rented for several years and received minimum maintenance. Please check it out carefully because with a price of $74,500, there must be a lot more wrong with it than simply the need for new landscaping, painting and carpet.

Clyde Realty   **476-8200**

255

A Frog

One kiss and he will turn into a handsome prince. Well, not exactly, but if you have that decorator touch and a few buckets of paint and rolls of wallpaper you can turn this neglected 3BR, 2-bath Tennessee stone ranch into one of the nicest homes in a desirable West Side neighborhood. Incidentally, the home comes with a 2-car garage, full basement, central air and is on an oversized corner lot. Priced for your magic wand at $132,500.

Clyde Realty   **476-8200**

If there are many ads in the newspaper where this ad will appear, the heading should read "Fixer-Upper—Frog."

256

Fixer-Upper—4BR

An unpleasant odor permeates this brick Traditional in lovely Westport. You'll probably discover the source when you clean up the debris, but please don't tell us. We recommend that clean-up of the 8 rooms, basement and double garage start with a shovel and dump truck. This is not for the faint of heart or persons with a weak back, but a bargain is possible at $79,500.

Clyde Realty   **476-8200**

The two important features of this home are found in the simple, but effective heading.

257

Almost
Livable—4BR

Of course, something will have to be done about fixing the roof and a few broken windows. The plumbing and heating systems look intact but should be checked out. If you want to make this home presentable, that's a different matter. On the positive side, anything you do will be an improvement. The location is great and the neighbors will applaud any effort to improve this decrepit brick Colonial, but they probably prefer total demolition. Where else can you find a house for $49,500?

Clyde Realty   476-8200

This ad, with its negative tone, is designed to excite the true buyer of fixer-uppers.

258

Needs Everything

Sorry, but we couldn't come up with anything nice to say about this 9-room, brick English Tudor in Middleton Downs. It has been a long time since this home has seen any owner's love and attention. At $79,500, it's a home very few will envy.

Clyde Realty   476-8200

The positive features emphasized in this ad are size, style, location and price. It will excite the buyer of fixer-uppers.

259

It Could Be Worse

The roof doesn't appear to leak, but just about everything else in this 3BR, 2-bath, brick English Tudor in Westwood is in need of mending. While it has expansive lawns, hedges and flower beds, you'll have to imagine how it will look trimmed without the weeds and bare spots and with flowers blooming. If you love to tinker, you have enough work for a lifetime. The only redeeming feature is the price, $89,500.

Clyde Realty   476-8200

260

World War III

was not fought in this 3BR, 2-bath American Traditional home on the West Side, but it is a logical conclusion based on the condition of the place. We don't know what happened, but if it can be broken, chances are it is. A builder told us the structure is sound, but you might want to consider starting its rehabilitation with a bulldozer. This will undoubtedly please the neighbors, who would be happy to see the only blight on an otherwise quality area removed. Not much of a house at a price to match—$69,500.

Clyde Realty   476-8200

For large newspapers, consider using the 2-line heading "Fixer-Upper/World War III."

261

Definitely Not Nice

In fact, it's a 3BR disaster.

Fix It Up

and it just might be quite livable. Anyway, you can buy this West Side Cape Cod for not much more than the lot value at $67,500.

Clyde Realty   **476-8200**

This ad gives no detail about the home or its problems. It's intended to intrigue the reader to call for details.

262

Minor Problems?

The air conditioner hasn't worked for 2 years, the roof leaks and when you slam the front door, the living room lights go on. Other than that, if you paint inside and out and replace the carpet, this 3BR, 2-bath, split level in Weston Acres would be almost respectable. We hope the price encourages someone—$76,500.

Clyde Realty   **476-8200**

This ad was written to make the property appear worse than it is. Get ready for lots of calls.

263

Seven Generations of Grime

have been lovingly preserved in this 3-bedroom West Side Victorian that looks as if it hasn't been cleaned since the Indian wars. It appears solid, but perhaps the grime is just holding it together. If you're looking for "original," this is certainly the place. Anyway, it's priced far less than a clean house at $92,500.

Clyde Realty   **476-8200**

This is an unusual ad for an older, "dirty" home where the primary problem is decorating.

264

Large and Scruffy—4BR

This 9-room, 1½-bath home on the somewhat fashionable East Side offers a great deal of nondescript space. If you're the fussy type, you'll probably want to fix the hole in the roof. The ideal home for the large and scruffy family at $79,800.

Clyde Realty   **476-8200**

You'll be surprised at the people who answer this type of ad. They won't be scruffy, but they will smell a bargain.

265

Revolting—4 BR

You have probably never seen a large American Traditional home with its classic lines in such revolting condition. We estimate it will take 3 men with large shovels several days to clean this place up—just so you can see what you've gotten into. The neighborhood would be highly desirable if it weren't for this mess. Take it off our hands for $89,500. Please!

Clyde Realty   476-8200

The positive features of this home are its 4 bedrooms, classic lines and the neighborhood.

266

The Worst Home in Southport

We have the winner in the ugly-house contest with this 3BR, 2-bath, brick Italianate Traditional set on a huge South Side lot. It needs everything, starting with soap and water.

The Best Buy in Southport

Because of its horrendous condition, you have the opportunity for the buy of a lifetime at $119,500.

Clyde Realty   476-8200

An ad with a split heading is very effective in this case.

267

A Little Shabby

but very comfortable is the best description of this 3-bedroom home in West Southport. There are two trees in the backyard to hold your hammock while you contemplate when and if you will repaint the house. There's a workshop in the garage if you ever decide to do anything, but planning is much better than doing. Even the price is pleasant at $69,500.

Clyde Realty   476-8200

This ad is unusually tactful, pointing out that while the house is a fixer-upper, it is presently very livable.

268

Filthy Old House

but it does have central heat and air. There are 3 bedrooms and a double garage. It ain't much, but where else can you buy a West Side home for $69,500?

Clyde Realty   476-8200

This is a short, but effective, ad.

269

The Basement's Damp

We aren't sure if the leaking roof has anything to do with it. This brick 3BR Cape Cod in Dorchester has definitely seen better days. In its favor, there is a nice 2-car garage with a paved driveway and some beautiful trees sprinkled among the weeds and bare patches of ground. Because of unusual circumstances, this home has been vacant for over a year, so check it out carefully because with a price of just $49,500, there must be a lot more wrong with it.

Clyde Realty   **476-8200**

This ad will excite the true buyer of fixer-uppers.

270

Abandoned

by people, but we understand a family of raccoons has taken up residence in the attic of this 9-room American Traditional. The garden is a shambles, and the lawn looks as if it has never seen a mower. It needs complete decorating, but the structure appears sound. At least Mr. Murdock of our office didn't fall through the floor, and he isn't a lightweight. The location is excellent, and for $69,500 you can make us and the owner happy.

Clyde Realty   **476-8200**

271

Sleeping Princess

If you are prince charming with a bucket of paint, you can awaken this 3BR, 2-bath Colonial beauty. All she needs is a little TLC. Set on one of the nicest wooded lots in Camelot Estates, this princess will return your love. Fairy-tale-priced at only $139,500.

Clyde Realty   **476-8200**

For a large city paper, the ad heading should clearly indicate that this home is a fixer-upper. A 2-line heading can be used: "Sleeping Princess. Wake Her with a Hammer."

272

Teenager in Trouble

This home is 14 years old and abandoned. With 3 bedrooms and 1¾ baths, this Skyway Estates rambling ranch has location, a huge lot and all the extras anyone would want, but it sits alone and neglected. It needs a good cleaning and a barrel of paint. If you have a flair for decorating, this is your chance to own a fine home for only $89,500.

Clyde Realty   **476-8200**

The above heading will attract attention. While it does not indicate that the house is a fixer-upper, the only problems appear to be cosmetic, so the property will be attractive to people who ordinarily aren't interested in fixer-uppers.

273

Allergic to Work?

If so, there is no need to apply for the position of owner of this neglected 3BR, 2-bath, brick split-level on a huge wooded site (you will need a machete to find the house) in Westhaven. This home needs work, starting with a shovel and ending with a paintbrush. If you have the guts and $79,500 with $8,000 down, call for an interview.

Clyde Realty   **476-8200**

Special thanks to Ian Price of Surfer's Paradise, Australia.

274

Miss Muffet

If you are frightened by spiders, don't come near this 3BR, 2-bath, Pennsylvania Colonial on a large wooded lot in Westbury. This home has been boarded up for years while tied up in legal procedures, so we don't know what you'll find inside. Miss Clancy, from our office, says she definitely heard chains clanking when she put up the For Sale sign. The price, however, is a haunting surprise at only $132,500.

Clyde Realty   **476-8200**

While this is really an ad for a fixer-upper, potential buyers might not understand this from the heading. The ad, however, can be effectively used in a small-town newspaper where all ads are likely to be read by house hunters. The following ad was written for the same house.

275

Ghosts!

If you are easily frightened, don't come near this 3BR, 2-bath Pennsylvania Colonial on a large wooded lot in Westbury. The home has been boarded up for years while tied up in legal procedures, so we don't know what you'll find inside. Miss Clancy, from our office, claims she definitely heard chains clanking when she put up the For Sale sign. The price, however, is a haunting surprise at only $132,500.

Clyde Realty   **476-8200**

The above heading will really attract attention to a home that has been vacant for some time.

276

An Orphan

Abandoned by its owners, this 3BR, 1½-bath, neglected Cape Cod needs family love and lots of TLC. While it has a double garage, fireplace, central air, hardwood floors and a full basement, it will take a lot of work to make it the showplace of Holiday Hills. It is, however, priced as a fixer-upper at $94,500.

Clyde Realty   **476-8200**

For a large paper, consider "Orphan—Fixer-Upper" as the heading.

277

Yuk! This Place Is Unbelievable

This 3-bedroom, West Side American Traditional appears to have been neglected from the day it was built. It will take a semi to haul away the junk in the backyard. Perhaps under all that dirt you might find shining splendor, but don't count on it. But then for $59,500, what do you expect?

Clyde Realty   **476-8200**

This was adapted from an ad by Ian Price, Surfer's Paradise, Australia.

278

Fixer-Upper

is a generous description for this 3BR, 2-bath ranch home that has seen better days. The toilets gurgle, paint is peeling and the carpet is threadbare. It's the worst house in an otherwise pristine enclave of fine homes in Westview Terrace. It will take real guts to attempt to bring this home back to life. The price of $97,500 reflects its near terminal condition.

Clyde Realty   **476-8200**

279

It Used To Be Nice

or so the neighbors tell us—that is, before renters moved into this 3BR, 2-bath Colonial. Right now you can see more bare earth than lawn, the shrubs haven't been trimmed in ages and the house has forgotten what a paintbrush feels like. On the positive side, it is the only rotten house in a great West Side neighborhood. The lot is large, there's an oversized 2-car garage, and the house appears basically sound. If you don't mind getting involved, it offers a unique opportunity at $139,500.

Clyde Realty   **476-8200**

280

You Finish—You Save

This 3BR, 2-bath Colorado Contemporary is almost ready to occupy. It needs some interior finishing, utility hookups, appliances, floor covering and decorating. Almost 2,000 sq. ft. of living space, a massive stone fireplace and a 2-car attached garage on an estate-sized lot in Northport are offered at a price you are unlikely to see again, $119,500.

Clyde Realty   **476-8200**

Homes that need finishing should be advertised in a manner similar to fixer-uppers if the buyer must do the work.

281

Fire Sale

This 3-bedroom ranch in Westview has suffered extensive fire damage.

Fix It Up

and you can save a bundle. Check this one out quickly at $59,500.

Clyde Realty   **476-8200**

Fire-damaged homes can be effectively advertised as fixer-uppers.

282

Damaged by the [Flood] [Earthquake]

The owners have left the problems of this 3BR, 2-bath Cape Cod in one of the finest West Side residential areas. While the home offers a double garage, separate family room, fireplace, screened porch and lavish use of tile and hardwoods, it needs work. If you can visualize what is needed in cleanup, repairs and redecorating, we believe this to be an unusual opportunity at $124,500.

Clyde Realty   **476-8200**

This ad is, of course, aimed at buyers of fixer-uppers who can visualize the home's potential. The extent of work needed is left uncertain to make readers call for details.

8

General Home Ads

You will have no difficulty quickly tailoring a number of the ads in this chapter to fit any home you have for sale. If you wish an ad tailored to a specific feature or simply want advertising language for that feature, use the Index to find the language or ad that meets your needs.

283

Sanctuary

Off a quiet lane on a wooded knoll stands a white clapboard, American Gothic, 3-bedroom home. When you enter the long drive, you will feel you are returning to a gentler period when you were safe and secure. The solid construction and workmanship of this fine home will delight you. There is a separate 2-car garage and storage shed on almost an acre, and it's priced for your family at $89,500.

Clyde Realty **476-8200**

This ad sells a mood. If a house has strong positive features, they should be stated. The above ad is probably for a 1-bath, older home.

284

High Fuel Bills?

When you see last year's heating costs, you'll appreciate this super-insulated, energy-efficient, better-than-new, 3BR, 2-bath split ranch in Newport. There is a 2-car garage and a farm-sized kitchen that will please any cook. You will love the huge beech and oak trees and specimen plantings. At $139,500, it's indeed a home you can warm up to.

Clyde Realty **476-8200**

This ad should be used during a cold winter snap. For southern areas, change the heading to "High Electric Bills?"

285

Don't Believe Us

We couldn't possibly be offering a 3BR, 2-bath, Quaker Colonial loaded with every extra you want and more on the nicest lot in Westbrook Estates for only $169,000. Call us today and try to prove us wrong.

Clyde Realty   **476-8200**

286

We Dare You

to view this 3BR, 2-bath Pennsylvania Colonial on a wooded, estate-sized setting in Fallbrook and fail to buy it. Your green thumb will begin to itch when you see the indescribable garden. There's a basement workroom that's a hobbyist's delight and the 2+++-car garage has room for everything you own. The clincher will be the price—only $139,500.

Clyde Realty   **476-8200**

287

We Lied

if we said this 3-bedroom Colonial is like new in a prestigious location. As a matter of fact, it's over 30 years old, and the neighborhood, while nice, is certainly not prestigious. If we were to be truthful, we would simply say, "It's a solid family home in a friendly neighborhood, and it's one heck of a value at $87,500 with a low-interest assumable loan."

Clyde Realty   **476-8200**

This ad has an attention-getting heading.

288

Want a House or a Home?

There's a difference. Why settle for an ordinary house when you can own this 3BR, 2-bath Westwood Colonial that will pay dividends for years in comfort and family happiness. Special features include family room, central air, 2½-car garage, spacious rooms, dream kitchen with every conceivable built-in and landscaping to win you a garden club award. Priced to sell quickly at $249,500.

Clyde Realty   **476-8200**

289

Going—Going!

And it will probably be gone in a few days. This is a 3BR, 1½-bath Cape Cod on an estate-sized, wooded lot in the highly desirable Hilldale School District. Special features include double garage, full basement with recreation room and photography darkroom, antique brick fireplace, central air and a very private dining patio. It won't last at $137,500.

Clyde Realty　　　**476-8200**

290

Mrs. Jones Was Intoxicated

with the beauty of this 3BR, 2-bath Nantucket Colonial. She loves the delightful garden and fabulous plantings. This house has everything on her wish list—premier West Side location, family room, full basement, built-in everything—and it's only

$10,000 Down

with below-market financing. If you ask her about this house, she will probably switch you to her own home since, if she can sell her place, *she* will be the buyer at $169,500.

Clyde Realty　　　**476-8200**

291

Garage Sale

Along with the oversized double garage, you get a 3-bedroom brick rambler on a quiet, tree-lined West Side street. There's room for a garden, and you'll love the dining patio shaded by two magnificent maples. This home has a full basement ideal for a rainy-day playroom or ? Special features include a huge, bright country kitchen; hardwood floors; and new Berber carpeting. A home for a lot of living at $89,500.

Clyde Realty　　　**476-8200**

292

Love for Sale

No, it isn't that kind of house; it is a home showing years of loving care. This fine 3BR, 2-bath Italian Renaissance residence with an oversized 2-car garage has been meticulously maintained. Exquisite flowers and shrubs, manicured lawns and gleaming woodwork all show the owner's affection. It's surely a home to return your love at $98,500.

Clyde Realty　　　**476-8200**

293

Someone Cared

and it is reflected in the immaculate condition of this 3BR, 1½-bath brick rambler with a full, finished basement and double garage in lovely Westmont. You will love the storybook garden, huge trees and toe-warming fireplace. You won't want to touch a thing, and it's yours at only $89,500.

Clyde Realty   **476-8200**

294

Frigid They Said

when they entered this 3BR, 2-bath brick English Tudor with central air. No more sleepless nights in a home that has everything including an intimate den, full basement awaiting your imagination, double garage and a garden to make your green thumb itch. A hot value in a cool house at $139,500.

Clyde Realty   **476-8200**

The above heading will attract attention to the ad.

295

A Cool Colonial

Central air conditioning makes summers enjoyable in this 3-bedroom, 2-bath Colonial. In a premier Woodland Hills location, this impressive residence has everything on your wish list plus a den or studio with private entrance, vegetable garden to make any farmer jealous, huge double garage and a price that won't require you to mortgage the children—$149,500.

Clyde Realty   **476-8200**

Feature air conditioning only when advertising in areas where many better homes do not have central air.

296

Pssst!

Want a hot deal on a cold house? The owner says, "Get what you can for this 3BR, 1½-bath, Westbrook Cape Cod with 2-car garage, new carpeting, dream tile kitchen and central air." For you there's a special price of $97,500, but don't tell a soul.

Clyde Realty   **476-8200**

297

A Good Ole Boy

would love this 3-bedroom Country Traditional with its farm-sized kitchen; down-home, rocking-chair front porch; fenced yard perfect for keeping hound dogs; and some very pretty trees and flowers. This is real country livin' in a small-town neighborhood right here in the city at a country price of $79,500.

Clyde Realty   476-8200

298

Business Is Rotten

because we can't keep anything in our inventory. When calls come in, we have to say, "We're sorry. We have nothing left." I know this 3BR, 2-bath home in Westchester will sell this weekend because it's priced at only $89,500 and the owners will supply below-market-rate financing. Why can't we get some property that doesn't sell like some of the other brokers?

Clyde Realty   476-8200

The above heading will attract attention.

299

First Offering

A 3BR, 2-bath California-style ranch in prestigious Oakbrook with a 2-car, attached garage; family room with native stone fireplace; and new Berber carpeting, but it's going to be your

Last Chance

since it will sell fast at the offering price of only $167,500.

Clyde Realty   476-8200

This is an unusual, attention-getting ad with a split heading.

A property that is new on the market will interest many buyers who feel there must be something wrong with a property that has been available for a long time.

300

First Curtain Call

This is the first time this 3BR, 2-bath, double-garage French Regency in Morningside Heights has been on the market since it was built. It includes everything on your wish list plus some things you never even knew you had to have. An exceptional opportunity at $198,500.

Clyde Realty   476-8200

This ad indicates that the first owner of the house is now selling it.

301

Never Shown

This 3BR, 1½-bath Tennessee stone ranch home has just become available. There is an oversized double garage, a full basement and 2 fireplaces on an estate-sized lot in the finest neighborhood of Southport. The best part is its price, at only $167,500.

Clyde Realty   476-8200

302

A Wrought-Iron Gate

leads you down a flower-bedecked walk to the soaring, double-door entry of this dramatic California Contemporary. This home features 3 bedrooms, 2½ baths, family room, pool, sumptuous hot spa and every amenity you can find in *Better Homes and Gardens*. Over 3,500 sq. ft. of living thoughtfully planned to provide you with the ultimate life-style at $329,500.

Clyde Realty   476-8200

303

Norman Rockwell

painted this house, or at least I think he did. This 3-bedroom American Traditional comes with a white picket fence; stone walk bedecked with flowers; and bright, happy rooms made for a family. There's even a big oak tree in the backyard with a tire swing. It's too perfect to last long at $89,500.

Clyde Realty   476-8200

304

Surrender to Comfort

Don't you deserve a 3-bedroom, brick split ranch in Morningside Heights with 1¾ baths; a double garage; and a huge, fenced yard with room for a garden? At only $98,500 and with a low-low down payment, it's easy to pamper yourself. Call.

Clyde Realty   476-8200

Give the square footage only when it is greater than one would expect.

305

"Maggie's Drawers"

When Maggie had this 3BR, 2-bath, double-garage Colonial built, she insisted on 24 feet of custom kitchen cabinets to hold all of her pans and dishes. She also insisted on double ovens and built-ins normally only associated with far more expensive homes. There's a huge family room with a river-rock fireplace, a patio that you'll agree is very special and a sunny garden spot on the oversized lot in one of the nicest West Side areas. It's your chance to own Maggie's house, drawers and all, for $132,500.

Clyde Realty   **476-8200**

"Maggie's Drawers" is a well-known military term for a miss on the rifle range.

306

Decorator's Own

3-bedroom, 2½-bath, brick Traditional with an attached 2-car garage, family room, central air and delightful patio in the very best Westlake wooded setting. New neutral Berber carpeting, soft colors and wall coverings you won't find in any store add color accents to make this a home to be envied at $247,500.

Clyde Realty   **476-8200**

307

Maxine and Marvin Slept Here

for 10 years, but Marvin was transferred to Phoenix, so they must regretfully take their bed and leave this 3BR, 2-bath, redbrick Georgian Colonial in the nicest area in all of Woodland Glen. The home features a tantalizing jacuzzi tub in the master bath, which is why the shower is practically new; walk-in closets; music room for little Ralph, who is learning to play the drums; and a kitchen any chef would fry for. Priced to get Maxine and Marvin on their way at $137,500.

Clyde Realty   **476-8200**

308

Millionaire's Home

Multimillionaire jetting off to faraway places wants to sell her 3BR, 2-bath, brick American Traditional in a prime close-in location. Features include a 2-car garage plus room to park an RV, hardwood floors, large screened porch and private back garden. Happily priced at $89,500.

Clyde Realty   **476-8200**

Many millionaires actually live in relatively modest homes. Many middle-class purchasers take pride in knowing that their homes were previously owned by millionaires or famous people.

309

Banker's Home

A quiet, tree-canopied street of fine homes is the site of this redbrick, 3BR, 2½-bath Georgian Colonial. This home exudes a quiet elegance with its high ceilings, paneled music room and antique brick fireplace. Decorated with soft tones, it is bound to please the most fastidious buyer. Other amenities include a 2+-car garage, zone-controlled heating and cooling, finished basement ideal for a home fitness center and landscaping you'll take pride in. This fine residence is proudly offered at $297,500.

Clyde Realty   **476-8200**

The fact that the above home was owned by a banker will give the house an image of unpretentious quality.

310

Lady
Saxophone Player

must sell her 3BR, cedar-shake, Westfield Cape Cod in order to seek fame and fortune. There are a garage, several magnificent hickory trees, a family of squirrels, a somewhat neglected garden and a kitchen big enough to seat an 8-piece band. The price hits a pleasant note at $129,500.

Clyde Realty   **476-8200**

311

Builder's Own

Constructed by a master builder for his own family, only the very best is featured in this Hillsdale Estates, 3BR, 2½-bath Nantucket Colonial. You will see this in the solid walnut paneling of the music room, Karastan carpeting and fine imported tile. This home exudes the very best set amidst landscaping that would be the envy of a garden club. Realistically priced at $279,500.

Clyde Realty   **476-8200**

People expect a builder's own home to be quality-built.

312

Tuba Player

out of breath and must sell this 3BR, 2-bath, New England-inspired town house located in an area of prestigious homes. There's a separate music room not quite soundproof, a private sun-bathing porch and a perfect garden spot. The price won't hit a sour note at $124,500.

Clyde Realty   **476-8200**

The hobby of a home's owner can be used to create a catchy heading.

313

Former Model Home

This 3BR, 2-bath Carolina Colonial in Brentwood Heights was upgraded beyond belief with every conceivable convenience and builder's option. Professionally landscaped and decorated by Wimsey Carter in soft earth tones, it is truly a delight to the senses. Special features include a split plan for privacy, 2+++-car garage, magnificent fireplace, wet bar, Eurostyle family kitchen, family room and a delightful dining patio. The best part is that it's priced no more than an ordinary home at $179,500.

Clyde Realty   **476-8200**

Mentioning the name of the decorator, even if not well known, makes a home more desirable.

314

Lucky House

A former owner won the lottery. This 3BR, 2-bath, brick American Traditional set on a lovely tree-lined street in a family area is your opportunity for years of pleasure. Pride of ownership shows in every aspect of this fine home. At $89,500, this is going to be your lucky day.

Clyde Realty   **476-8200**

If a former owner was lucky, it will entice buyers who take luck very seriously.

315

Mr. & Mrs. Clean

are moving. Their 3BR, 1½-bath, West Side Cape Cod set amidst immaculate landscaping is available for the first time. This home offers a double garage; full basement; stone fireplace; and French doors opening onto a covered patio, perfect for dining or relaxation. Wear your white gloves and check it out. You won't find another like it at $147,500.

Clyde Realty   **476-8200**

316

Orthodox Druid

wishes to sell this 3-bedroom, West Side, Colonial Manor House so she can commune with nature. Actually, this home is in like-new condition, as I think the owner spent most of her time tending her magnificent flower, vegetable and herb gardens. There's a delightful conservatory perfect for an artist's studio. If you buy the house, don't cut down the big oak in the front yard, as the owner indicated that it's her great grandfather. Priced to send the owner away quickly at $189,500.

Clyde Realty   **476-8200**

This ad will attract attention and much discussion, but make sure you have an owner with a slightly twisted sense of humor who agrees to the ad.

317

Mrs. Higgins Was Mortified

when she discovered that the last visitors to her 3BR, 2½-bath, double-garage Colonial had walked on the sparkling ceramic-tile floor and soft Berber carpeting with dirty shoes. She says that she won't sell her dream home to people like that. If you really want a home that surpasses everything you have seen, in an estate setting and for $187,500, then you better wipe your feet first.

Clyde Realty **476-8200**

319

Music Lovers Wanted

The piano stays with this 3BR, 2-bath Dutch Colonial sheltered by towering maples on the nicest street in Southport. The home offers a full basement big enough for your recitals, a large great room with fireplace, hardwood floors and a delightful dining patio. Even the price is in tune at $164,500.

Clyde Realty **476-8200**

The ad body in the above could also say "There is a separate music room in this. . . ."

318

Muscle Man

You can keep those deltoids in shape in the fitness room and sauna of this 3BR, 2-bath Cape Cod on one of the most desirable streets in Westchester Estates. Included are a family-sized kitchen with breakfast nook, formal dining room, and a 30-foot living room with a massive orchard stone fireplace. There is an estate-sized, fenced and gated yard. Priced at a relaxing $169,500.

Clyde Realty **476-8200**

320

The Great American Novel

is waiting to be written in the large, sun-drenched studio of this 3BR, 2-bath Tennessee stone ranch set on a secluded, tree-lined street in Westhaven. Beneath a towering oak, it is truly the place for quiet contemplation. Your escape from the world at $139,500.

Clyde Realty **476-8200**

321

Photographers Do It in the Dark

This 3BR, 2-bath American Traditional has a large basement darkroom perfect for the professional or dedicated amateur. Other features include a private patio off the family room/kitchen, a spectacular flower garden, several magnificent oak trees and a friendly family neighborhood. Develop this opportunity at $149,500.

Clyde Realty   **476-8200**

322

Mint Julep Time

The veranda of this classic, columned Southern Colonial is the perfect spot to end the long days of summer in gentle relaxation and conversation with family and close friends. You'll look out upon a huge emerald lawn with lovingly cared-for flowers, on a quiet street reflecting an elegant way of life. The house is only 7 years old, but the architect captured the ambiance of the old South. Included are 3 bedrooms, 2½ baths, a den with its own entry, a pool with hot spa and every amenity you can possibly want. Offering the good life at $389,500.

Clyde Realty   **476-8200**

323

Turn Off the Lights

and see what develops. Photographers will love this 3BR, 2-bath, almost-new ranch in Pacific Heights. There's a darkroom in the basement and a yard full of colorful plantings and shrubs. Picture yourself as the owner for $149,500.

Clyde Realty   **476-8200**

324

Absolute Privacy

Set back behind a screen of trees and flowering bushes, this 3-bedroom American Traditional cannot be viewed from the quiet street. You can swim in nature's garments in the in-ground, sparkling pool. You'll love the family-sized organic garden, apple and pear trees and the huge workroom or studio in the oversized garage. It's the home you dreamed of and deserve at $198,500.

Clyde Realty   **476-8200**

People who like privacy are interested in self-sufficiency and are likely to be health conscious.

325

Why Settle for Vanilla

when you can have it all—charming breakfast patio; an estate-sized lot in a neighborhood you only dream of; and this 3BR, 2-bath, cedar and stone Colorado Contemporary offering a forever view through walls of glass. You will be delighted with the kitchen of tomorrow and will relax in the paneled music room. At only $193,500, you need not settle for the ordinary.

Clyde Realty   **476-8200**

326

Yak! Yak!

You'll need a Sherpa guide to climb the driveway, but your journey will not be in vain. Sweeping views and space to spare are just two of the virtues of this 3BR, 2½-bath former model home. If you have ever missed an exceptional opportunity before, you better call immediately. With a price of $149,500, it's unlikely we'll repeat this ad.

Clyde Realty   **476-8200**

Special thanks to Ian Price of Surfer's Paradise, Australia.

327

Expect
To Be Impressed

when you enter this 3BR, 2-bath European Renaissance masterpiece. From the lush landscaping to the European-inspired kitchen, this home offers everything on your wish list including a quiet, sun-lighted studio to delight any artist. An opportunity not be missed at $179,500.

Clyde Realty   **476-8200**

328

What's Not To Like?

This 3BR, 2-bath California-inspired ranch features a separate family room for informal entertaining and a living room with a view of a wonderland of flowering shrubs and stately maples. There's even a picnic-perfect patio and full basement ideal for a rainy-day playroom or workshop. Of course, there's also a double garage. As much as you will like this house, you'll love the price even better—$119,500.

Clyde Realty   **476-8200**

If the newspaper in which you advertise doesn't have a heading category for a specific area and the area is desirable, mention it in the ad heading. For example, "Westwood, What's Not To Like?"

329

Grab the Phone

Tomorrow may be too late. This 3-bedroom Cape Cod in the Hilldale School District won't last long because it has a double garage, full basement, delightful garden and is priced at only $119,500.

Clyde Realty   **476-8200**

This is a short, but effective, ad.

330

Grab Your Reeboks

and run to see this 3BR, 2½-bath ranch on the nicest street in Westhaven. With a 2+-car garage, landscaping your friends will envy, soaring ceilings, large bright rooms, family room, fireplace and everything else on your wish list, you better get here fast, as it won't last at $187,500.

Clyde Realty   **476-8200**

331

Question

Where can I find a 3BR, 2-bath home in a prime Fox Point location with a fireplace and 2-car garage for under $150,000?

Answer

We have the house and can throw in a finished basement recreation room, lovely garden and an over-sized wooded lot for just $147,500 if you call now!

Clyde Realty   **476-8200**

332

No Place Like Home

when home is a 3-bedroom, New England clapboard Colonial set back off of a quiet street in a village setting. You'll fall in love with the prize-winning roses and will feel compelled to sample an apple from one of 3 trees. There is an oversized garage with room for generations of collectables. All it needs is you at $79,500.

Clyde Realty   **476-8200**

333

Spellbound

is the way you will leave this stunningly conceived, lovingly maintained 3-bedroom American classic. From the leaded-glass entry with slate tile to the great room with polished oak floors and extensive use of hardwood trim, you'll appreciate the quality of this fine residence. The mature landscaping rivals any you have ever seen. Call, and we'll prove that for $89,500 you can have a home that has not known compromise.

Clyde Realty   **476-8200**

This ad can be easily modified for a newer home.

334

As Good As It Gets

You can have a rocking-chair front porch, an intimate dining patio, sundrenched kitchen, 3 king-sized bedrooms, 2 full baths, double garage, room for an RV, choice neighborhood and a price under $100,000 with less than 10 percent down. It doesn't get any better than this.

Clyde Realty   **476-8200**

335

Beer and Pretzels

may be described by some as cocktails and hors d'oeuvres, but when we say this 3BR, 2-bath, white clapboard Pennsylvania Colonial on a wooded half-acre estate site in Westport is magnificent, it's great by anyone's standards. This fine residence offers an antique brick fireplace, a den paneled in rich cherry, central air, a kitchen surpassing anything your friends have ever seen and a huge screened porch for summer relaxation or entertaining. First one to the phone will be the winner at $187,500.

Clyde Realty   **476-8200**

336

House

Bedroom—Bedroom—Bedroom—Bath—Bath—Garage—Garage—Family Room—Den—Porch—Fruit Trees—Garden—View—Price, $159,900.

Clyde Realty   **476-8200**

Of course it is a 3BR, 2-bath house with a double garage. The ad will be deciphered by the readers.

337

They Wouldn't Believe Me

when I told them we had a newer, 3BR, brick, 2-bath ranch home with double garage, central air, and room to park their RV on the West Side for only $89,500. Maybe I was lying, but just suppose I wasn't. Call Cliff Henderson at

Clyde Realty   **476-8200**

Note that this ad names a particular salesperson.

338

We Want Your Money

and you will certainly get your money's worth with this 3BR, 2-bath Italian Traditional set on a corner site in desirable Westlake Hills. Special features include a formal dining room, huge kitchen with tons of imported tile, walk-in closets, a tasteful neutral decor, dining patio and landscaping that will be the envy of the garden club. For all this, we only want $179,500, and we will be satisfied with $15,000 down.

Clyde Realty   **476-8200**

This ad will generate interest.

339

If It Ain't Broken

don't fix it. This 3BR, 1½-bath Cape Cod in Weston Heights is perfect the way it is. It has landscaping to turn your friends green with envy; new Berber carpeting; drapes in soft, neutral tones; a fully finished basement ready for your hobbies, entertaining or as a fitness center; and a great deal more. It's ready for you at $89,500.

Clyde Realty   **476-8200**

340

Buy

Buy Location—Midvale School District
Buy Size—3BR + den, 2 baths
Buy Style—French Regency
Buy Terms—90 percent financing available
Buy Price—$169,500

Clyde Realty   **476-8200**

341

Don't
Waste Our Time

if you're not a serious buyer. However, if you are and want a 3BR, 2-bath, double-garage, sprawling American ranch home on a huge lot in prestigious Meadow Wood, then we can help. This home has a huge family room, tiled country kitchen and a perfect garden area. It's better than new and realistically priced at $189,500.

Clyde Realty   **476-8200**

A negative heading attracts attention. (See chapter 19 for negative ads.)

342

The American Dream

You can have a white 3BR Cape Cod home set on a quiet, tree-canopied street amidst flowering shrubs and stately walnut trees and neighbors who care and share your joys, hopes and concerns. It's truly an investment in your peace of mind at $129,500.

Clyde Realty   **476-8200**

This ad appeals to the buyer's emotion, rather than emphasizing the house itself.

343

If You Have
Looked Around

you will immediately buy this 3BR, 2½-bath, West Side stone rambler. From location, condition, decorating and amenities too numerous to mention, you will realize this is indeed a rare offering at $139,500.

Clyde Realty   **476-8200**

344

You Just Found It

The perfect home: 3 king-sized bedrooms, 2 gleaming tile baths, an oversized double garage, a neighborhood you dream about and a huge lot with room for a garden and a pool. Everything about this fine residence is impressive except the price, $149,500.

Clyde Realty   **476-8200**

345

Were You the One

who called about this 3BR, 2-bath Colonial on the huge wooded lot in Westport available with only $5,000 down?

We Goofed

when we told you it was sold, as it is still available. We also failed to tell you about the double garage, central air, family room and full basement. By the way, the price has been reduced to $187,500.

Clyde Realty   **476-8200**

See the following ad for a slightly different treatment.

346

Are You the One

who called on the 3BR, 2-bath, brick Traditional in Southby Hills and was told it was sold? The sale fell through so it's available again. We didn't tell you that the basement is fully finished, there is a built-in workbench in the double garage, a jacuzzi tub in the master bath, a patio ready for a barbecue, 4 fruit trees for pies and home canning as well as a sunny garden spot. This is your second chance at $137,500.

Clyde Realty   **476-8200**

347

Take Your Choice

We have 4 3-bedroom ranch homes with attached garages. All have great West Side locations, and all are priced under $90,000. Call now to get the first pick.

Clyde Realty   **476-8200**

This is a simple way to show that you offer a choice.

The words "first pick" add a sense of urgency to this ad.

348

West Side—5 Homes

We have 5 3BR, 2-bath homes all with double garage and basement in desirable areas and all are priced from

$90,000 to $98,500

They have different features such as fireplaces, central air, recreation rooms, family rooms, wet bars, dens, and so forth. Call for your private tour of these fine homes, but we warn you, you will like them all, so the choice won't be easy.

Clyde Realty   **476-8200**

Use this unusual approach when you have a number of similar homes or a number of homes in the same area. The ad is very effective.

349

A Tough Decision

You'll have a problem deciding which of these 2 fine 3BR, 2-bath homes in Oregon Highlands to buy. One is a Dutch Colonial, and the other is a California Contemporary. They have some different features, but they are priced identically at

$187,500

Call now, and we will let you make the decision.

Clyde Realty   **476-8200**

350

Prices Are Too High

but they are going to get higher. In a few years you'll be telling your friends that you nearly purchased this 3BR, 2½-bath French Regency on almost a half-acre in Westwood for only

$197,500

You'll tell them about the paneled den, 2 fireplaces, delightful dining patio, huge garden area and the breathtaking landscaping. If you want to tell this story, call today, but don't bring your checkbook.

Clyde Realty   **476-8200**

351

Sorry!

You'll probably be too late to buy this 3BR, 2-bath Pennsylvania Dutch Colonial on the nicest street in Newport. At only $129,500, you know it will be sold to the first buyer who sees it.

Clyde Realty   **476-8200**

Very little is said about the house. This ad will bring in calls from people wanting more information.

352

Leave a Message

We'll be out showing this 3BR, 2-bath, brick New England Traditional on a quiet, wooded cul-de-sac in Westbury Heights. The customers will love the family room with its view of a wooded ravine—home to chipmunks, squirrels and a friendly raccoon. The huge garage, full basement, walk-in closets and solid oak woodwork will surely influence them in their decision to buy. When we call back, we might just tell you the house is sold. For your general information, if you call early, you can have it for $179,500.

Clyde Realty   **476-8200**

353

A Perfect 10

She shows well with her heart-stopping face, beautiful lines and perfect proportions. This 3-bedroom, 2-bath Colonial Ranch was designed with your family's comfort in mind. It has a toe-warming, native stone fireplace; farm-style kitchen with room for the whole crew and their friends; family room for relaxation; and a living room large enough for a grand piano. The 2½-car garage offers plenty of storage space. Whatever is on your wish list, we bet this beauty has it. Priced for you at $189,500.

Clyde Realty   **476-8200**

354

Have a Great Summer

on the picnic-perfect, shaded patio of this 3BR, 2-bath West Side Traditional. You'll love the huge trees and sunny garden spot, the double garage with room for a workbench, the full dry basement that awaits your imagination and the bright feeling of spaciousness. Look and you're going to own at $129,500.

Clyde Realty   **476-8200**

355

The Next To Go

This 3-bedroom, 2-bath French Provincial in Clayton Hills will be sold in a matter of days. The home has parklike grounds, is in pristine condition, has a huge family room and is located on a quiet cul-de-sac. We think it is the best buy on the market at $149,500.

Clyde Realty   **476-8200**

356

Like To Sit

and watch your neighbors run, jog and bike? The covered front porch of this 3BR, 2½-bath Victorian-inspired masterpiece is just the spot for watching. Shaded by giant beech and maples, this is indeed a tranquil spot. The wide, quiet, tree-lined street seems to act as a magnet to exercise freaks. Be strong, or you could be drawn into the madness. All yours at a lazy $189,500.

Clyde Realty   **476-8200**

"Victorian-inspired" means it is of fairly recent vintage but built in the Victorian architectural style.

357

Off a Quiet Road

is the home of your dreams. This 3BR, 2-bath American Traditional is guarded by giant hemlocks that stand like sentinels to the world. You'll revel in the warmth of the wood paneling and comfort of the rose brick fireplace. A captivating, beautiful home with everything you can possibly want or need. This retreat from stressful living can be yours at $187,500.

Clyde Realty   **476-8200**

358

This Ad Will Not Be Repeated

as this spacious 3-bedroom, 2½-bath, split-level Arizona Contemporary is bound to sell to the first viewer. Definitely better than new, this is a home to capture your vision of tomorrow with every contemporary comfort imaginable. Irresistibly priced at $149,500.

Clyde Realty   **476-8200**

359

Ben Franklin Said

don't be "penny wise and pound foolish." Sure, this newer 3BR, 2-bath Colonial ranch on a quiet street in Westhaven costs more than some other homes, but compare what you get for those few extra dollars. It has the most sought-after location, an oversized double garage, professional landscaping, upgraded appliances and carpet, matched hardwood floors and trim, soaring ceilings, an orchard stone fireplace, zone-control heating and cooling, walk-in closets, jacuzzi tubs and so much more. Ten years from now, your friends won't believe you only paid $198,500.

Clyde Realty   **476-8200**

360

Don't Want To Be Envied?

Then don't buy this 3BR, 2½-bath French Regency in exclusive Pinewood Estates. This house stands out even among the fine homes in the area because of its classic lines. It has amenities normally only seen in magazines. Whoever buys this home is bound to be envied by their friends. Not as expensive as your friends will imagine at $279,500.

Clyde Realty   **476-8200**

The ad, of course, appeals to those who want to impress others.

361

Just the Facts

This one-of-a-kind 3BR, 2-bath, split-level ranch has everything you want and some things you haven't even considered, but once you see them, they will be high on your want list. There is a 2½-car garage, a large hobby area on the lower level, 2 fireplaces, and built-in everything (including a central vacuum system and intercom). To describe the landscaping as awesome would be an understatement. The best part is that it is priced no more than an ordinary home at $169,500.

Clyde Realty   **476-8200**

362

There Is a Difference

between Ho Hum and Wow! This 3BR, 2-bath Colorado Contemporary with knee-to-ceiling walls of glass, cantilevered decks, forever views and the ambiance of light and space that seemingly makes nature one with the living areas is a one-of-a-kind masterpiece. The only thing ordinary is the price—$289,500.

Clyde Realty   **476-8200**

363

Low Taxes

One of the lowest tax rates in the state and only 40 minutes from the civic center are just 2 of the advantages of this 3BR, 2-bath split-level ranch on its almost half-acre, wooded site. The house appears practically new, the neighbors are friendly, the schools are great and low-down FHA financing is available. Hey! What more do you want for $114,500?

Clyde Realty   **476-8200**

364

Appreciate the Appreciation

The value on this 3BR, 2-bath West Side home with a double garage should soar. Besides providing an investment, the home is a very pleasant place to live with its large fenced yard, fruit trees and lovely garden. There is new carpeting, and it's ready for your furniture. In a few years, you'll brag that you only paid $89,500.

Clyde Realty   **476-8200**

This ad shows that a home purchase represents an investment as well as the fulfillment of family needs.

365

Going! Going!

You can have a 3-bedroom home on the nicest street in Westmont that's not priced beyond your means. This one will be *gone* at $179,500.

Clyde Realty   476-8200

This ad's primary selling point is price. Ads like this can be used when a home is priced for less than most of the other homes in an area.

366

Fast Eddie

might have a chance to be first to our office to buy this 3BR, 2-bath, double-garage, executive ranch in Brynwood Acres. If he wins the race, his reward will be one very fine home at only $119,500.

Clyde Realty   476-8200

The following ad uses a different treatment for the same home.

367

Beat It!

You can try, but you won't find a 3BR, 2-bath, double-garage, executive ranch home in Brynwood Acres for a lower price than we are asking—$119,500.

Clyde Realty   476-8200

368

Leave It to Beaver

Hey! His home and neighborhood really do exist, and they can be yours. You'll love this 3BR, 1¾-bath, two-story, white clapboard Colonial with its wide, covered porch; picket fence; and quiet tree-canopied street. It's as if a whole neighborhood was taken from the past and lovingly preserved for your future. This is definitely a *must see* at $89,500.

Clyde Realty   476-8200

This ad mostly sells image. Very little is said about the house itself. The purpose of the ad is to whet the reader's appetite for more information.

369

Never Again

will you find a 3BR, 2-bath ranch home with a double garage and full basement on an oversized lot in the Hillsdale School District for only $92,500.

Clyde Realty   476-8200

This is a short and effective ad. If a school district is considered extremely desirable, a still more effective ad is

Hillsdale School District

Never again will you find. . . .

370

Escape the Ordinary

This 3BR, 2-bath, brick American Traditional is resplendent in unique details—from the carved cherry balustrades to the stained-glass panels beside the door. Set in a neighborhood where pride in one's home is clearly evident, this fine residence is superior in every aspect but price. Offered at a very reasonable $89,500.

Clyde Realty   **476-8200**

It is very likely that this is an older home in an established neighborhood.

371

3-Bedroom— 2-Bath Home—Free

with purchase of double garage at

$179,500

The home is a French Regency designed by Cathbert Reynolds, located on an estate-sized, wooded site in Longview Acres. It has all the amenities you want, including music room, delightful patio and curved concrete drive. This home deserves your immediate attention.

Clyde Realty   **476-8200**

If a home was designed by an architect, mentioning his or her name adds prestige even when the architect is not well known.

372

Don't Get Too Excited

If the owners see how much you want this 3BR, 2½-bath American Traditional on an estate-sized lot in Westwood, they are liable to raise the price. With the huge family room, exotic plantings and dramatically proportioned rooms, what's not to like? Just seem mildly interested and you should be able to buy this masterpiece for only $179,500.

Clyde Realty   **476-8200**

373

Historic Home

It was just 1 year ago that Homer Clapmeyer invented the electric paper clip while staying as a guest in this 3BR, 2-bath modern American classic in Westwood Heights. He used the workroom in the 2½-car, attached garage to build his prototype, which was tested before dozens of relatives in the huge family room. Today his name is a household word. This is your chance to own a bit of American history for only $97,500.

Clyde Realty   **476-8200**

This ad is a spoof on ads for historic homes often found in southern and eastern papers. It will definitely cause much discussion.

374

You've Got It—

the finest area in Westwood; a 3BR, 2½-bath Colonial with a 3-car garage; and landscaping to be envied.

Flaunt It

Entertain your friends on the huge patio terrace with a bubbling fountain and screen of greenery. The finished full basement is ideal for an office party. Everyone will think you paid much more than $179,500.

Clyde Realty   **476-8200**

375

Want a Steal?

Then we suggest you contact someone else. But if you want to buy the nicest 3BR, 2-bath American Colonial in Clydesdale Estates at a fair price with below-market financing, then consider this fine home. Of course it has a fireplace, family room, covered patio, 2½-car garage and all the built-ins. What makes it special is the warmth of the authentic colonial design and spaciousness of the bright interior with its free-flowing floor plan. Fairly priced at $189,500.

Clyde Realty   **476-8200**

376

Pyromaniac

You'll love the 2 antique brick fireplaces in this 3BR, 2-bath California-style ranch on an estate-sized, wooded lot in Weston Hills. You'll enjoy watching the hot coals and licking flames on those cold wintry nights. Come summer, you can burn dinner in the stone barbecue on the delightful dining patio. Incidentally, this home includes a full basement; family room; hardwood floors; double garage; and a sun-drenched, country-style kitchen. It's a hot property we won't be able to hang onto for very long at $137,500.

Clyde Realty   **476-8200**

377

Split Personality

Do you want a warm home for family living as well as a home suitable for entertaining on a grand scale? We can satisfy both of you with this 3BR, 2½-bath, Arizona-style ranch home in prestigious Weston Hills. You'll love the quiet, paneled den with its own fireplace and the huge great room and flowing floor plan. A family room off the huge country-style copper, tile and brick kitchen has its own barbecue. The covered patio overlooking the garden is the perfect spot for relaxation and quiet dining. The price will please both your personalities at $197,500.

Clyde Realty   **476-8200**

378

The End

of your house hunting. Own a 3-bedroom, 2-bath Colonial with a large double garage in the most prestigious area of Westwood. This buy demands your immediate attention at $159,500.

Clyde Realty   **476-8200**

379

We're Not Paranoid

It's a fact. Everyone hates us for offering a 3BR, 2-bath sprawling ranch home with a 2½-car garage, fireplace and family room in prestigious Weston Hills for only $189,500. They're talking behind our backs, saying we're lowering property values. Even the purchasers will hate us because they won't be able to brag about how much they paid. Want to yell at us? Call.

Clyde Realty   **476-8200**

380

The Good News

is we have a 3BR, 2½-bath Colonial ranch with a 2-car garage in the Midvale School District for only $147,500.

The Bad News

is if you're not the first person at our office, you'll surely be disappointed.

Clyde Realty   **476-8200**

381

Is Your Wife Running Around

looking for that perfect 3BR, 2-bath Colonial ranch with a 2-car garage that's only a close walk from a quality grade school for less than $150,000?

Tell Her To Stop

because you found it, and the price is only $147,500.

Clyde Realty   **476-8200**

This ad is a positive attention getter.

382

Thomas Wolfe

said, "You can't go home again," but this 3BR, 1½-bath New England Cape Cod proves him wrong. It's located on a quiet, tree-canopied street where children still rollerskate on summer afternoons, people still take evening strolls and homes still have front porches where families gather to talk. The old neighborhood is there waiting for you at $137,500.

Clyde Realty   **476-8200**

A similar approach is taken by the next ad.

383

"You Can't Go Home Again"

Thomas Wolfe didn't know about this 3-bedroom brick Traditional on a quiet, tree-lined street where neighbors still call each other by name and children feel safe. He didn't know about the rocking-chair front porch or the apple tree in the backyard just made for climbing. Call today because for $69,500, you can go home again.

Clyde Realty   **476-8200**

This ad sells the very pleasant image of an older home in a safe, established neighborhood.

384

Crackerjack

and the surprise is the price. This 3-bedroom Colonial ranch in the nicest South Side neighborhood is offered on a first-come, first-served basis at $89,500.

Clyde Realty   **476-8200**

The words "first-come, first-served" lend a sense of urgency to the above ad. This unusual heading invites people to read on.

385

How Sweet It Is!

We know of a 3BR, 2-bath Colonial with a double garage on the West Side and a price less than

$100,000

And that's not all. The financing is unbelievable.

Clyde Realty   **476-8200**

386

Everything
You Want Even If
You Want Everything

This 3BR, 2-bath American Colonial offers a large family room, private den or music room, 3-car garage, full basement and amenities you didn't even know existed on 1 full acre in the most desirable area of Southport. Expect the best, and you won't be disappointed at $249,500.

Clyde Realty   **476-8200**

387

Waste Not—Want Not

This 3-bedroom Newport Colonial with double garage uses every bit of space with its open-flowing, sensible floor plan. You'll love the way the family room uses brick to become a natural extension of the brick and copper kitchen. One look and you will know it was designed for your family. It's proudly offered at $89,500.

Clyde Realty   **476-8200**

If there is more than 1 bath, it should be included in an ad (e.g., "3-bedroom, 2-bath").

388

Keep Your
Mother-in-law Away
Don't Buy This House

The problem with this 3BR, 2½-bath Connecticut Colonial is that there are 2 master suites. One of them is perfect for a mother-in-law. After one look, your mother-in-law will move in and won't ever leave. She'll love the quiet, tree-lined streets and huge kitchen with room for 2 cooks. She will want to turn your paneled den into a bright sewing room. Be smart, call her other children and tell them about this terrific house available now at only $149,500.

Clyde Realty   **476-8200**

389

The Family Jewels

won't have to be pawned to buy this spectacular 3BR, 2½-bath, stone and glass Arizona Contemporary on its hillside site. The price is only

$249,500

and this includes the 3-car garage, over an acre of land and a view that goes on forever. This fine residence, designed by Archibald Slottem, demands your immediate attention.

Clyde Realty   **476-8200**

390

What Price Happiness? $124,500

for a 3BR, 2-bath, Western-style ranch home on a half-acre in a quiet, small-town atmosphere of suburban Westhaven. The home features a double garage, huge family room, cut-stone fireplace as well as hardwood floors and trim. With this better-than-new home, your wish list of special features will be fulfilled. There's even a great area for a garden. For a happy family, call.

Clyde Realty   **476-8200**

391

Attention Artists!

Do you ever dream of having a very special studio filled with light and high ceilings so you won't feel cramped? What about a place to work or just relax and contemplate? This 3BR, 2-bath home in Hillside Terrace offers just such a special place. The former owner used this conservatory to raise exotic flowers. One look and you'll grab your easel. It's a very special home for you at $189,500.

Clyde Realty   **476-8200**

Many people consider themselves to be artistic. In this ad, the description of the studio is used to elicit a response from readers.

392

The Lazy Days of Summer

can be enjoyably spent on the covered front veranda of this 3-bedroom New England Traditional set on a quiet, tree-shaded street in Belville. If you decide to go inside, you'll be greeted by gleaming oak floors and solid maple woodwork that has a special softness about it. High ceilings and bright rooms add a sense of happiness to the whole house, but the front porch is still a very special spot. Priced at an unusually affordable $93,500.

Clyde Realty   **476-8200**

393

You Won't Be Impressed

by the price of this 3BR, 2-bath stone and glass Contemporary offering a breathtaking vista of mountains and valleys. After all, it's priced no more than one pays for a better tract home. When anyone asks what the house cost, you'll have to lie. Tell them a half million, and they'll be suitably impressed. This unique home looks like a *million* with its huge soaring ceilings and spacious floor plan. It's a home built for entertaining and impressing others. We're sorry we can't ask more, but all the owner wants is $249,000.

Clyde Realty   **476-8200**

394

What's Not To Like

about this 3BR, 2-bath French-inspired hillside villa overlooking the city? It offers European charm with a floor plan designed for entertaining. You will love the intimate private patio just off the family room. Of course all the usual amenities you expect in one of the grand homes are present. It is priced to like at $149,500.

Clyde Realty   **476-8200**

395

Oddball

If you're not afraid to be different from the crowd, you'll love this spacious, geodesic dome located on a huge site with a wooded view in lovely Clifton Hills. With 2 bedrooms, a loft, 2 baths and an open floor plan, this architectural masterpiece offers the ultimate in lifestyle at a very affordable $149,500.

Clyde Realty   **476-8200**

396

A Little Weird

If people consider you "different," you'd appreciate this very unordinary 2-bedroom home in a wooded setting. Built by a millionaire as his private hideaway, it is a recreation of a fourteenth century English woodcutter's home with natural stone, massive beams and a fireplace big enough to roast an ox; but it has every possible modern convenience. It's a home that must definitely be seen, and we believe it is a rare opportunity at $73,500.

Clyde Realty   **476-8200**

This ad has an attention-getting heading that will cause buyers to read the entire ad.

A home built by a millionaire, well-known person or person in a prestigious position or profession adds an aura of quality to a home.

397

It's Plain

This home is a solidly built, brick and cedar, 3-bedroom ranch with a full basement and double garage situated in a West Side family neighborhood. No soaring ceilings or walls of glass here. It does have several nice fruit trees and room for a garden. There's nothing far-out about the price—$89,500.

Clyde Realty   **476-8200**

This ad makes a virtue out of a simple tract home.

398

It's Sold

or it will be soon as you see this 3BR, 2-bath, double-garage, white clapboard Colonial on its wooded, estate-sized setting in Meadowbrook. At $89,500, there will be absolutely no reason to hesitate.

Clyde Realty   **476-8200**

399

A Special Neighborhood— A Special Home

This 3BR, 2-bath, double-garage, brick American Traditional was made for your family. Located in a quiet family neighborhood, this house has all the built-ins, central air, full basement ideal for a family playroom, new carpeting and almost 2,000 sq. ft. of living space for an affordable $139,500.

Clyde Realty   **476-8200**

Use square footage only when it is larger than expected.

400

THIMK!

and you will realize this 3BR, 2-bath Cape Cod with a 2-car garage on a wooded lot in Westhaven is a fantastic opportunity at $89,500.

Clyde Realty   **476-8200**

The intentional mispelling in the heading will be pointed out by callers.

401

Don't Touch a Thing

This immaculate, 3BR, 2-bath, double-garage split ranch on a wooded lot in Westhaven is perfect just the way it is. You'll love the finished recreation room, orchard stone fireplace and landscaping that is the envy of the neighborhood. You won't match the price of $129,500.

Clyde Realty   **476-8200**

See the following ad for a slight variation on the above.

402

Don't Touch

a thing. This 3BR, 2-bath Pennsylvania Colonial in Westmont is perfect the way it is. There's a huge chestnut tree in the front yard, white clapboard siding, double garage, sunny garden spot, finished basement recreation room, paneled family room, 2 fireplaces and a kitchen that will turn any chef green with envy. The first one to see it is surely going to buy at $189,500.

Clyde Realty   **476-8200**

403

Dine Out Tonight

on the delightful patio of this 3-bedroom, 2-bath Weston Hills ranch home sheltered by an ancient Chestnut tree. You'll love the myriad of flowers that sets the large fenced yard ablaze with color. This home offers bright, spacious rooms; a warm family room; antique brick fireplace; central air; 2+-car garage; and the finest location in prestigious Orchard Ridge at only $189,500.

Clyde Realty   **476-8200**

404

Rembrandt Couldn't Paint

a prettier picture than this white clapboard Colonial set among tall maples in an idyllic Woodland Estates area. Included are 3 bedrooms, a den, 2 baths, a screened porch, a 2-car garage, a full basement and a kitchen to excite any chef. You can put your family in this picture for $129,500.

Clyde Realty   **476-8200**

405

Ask George

Johnson of our office what the best buy on the market is in a 3BR, 2-bath, Weston Hills ranch home with a 2-car garage, and he will tell you about this exceptional opportunity on an estate-sized, wooded lot. The home offers soaring ceilings, a family room, a fireplace, a Eurostyle kitchen and the most delightful dining or relaxation patio in town. George says it will sell fast at $119,500.

Clyde Realty   **476-8200**

Using the comments of other salespeople in your office adds a friendly, personal touch to your ads.

406

You Won't Strike Out

With this 3BR, 2-bath Weston Heights Cape Cod. It's better than new on an estate-sized, wooded lot and features a 2-car garage, screened breezeway, hardwood floors, tribe-sized country kitchen and a picnic-perfect patio. A home run at $119,500.

Clyde Realty   476-8200

407

You Will Score Points

when you show your family this 3BR and den, 1¾-bath Cape Cod surrounded by flowers and stately maples in the quiet, friendly community of West Bend. This home features a 2+-car garage, full basement, family room, delightful veranda and sun-drenched country kitchen on an estate-sized lot. Don't tell them it's priced at only $119,500. They'll think you're spending far more.

Clyde Realty   476-8200

408

Attention Lottery Winner

Now that you have struck it rich, you'll want the finest home money can buy. We think we have it in this 3BR, 2½-bath, white-clapboard, New England Colonial on a wooded estate setting in Northport. It has a warm, paneled den; family room; formal dining room; eat-in country kitchen; large patio, perfect for garden parties; and even a 3-car garage for those new cars you're going to buy. The only flaw in this home is the price—it's only $219,500. If you want to spend more for this kind of quality, you'll have to go elsewhere.

Clyde Realty   476-8200

409

We Cannot Tell a Lie

This 3BR, 2-bath, split-level with a 2-car garage and large maple tree in the front yard is just like every other house on the block. The only difference is some homes have garages on the left and some on the right, and the brick trim varies. They all have family rooms and ceramic tile in the baths and kitchens. What is different about this house is it's for sale. Seldom are these homes put on the market. This is your chance to live in a friendly, family-oriented, village-type environment for only $119,500.

Clyde Realty   476-8200

This is an unusual treatment for a tract home where the other homes in the area are almost the same.

410

Circle and Call

about this 3BR, 1¾-bath, double-garage, brick Traditional on a choice corner lot in the McKinley School District with finished basement recreation room, central air and hundreds of beautiful flowers. FHA low-down financing is available, and the full price is only $89,500.

Clyde Realty   **476-8200**

411

Bang!

Now that we have your attention, let us tell you about this 3BR, 2-bath, Westport Contemporary on a wooded hillside lot offering a terrific view of the city. This home has wraparound decks; 2-car, heated garage; soaring ceilings; zone-controlled central air; walls of glass; native stone fireplace; huge family room; basement hobby room; Euro-style kitchen; and decorating that will knock your socks off and all at the dynamite price of $189,500.

Clyde Realty   **476-8200**

412

Almost Perfact

This 3BR, 1¾-bath Massachusetts Colonial with white clapboard and authentic moldings set on a tree-sprinkled, double-size lot in West-brook has a double garage and a delightful summer porch. About as close to perfection as you can get at $97,500.

Clyde Realty   **476-8200**

The ad has an attention-getting, mis-spelled heading.

413

Wanted! A Live

buyer for this 3-bedroom Cape Cod in a delightful West Side neighborhood of quiet streets and well-cared-for homes. Features include solid hardwood floors, fireplace, 2-car garage, and it's only a short walk to schools. Reward yourself at $79,500.

Clyde Realty   **476-8200**

414

Smell the Flowers

and relax on the tree-shaded patio of this 3BR, 1½-bath, double-garage Virginia Colonial on the friendliest street in Westhaven. All modern conveniences—such as central vacuum, intercom, trash compactor, and built-in microwave—will give you the time to relax. Priced to enjoy at $189,500.

Clyde Realty   **476-8200**

416

For Your Senses

both aesthetic and common. With the best West Side location, 3 bedrooms, 2½-baths, a 3-car garage and a split plan for utmost privacy, this Traditional, California-style ranch meets all your requirements. It radiates warmth and beauty at a price that won't shock you— $189,500.

Clyde Realty   **476-8200**

415

Beauty (No Beast)

This 3BR, 2½-bath English Tudor on an estate lot in Meadowbrook will take your breath away. You never thought it was possible to own such a fine residence in a quality area for only $149,500.

Clyde Realty   **476-8200**

This is a short, but effective, ad.

417

Take the Cure

from the house-hunting blahs. Now we have a home as individual as you are. This 3BR, 2½-bath California Regency estate on the most prestigious site in Westmont offers over 3,000 sq. ft. of luxurious living. You'll delight in the fantasy master suite with sensuous Roman spa, dream kitchen and private music room. Of course, there's a 3-car garage, family room and all the extras you dream about. Priced to end your looking at $695,000.

Clyde Realty   **476-8200**

418

California Dreamin'

Milwaukee livin'. This is a sprawling California-style, 3BR, 2-bath ranch home with a fireplace and a huge family room with sliding glass doors that open to a delightful covered patio. Hey! It doesn't get any better than this at $149,500.

Clyde Realty   **476-8200**

419

California Living in Milwaukee

This 3BR, 2-bath, California-style ranch home is set in a veritable botanical garden with flowering shrubs and plants. The sliding glass doors in the family room open to a private dining patio for your enjoyment or entertaining. An in-ground pool, the envy of any Californian, brings the beach to your own backyard. Priced no more than an ordinary home at $189,500.

Clyde Realty   **476-8200**

420

Small-Town Safe

This home is surrounded by quiet streets and neighbors who seldom lock their doors. It's a place where children play and friends stroll the walks without care. You'll love this 3-bedroom American Traditional on almost a half-acre with apple and pear trees and a perfect garden spot. A full basement; 2-car garage; and large, bright rooms are ready for you. Best of all, it's small-town priced at $79,500.

Clyde Realty   **476-8200**

421

Extra! Extra!

You can read all about it, but words can't express the charm of this 3BR, 1¾-bath, white-clapboard Cape Cod set back from the street in a haven of oak and hickory trees. There is a finished recreation room in the full, poured basement, and a screened breezeway adjoins the 2-car garage. This picture-perfect home for your future is waiting for you at $114,900.

Clyde Realty   **476-8200**

422

Reward

If you check out and buy this 3BR, 2½-bath, Spanish Renaissance estate on a coveted tree-lined street in Westbridge Estates, you'll be rewarded with a lifetime of happiness. You will be impressed by the high ceilings and spacious rooms. The long covered porch; huge beams; tons of tile; and dedicated craftsmanship will make this a residence loved by you and envied by others. Priced at $385,000, call now or someone else will claim your reward.

Clyde Realty   **476-8200**

423

Reward

yourself with the home your family deserves. This 3BR and den, 2½-bath, sprawling California ranch in prestigious Hawthorne Hills is the home you always dream about. Two fireplaces; a huge family room opening to the patio, spa and pool; and a kitchen to make any man want to cook are just a few of the features in this stunning residence. You've worked hard; now take your reward at $249,500.

Clyde Realty   **476-8200**

424

Wanted!

A family to fill this 3BR, 2-bath Garrison Colonial on a quiet, tree-canopied street in Hawthorne. While close to schools, shopping and public transportation, there's still a small-town, friendly atmosphere where neighbors greet one another by name. It's a delightful home with large, sun-filled rooms; a basement workroom or an ideal photographer's dark room; 2 fireplaces; a huge garage; and an ambiance of casual dignity. It's a home any family would love at an affordable $169,500.

Clyde Realty   **476-8200**

425

Your Second Chance

This Crafton Hills, 3BR, 2½-bath Arizona Contemporary was sold 3 days after we put out the "For Sale" sign. An unexpected situation put this home back on the market. With walls of glass, magnificent vistas and over 2,800 sq. ft. of living space, we expect this architectural masterpiece to be gone in another 3 days. Call now, as opportunity seldom knocks twice. Priced for you at $219,500.

Clyde Realty   **476-8200**

426

Play It Again Sam

It's back on the market, but not for long. You'll have to move quickly to get this 3BR, 2-bath, South Side California ranch at only $139,500.

Clyde Realty   **476-8200**

Other possible headings for the above 2 ads are: "Sale Failed," "Fell out of Escrow," or "Buyer Backed Out." Obtain the owner's permission before any information on past dealings is revealed. As an agent, you have the duty of confidentiality.

The following ad uses the same heading, but has a slightly different treatment.

427

Play It Again Sam

We thought we had this 2-bedroom and den, New England Cape Cod in Waterbury Heights sold. It was love at first sight when the buyers walked into this sun-filled home and saw the generously proportioned rooms, a fireplace of ancient brick, the family-sized kitchen opening onto a dining patio, and the workroom off the double garage. They were close but just couldn't come up with the financing. Priced at $150,000, this fine home will not be available long.

Clyde Realty   **476-8200**

428

Available Again

We sold this fine home in just 3 days, but the buyer was unable to complete the purchase. With a prime West Side location, this truly impressive 3-bedroom Colonial ranch will not be available very long. First come, first served at $119,500.

Clyde Realty   **476-8200**

429

Unsold

We thought this 3BR, 2-bath Westview Cape Cod sold the first week, so we stopped advertising it. Somehow the sale fell apart, and the owner wants it sold. Set on a large wooded lot, this home offers a full basement, a 2+-car garage, hardwood floors, a delightful patio, and it's priced to move quickly at $94,500.

Clyde Realty   **476-8200**

430

Sold in Three Days

That's what happened with the last property we advertised in the highly desirable Wingate Estates, and this 3BR, 2-bath American Colonial is even nicer. The home boasts 3 king-sized bedrooms; walk-in closets in the master suite; a jacuzzi tub; a dream kitchen; a family room that opens onto a covered patio, perfect for dining or just relaxation; and model-home landscaping. Priced at $187,500, it will probably go to the first caller.

Clyde Realty   476-8200

This ad can be easily tailored for a condominium.

431

We Were Wrong

All of our salespeople believed this 3BR, 2½-bath Quaker Colonial on a huge wooded lot would sell in just a day because of the low price and fantastic terms available. This home shows like a model and even has a den with a separate entry—ideal for a home office—and a huge, screened and glassed, 3-season porch that would make an excellent studio. Perhaps we should raise the price as $169,500 might seem too good to be true.

Clyde Realty   476-8200

432

What Happened?

This 3BR, 2-bath Colonial in Westport should have sold from the first ad, but we didn't have a single response. With the 2-car garage; fireplace; family room; full basement; professional decorating; huge, wooded lot; and skipping distance to Midvale School, we expected buyers to be beating on our doors. After all, we're only asking $179,500.

Clyde Realty   476-8200

This is an unusual approach that creates interest in a home when your first ad failed to produce calls.

433

It's a Mystery

why this 3BR, 2-bath, College Heights split-level with heated garage is still on the market. We thought that with the estate-sized lot, central air and all the built-ins, this home wouldn't last 3 days. Mr. Hendricks of our office thinks the problem is that it's too good a deal. People don't want to see it because they think that at $179,500, it's too good to be true. Let us prove them wrong.

Clyde Realty   476-8200

434

Close to Everything for Next to Nothing

This 3-bedroom West Side Traditional is located within walking distance to train, shopping and schools. It has a double garage, full basement, hardwood floors, central air and a price you won't believe—$79,500.

Clyde Realty   **476-8200**

435

The Sky's the Limit

The soaring cathedral ceiling adds a feeling of spaciousness to this 3BR, 2-bath, Arizona-style Contemporary in Highland Estates that has a view that goes on forever. You'll want to light the barbecue when you see this treetop, cantilevered deck. The feeling of being as one with nature can be yours for $219,500 if you act now.

Clyde Realty   **476-8200**

436

Topless

Ceilings seem to soar forever in this 3BR, 2½-bath, Mediterranean Renaissance residence in Belwood Heights. Other amenities include a 3-car garage, magnificent fireplace sheathed in marble, Grecian tile, gallery dining room and everything on your wish list. Down-to-earth priced at $249,500.

Clyde Realty   **476-8200**

437

Inside and Out

This 3BR, 2-bath, split-level ranch in Westbury Heights is as close to perfect as you'll ever find. From the oversized 2-car garage to the friendly neighborhood of fine homes, you won't want to change a thing. Even the price is pleasant at $119,500.

Clyde Realty   **476-8200**

438

If You
Ain't Seen This

you ain't seen the best. This 3BR, 2-bath Colonial with a double garage on an estate-sized, wooded lot in the prestigious community of Meadowbrook has no equal at $149,500.

Clyde Realty   **476-8200**

439

It's a Mistake

to buy a new home until you've seen this 3BR, 2-bath Colonial in a very desirable West Side family neighborhood. It has a double garage; mature landscaping, including a century-old chestnut tree that shades the dining patio; screened porch; and a basement ideal for the hobbyist or as a rainy-day adult or children's playroom. You get a great deal more, and it's priced less than new at $139,500.

Clyde Realty   **476-8200**

440

Watch the Squirrels

from the cedar deck of this 3BR, 2-bath California-style ranch with a huge family room, fireplace and cathedral ceilings. It has over 2,000 sq. ft. of sheer luxury on an estate-sized lot with ancient oaks loaded with acorns. There's even a perfect branch from which to hang a swing. This is a home to be proud of at $179,500.

Clyde Realty   **476-8200**

441

Country Quiet

and the conveniences of city life are available with this 3BR, 2-bath, California-style rambling ranch on almost a half-acre of professional landscaping. You'll love the feeling of privacy, the state-of-the-art kitchen, large family room, fireplace and 2½-car attached garage all waiting for you at $147,500.

Clyde Realty   **476-8200**

442

Time Warp—

a 3BR, 2-bath, white clapboard Colonial on a tree-shaded, estate-sized lot that looks as if it were preserved from a gentler era. Amenities include a double garage, screened garden porch, magnificent fireplace and a generous use of gleaming hardwoods. Available for your family's future at $179,500.

Clyde Realty   **476-8200**

This is not necessarily an old house. It could be a newer home built in an older style.

443

Real Bad

The greatest by far, this 3BR, 9-room, double-garage ranch has a built-in stereo system that rocks the house, a separate music room, a huge lot with all sorts of green stuff and a location you only dream about. Proudly offered at $129,500.

Clyde Realty   **476-8200**

In music circles, "real bad" refers to "great." This type of heading almost demands the ad be read.

444

Chalet in the Woods

This is a cedar and stone masterpiece, and it's as modern as the setting is rugged. There are 3BR, 1¾ baths, heated 2-car garage and over an acre that has been magnificently landscaped by mother nature. It's commuting-close at far less than you'd pay in the city—$239,500.

Clyde Realty   **476-8200**

"Landscaped by mother nature" means that the site has not been professionally landscaped.

445

Prepare To Be Envied

It's inevitable that your best friends will turn green with envy when they see your 3BR, 2-bath, shuttered American Colonial in an estate-sized lot in Westbridge. They'll be impressed with the immense rooms, elegant woodwork and professionally designed grounds. All the extras are here: central air, family room, 2 fireplaces and finished basement ideal for a home fitness center and family game room or photographer's darkroom. Your friends will think you paid far more than $179,500.

Clyde Realty   **476-8200**

When people buy a new home, it is usually a step up from their previous home and that of many of their friends, so this ad need not be confined to luxury homes. It appeals to those whose income has recently increased significantly.

446

Don't Do It!

If you ignore this ad, you'll miss the chance for a 3BR, 2-bath ranch home in a prime West Side location with a double garage, family room and central air for only $93,500.

Clyde Realty   **476-8200**

447

Work at Home

in a 3-bedroom home with a like-new, 24 by 48-foot, insulated steel shop building with a 10-foot overhead door on 1 acre. It's ideal for a home-based business or hobby shop. This home has plenty of room for a garden, and you're going to love it. A fantastic opportunity at $77,000.

Clyde Realty   **476-8200**

Many rural homes include large, metal buildings or barns.

448

Room for an RV

and a boat, several cars, plus a truckload of bikes and even a workshop in the huge, 26 by 40-foot, insulated metal building with 10-foot-high doors comes with this 3BR, 2-bath split ranch with a 2-car garage on over a half-acre of beautifully landscaped grounds in West Hills. Let your imagination run wild! The possibilities are endless, and the price is a moderate $129,500.

Clyde Realty   **476-8200**

Homes often have large storage buildings that can be used to draw attention to an ad.

449

In a Friendly Village

on a quiet, tree-lined street, this white clapboard, Traditional, 3-bedroom bungalow with its large country kitchen, huge front porch, full basement with 20 by 32-foot garage/workroom, and perfect garden spot is waiting just for you. It has a new natural gas furnace and roof and is only 45 minutes from the city. Small-town priced at $99,500.

Clyde Realty   **476-8200**

450
Country in the City

You can have a 3-bedroom, American Gothic, farmhouse-style home; an oversized garage/workroom; and a large lot on a quiet street with a garden the envy of any farmer and a huge chestnut tree in the front yard. In a very special neighborhood, this will be the first home you'll want to see. Best of all, it's country-priced at $79,500.

Clyde Realty   **476-8200**

Any older frame or brick home can be described as "farmhouse-style."

451
Somebody Cared

and it is reflected in the immaculate condition of this 2BR, 1½-bath Cape Cod with attached, double garage and breezeway patio. You will marvel at the finely manicured lawn, lovingly cared-for flower beds and the fine specimen trees. In a neighborhood you'll love, this is what you dream of, at $114,500.

Clyde Realty   **476-8200**

452
Bring the Moving Van

You'll want to move right in to this 3BR, 2-bath, Morningside Heights Colonial ranch. Besides its super location, you'll love the pool-sized yard with room for an RV, 2+-car garage, hardwood floors, Eurostyle kitchen, and the full basement offering limitless possibilities. The price is not a misprint. It is only $119,500.

Clyde Realty   **476-8200**

453
Au Naturel

This 3BR, 2-bath, double-garage Arizona Contemporary appears as one with nature. Redwood decks, delightful dining patio and knee-to-ceiling walls of glass meld the living area with the natural environment. You'll marvel at the feeling of light and spaciousness of the free-flowing floor plan and special intimate areas. Unpretentious luxury at $189,500.

Clyde Realty   **476-8200**

454

Feels Like Home

Step inside this 3BR, 2-bath, white-clapboard American Traditional, and you'll be absorbed by the warmth of a happy home. It has large, light, airy rooms; mellow, polished woodwork; a large, family-sized kitchen; and even a sun parlor perfect for a sewing room or studio. Also included are a 2-car garage and a great spot for a garden. All this for only $79,500.

Clyde Realty   476-8200

455

Hey! Big Spender!

You won't have to empty your wallet for this 3BR, 2½-bath, California-style ranch on a wooded half-acre site in desirable Westlake Village. Even though there's a circle drive, a 2++-car garage, landscaping to be envied, a family room with a fireplace and central air, you can still be the owner for only $179,500.

Clyde Realty   476-8200

456

Curb Appeal? No!

Actually this 3BR, 2-bath ranch home with double garage doesn't look very impressive from the outside, but once you pass through the double door entry—wow! This home has soaring ceilings; soft, natural lighting through clerestory windows; and a flowing floor plan of space and function skillfully combined for the lifestyle you dream of. Indeed, this is an impressive residence in every way but the price, $169,500.

Clyde Realty   476-8200

457

Private Bird Sanctuary

The owners of this 3BR, 2½-bath, double-garage Colonial reportedly identified over 80 varieties of birds on their nearly half-acre property—everything from chickadees and hummingbirds to quail and a red tail hawk. The screened and glassed porch is their favorite bird-watching spot. You won't be disappointed if you circle this ad and call.

Clyde Realty   476-8200

458

For the Birds

There are usually several hummingbirds at the well-frequented feeders on the 1-acre grounds of this 3BR, 2½-bath Southern Colonial with fluted soaring pillars. Set amidst a myriad of blooming flowers, this house captures the gracious ambiance of colonial Virginia with all the conveniences of today. You'll love the large den with French doors that open onto the garden. There's room for a pool and courts. Definitely top drawer, except for the price—$325,000.

Clyde Realty   **476-8200**

459

A Goldfinch and a Hummingbird

were at the feeders when we visited this 3-bedroom, brick American Traditional on a large corner lot. The backyard is a delight with colorful plantings and a family vegetable garden. The house includes a 2-car garage, full basement, hardwood floors and best of all, you'll fall in love with the quiet, friendly neighborhood of well-kept homes and lawns. This is a great family or retirement home at only $77,500.

Clyde Realty   **476-8200**

Not much is said about what is probably a 1-bath, smaller, older home.

460

Groovy to the Max

This 3BR, 2-bath split ranch with its 2-car garage really has it all—prestigious West Side location, huge corner lot, family room, fireplace, central air and only 2 quiet blocks to a grade school. Old Mr. Higgins of our office describes this home as a regular "Jim Dandy" at $139,500.

Clyde Realty   **476-8200**

461

If I Had a Hammer

I'd fix the front gate on this 3-bedroom American Traditional in a villagelike neighborhood of fine homes. Other than the gate, this home is in move-in condition. You'll love the bay windows and hinged window boxes for storage (remember *Arsenic and Old Lace?*). The woodwork shines, and every spacious room seems to catch the sun. Of course, it comes with a garage, garden and even a small garden shed. A bright future for $89,500.

Clyde Realty   **476-8200**

The ad heading makes this home appear to be a fixer-upper, which it is not.

462

Throw Away the Paper

You don't have to look any further. We have a 3BR, 2-bath, double-garage Colonial with full basement on a wooded, estate-sized lot in a prime West Side neighborhood for only $149,500.

Clyde Realty   **476-8200**

463

Fairy Tale

"They lived happily ever after in this 3-bedroom, brick and cedar cottage beneath a towering chestnut tree." We can't guarantee the "happily ever after," but we do have the fairy-tale cottage on a quiet, tree-lined lane. It has a sunny spot perfect for a garden and a garage with a workroom. If you can take care of the "happily ever after," this is a dream come true at $89,500.

Clyde Realty   **476-8200**

If there is more than 1 bath, it should be stated. If the garage is for 2 cars, it should also be stated.

464

"How Could You Afford It?"

your friends and relatives will say when they see this 3BR, 2½-bath, center-entrance Colonial in Weston Hills with its 2½-car garage and huge, wooded site. They will be amazed at the private, paneled den; huge basement recreation room; 2 fireplaces; formal dining room; and central air. The quality will show that this is definitely the home of a bank president or doctor. Don't tell them you only paid $137,500.

Clyde Realty   **476-8200**

This ad will fit a large home 30 to 50 years old in an area of similar homes.

465

Stop Reading

and call now to become the owner of this 3BR, 2-bath, Morningside Heights, brick and cedar American Traditional. You'll find that it has all your wants and a great many more at a price of only $124,900. But keep in mind, others are also reading this ad.

Clyde Realty   **476-8200**

466

Telephone Your Future

A simple call will show you how easy it is to have the security of owning this 3BR, 1¾-bath Cape Cod with double garage and full basement on a large, wooded lot in the nicest family community. You'll learn about the low down payment and financing tailored to your particular needs at a price of only $114,000. Stop reading and call.

Clyde Realty   **476-8200**

467

Been Very Good?

Then you deserve to pamper yourself with this like-new, 3BR, 2-bath split ranch with a 3-car garage in Meadow Wood. There's no need to list the special amenities, as this house has them all. It's a real treat to your senses and your pocketbook at $189,500.

Clyde Realty   **476-8200**

468

Nothing To Do

This pristine, 3BR, 1¾-bath, double-garage, West Side raised ranch is ready for you. Newly decorated in neutral tones, it needs only your furniture. You'll love the huge family room and the feeling of bright spaciousness. It's priced for you at only $79,500.

Clyde Realty   **476-8200**

469

Don't Buy

until you see this 3-bedroom, 2-bath, double-garage Kentucky Traditional on almost 1 full acre in the finest West Side area for only $139,500.

Clyde Realty   **476-8200**

470

Suburbia in the City

A quiet, tree-lined street of well-kept homes and neighbors who know each other by name give this 3BR, double-garage Colonial on a large wooded lot a countrylike ambiance. Offering a lifestyle of the suburbs without the commuting for $129,500.

Clyde Realty   476-8200

If a home has more than 1 bath or a fireplace, it should be stated in the ad.

471

Massive Oak Beams

an orchard stone fireplace, random-plank hardwood floors and soaring ceilings make this spacious cedar and glass, 3BR, 2-bath hillside chalet in Westmoreland a home that will touch your heart. This is a place you'll love coming home to at $139,500.

Clyde Realty   476-8200

An architectural feature can be used to make an effective heading.

472

Pack Rat Special

This 3BR, 2-bath West Side Colonial comes with double garage; basement; and an attic full of boxes, parts and we don't know what all. For someone who loves to save things rather than throw them away, the saving has been done for you, and it's all included at $119,500.

Clyde Realty   476-8200

This ad turns the fact that the owners or renters have left an accumulation of junk on the property into a tongue-in-cheek asset.

Although not a fixer-upper ad, it will attract many of the same callers fixer-upper ads attract.

473

Clear, Cold Water

Your own deep well and water clear of chemicals come with this 3-bedroom American Gothic farm home. You'll be impressed with the handsome detailing, high ceilings and mantled fireplace. There's an immense garage/workroom big enough for all your needs. It all comes on your own half-acre, and it's only a short commute to the city. Definitely not to be overlooked at $139,500.

Clyde Realty   476-8200

474

Disappearing Act

The owners have left only a pile of fuzz balls in the spot where their refrigerator once stood. This 3BR, 2-bath, Lorraine Heights Cape Cod couldn't be any emptier. They even took the rope swing from the huge apple tree in the backyard. This house is generally pretty clean, and except for problems a good mowing will solve, so is the yard. Once you see it—presto! You'll be the new owner at $119,500.

Clyde Realty   **476-8200**

9

Golf and Tennis Homes

The fact that a home is located in a golf or tennis development or is close to courts or course is a strong plus that generally can be used as the central focus of an ad. Such ads are listed under condominiums, and several of the vacation home and time share ads also emphasize golf and tennis. In this section, the golf and tennis ads are for single-family homes.

475

Fore

You can own a 2BR, 2½-bath, single-family home only a 7 iron from the fairway. Take your golf cart from the 3-car garage right to the first tee in minutes. Paradise is here at the championship 27 holes of Wedgewood Greens, and it's available for you at an affordable $169,500.

Clyde Realty   **476-8200**

If a home is on the fairway, it should be stated.

476

Tell Your Wife

that this 3BR, 2-bath, double-garage Colonial is in the Midvale School District, which many regard as having the best schools in the county. Tell her about the new regional mall only 15 minutes away. Tell her about the maple cabinets in the country-sized kitchen, the finished basement and the estate-sized lot with all of its exotic plantings.

But Don't Tell Her

about the 6 championship golf courses within a 15-minute drive. At least the house is honestly priced at $234,500.

Clyde Realty   **476-8200**

477

Below Par

Your score will sink when you have a championship golf course in your backyard. You'll love the twin master suites, the huge living and family area and delightful patio for entertaining or relaxation. If you think you have seen the best, be prepared to see what is available right now for only $189,500.

Clyde Realty   **476-8200**

The above ad has an attention-getting heading.

478

Score Low— Live High

with a 2BR and den, 2-bath home right on the 7th fairway of Avondale. A 2-car garage and every conceivable extra are included in this professionally decorated home. The exquisite furnishings are included at only $149,500.

Clyde Realty   **476-8200**

479

Birdie Lovers

A chip shot away from a Pete Dyer championship course, and you are home. This 3BR, 2½-bath, single-family residence is the perfect spot for the golfer. Your own jacuzzi tub, a delightful patio to entertain your friends or to relax or dine, a family room with a special wall made to hold your trophies and room in the garage for 2 cars and a golf cart. A millionaire's lifestyle for you at $219,500.

Clyde Realty   **476-8200**

This ad is for a home located off a course.

480

Tee Off

practically from your own backyard with this 2BR, 2½-bath, single-family fairway home on a course designed by Jack Nicklaus. From your patio you can greet your friends as they make their rounds. A great place to entertain or just relax at a very affordable $189,500.

Clyde Realty   **476-8200**

Very little information is given about the above home. The ad emphasizes a particular lifestyle.

481

Fore You

We have a near-new, 2BR, 2-bath, single-family home on the 7th fairway for the price of a condominium. You'll love the privacy, the view from your glassed-wall living room and dining patio and the feeling of bright spaciousness. Decorated in the light cheerful colors of the Southwest, you won't be teed off at the price, $149,500.

Clyde Realty   476-8200

This ad shows the advantage of a single-family home versus a condo.
An alternative heading is simply "4."

482

"Love" in the Afternoon

You have your choice of 6 courts as the owner of this 3BR, 2-bath, Southwest Contemporary, single-family home in Hidden Palms Estates. A home that has it all: family room, 3-car garage, soaring ceilings, every conceivable built-in plus friendly neighbors in a premier gate-guarded community. It will be first come, first served at $197,500.

Clyde Realty   476-8200

Again, this ad is an attention getter.

483

Tennis Anyone?

You'll never wait again with your own championship court that comes with this 3BR, 3½-bath French Provincial on the nicest street in Morningside Heights. The home is as impressive as the address with its leaded French doors, rich paneling, dramatic living areas and French country kitchen. The professionally maintained grounds are the envy of any horticulturalist. At $478,500, life just doesn't get any better than this.

Clyde Realty   476-8200

484

Game—Set—Match

Does having your own lighted championship tennis court interest you? Then consider this.

4BR Colonial

with its paneled den, screened summer porch and authentic detailing on a full acre sprinkled with giant chestnut and beech trees. At $319,000, it will be "Love."

Clyde Realty   476-8200

This heading says "Tennis."

10

Holidays

Ads can be written to correspond specifically to a particular holiday. While such ads may appear timely, they aren't necessarily more effective than ads written without regard for the time of year. The ads in this chapter are intended to be published around certain holidays.

485

Martin Luther King, Jr.

had a dream that we share of all people living together as equals with equal rights and opportunities. We want the world to know we subscribe to and practice Equal Housing Opportunity.

Clyde Realty   476-8200

While not an ad for a specific property, it is an appropriate ad for Martin Luther King Day. It lets readers know they can expect fair and equal treatment in their housing needs.

486

Ground Hog Special

Don't hide from the world. Winter is about over, and summer can't be far behind. Get ready with this 3BR, 1½-bath Cape Cod complete with a rose garden that's the pride of the neighborhood with colorful flowers about to pop through the ground. There is a screened porch that's ideal for lazy-day relaxation or even entertaining, a double garage, full basement and central air for those sultry days ahead. It's available now at a price any ground hog will love, $119,500.

Clyde Realty   476-8200

487

Emancipation Special!

This 3BR, 2½-bath, West Side home, with its impressive, European-inspired architecture, features every conceivable labor-saving device from a central vacuum system to a refrigerator with automatic ice dispenser, trash compactor, easy-care tile in baths and kitchen, dishwasher, washer, dryer and garbage disposal. There are devices for everything, except changing junior. Drag your spouse over to see the real freedom possible at $184,500.

Clyde Realty   476-8200

This ad is intended to appear around Lincoln's Birthday.

488

Keep Your Valentine

in this 3BR, 1½-bath Cape Cod on a quiet, tree-lined street in Westwood. She will love the hardwood floors; soft, neutral decor; country-sized, sun-drenched kitchen; full basement ideal for a rainy-day playroom; child-safe, fenced yard; and even the double garage. There's room for a garden, and the price won't break your heart at $89,500.

Clyde Realty   476-8200

489

Cherry Tree Special

In honor of George Washington, we axed the price on this 3BR, 2-bath, West Side Colonial with a fabulous family room and large screened porch. We cannot tell a lie. At $147,500, it's an exceptional purchase.

Clyde Realty   476-8200

490

George Washington Special

A cherry tree is included with this 3-bedroom, 2-bath Delaware Colonial. This home has a huge double garage, a "whatever" room for sewing or whatever, and a delightful breakfast patio. Hatchet-priced at $139,500.

Clyde Realty   476-8200

Most homes have a patio area. "Breakfast patio" gives the patio added desirability.

491

St. Patty Special

This shamrock green Traditional, in an almost village setting, comes complete with 3 bedrooms, 2 baths, double garage, fireplace, old-world garden and even a friendly leprechaun. The price, however, won't turn you green: $137,500.

Clyde Realty   **476-8200**

492

For the Easter Parade

This eye-turning, newer, 3BR, 1½-bath Cape Cod with double garage, on a wooded lot with room for a garden in friendly Glen Allyn, has a yard ablaze with colorful plantings, a rich green lawn and has had a fresh coat of paint. Inside, the spacious, sun-drenched rooms have an ambiance of happiness. What better place for your family to come home to. $89,500.

Clyde Realty   **476-8200**

493

Liberate Mother

We can free you from household drudgery with this 3BR, 2-bath Westhaven Contemporary that includes every conceivable labor-saving built-in from a central vacuum system to a garbage compactor. Priced for Mother's Day at $139,500.

Clyde Realty   **476-8200**

This ad can be modified to say "Priced for Labor Day ..."

494

Give Father a Lawn Mower

and the rich, green lawn surrounding this 3BR, 2-bath, white-clapboard Cape Cod set between giant maples on an estate-sized lot in prestigious Midview Heights. This home offers a large double garage with workroom, full basement, antique brick fireplace, oversized country kitchen, formal dining room and patio just made for Dad to relax. The price of $127,500 won't shock Dad.

Clyde Realty   **476-8200**

This Father's Day ad can be used any time of the year.

495

Father's Day Special

He will love the lion-sized, paneled den in this 3BR, 2-bath split ranch in Westwood. There's room in the ample family room for a billiard table or even ping pong. He'll love playing chef on the patio. Only a short drive to golf and fishing, this is a place any Dad will want to call home. Best of all, he won't explode when he finds out that the price is only $187,500.

Clyde Realty   **476-8200**

496

Independence Day

Say farewell to your landlord when you see this lovely 3-bedroom, North Side Cape Cod that can be purchased with only $3,000 down and

Net Payments Less Than Rent

Call now, and we will show you that you can be an owner.

Clyde Realty   **476-8200**

497

Firecracker Special

Your independence day will come as the owner of this near-new, 3BR, 2-bath, stone and cedar split ranch in the best possible West Side location. Every conceivable labor-saving convenience and built-in has been incorporated into this home. Special features include a soaring entryway, huge family room, lovely patio and professionally designed landscaping that will be the envy of your friends. Best of all, the price won't blow you away—$98,500.

Clyde Realty   **476-8200**

498

4th of July Special

This Vermont Colonial exemplifies all our country stands for. Solidly and honestly built with clean, unpretentious lines, this is a home for your independence. There are 3 bedrooms, 1¾ baths and a very private den. Special features include a sun porch, double garage and central air. Priced to please any Yankee at $214,500.

Clyde Realty   **476-8200**

The price is not given in this ad nor is it needed since it is selling terms. The ad can actually be used year-round.

499

Red, White and Blue

This 3-bedroom Colonial is as American as the 4th of July. Set on a wooded lot with a double garage, this home has a full basement with finished recreation room, screened gazebo and is in a neighborhood where pride in one's home is very evident. An exceptional offering at $114,500.

Clyde Realty   **476-8200**

This ad can be used any time of the year but is most appropriate before July 4th.

500

No Labor Day

When you are the carefree owner of this 2BR, 2-bath executive end unit in prestigious Catalina Palms. While you have the spaciousness and privacy of a single-family home, others do your bidding as to lawn, flowers and exterior maintenance. With all that time on your hands, consider spending some of it by the pool and spa or perhaps on the 18-hole golf course. If you are too busy being lazy, get your spouse to call us for a private showing. Incidentally, the price is only $135,500.

Clyde Realty   **476-8200**

This ad is designed for condominiums or cooperatives.

501

On Columbus Day Discover Westport

This is a community of quiet streets, friendly people, fine homes and schools to be proud of. Discover a 3BR, 2-bath Cape Cod set on a tree-shaded cul-de-sac midst park-like grounds. Discover the spacious rooms, large family room and delightful dining patio. Best of all, discover that the price is only $139,500.

Clyde Realty   **476-8200**

502

Halloween Special

Contrary to common opinion, Mr. Fredericks, of our office, doesn't wear a mask, but he has informed us you need not be scared since the 3BR, 2½-bath Pennsylvania Dutch Colonial in Almond Acres—which he has just listed—is only priced at $176,500.

Clyde Realty   **476-8200**

503

Pumpkin Patch Special

Charlie Brown might wait for the Great Pumpkin forever, but you need wait no longer if you're looking for a 3BR, 2-bath ranch home in Sussex Heights for less than $150,000. You better act fast.

Clyde Realty   **476-8200**

504

Pilgrim's Pride

This 3BR, 2-bath New England Colonial is definitely not a turkey. There is a 2-car garage, hardwood floors, 2 fireplaces, a quiet den with soft maple paneling, built-in bookcases and a kitchen to excite any chef. A purchase your family will be thankful for at $169,500.

Clyde Realty   **476-8200**

The heading "Not a Turkey" can be used with almost any ad for Thanksgiving.

505

No Room in the Stocking

for this 3-BR, 2½-bath French Colonial on a very special wooded lot in Westhaven, but it's the best present you can ever give your family. You'll love the sumptuous, marble-sheathed master bath with its Roman spa; the richly paneled den; the lovely family room; and this home's general feeling of spaciousness and quality. By no means an ordinary house, it is proudly offered at $239,500.

Clyde Realty   **476-8200**

This is an ad for the Christmas season that can be tailored for any home.

506

It Won't Fit

in the stocking, but what better present for your family than this 3BR, 1½-bath, white-clapboard Cape Cod on a large wooded lot in Northport. They will love the huge double garage with room for bikes and trikes, screened porch for summertime play or just relaxation, full basement with room for everything, corn-popping fireplace and even central air. Priced for your family at $139,500.

Clyde Realty   **476-8200**

507

Scrooge Special

On a large wooded site in Northport sits a white-clapboard, 3BR, 1½-bath Cape Cod with a double garage, screened porch, family room, full basement, fireplace and central air. Buy this home for your family before Christmas, and you won't need to buy any other presents. The best part is it's priced for a miser at only $139,500.

Clyde Realty   **476-8200**

509

New Year's Party

with all your friends can be held in the basement recreation room of this 3BR, 1½-bath New England Colonial on a quiet, tree-lined street in Westport. Decorator-perfect, all it needs is your moving van. Start celebrating early because the price is only $119,500, with great terms.

Clyde Realty   **476-8200**

508

Red-Stocking Special

The huge orchard stone fireplace in this 3BR, 2-bath Vermont Traditional in Arlington Heights has room for a dozen Christmas stockings. The living room can hold the largest tree around and have space left for a dozen small children and their presents. You'll love the oversized garage with room for all the bikes and trikes. At only $179,500, it is the perfect opportunity for you to play Santa Claus for your family.

Clyde Realty   **476-8200**

11

Homes with Acreage

Homes with several acres located beyond the suburbs are attractive to many buyers including people who want to get back to the soil to raise their own food, people who want privacy, survivalists, and those seeking a more relaxed and/or safer way of life for themselves and their families.

A home with acreage is particularly attractive to retirees and to people looking for vacation homes. Many of the ads in chapter 30 (Vacation Homes) can be easily adapted for homes with acreage.

Ads aimed at horse owners are shown in chapter 12.

511

You Can't Get Here

very easily. To say this 3-bedroom Nantucket Colonial is secluded is an understatement. It is so remote that when you see something moving, you can be certain it is wearing a fur coat. The home has been excellently maintained, and it is a real showplace if showing it to raccoons, deer and squirrels counts. There is a 2-car garage and almost 5 acres of woods, so grab your compass and see how much isolation you can buy for $89,500.

Clyde Realty   476-8200

This negative approach can be very effective for buyers who welcome seclusion or love nature.

510

Believe in Fairy Tales?

If you don't, then forget about this stone, 2-bedroom cottage nestled in a wooded glen on 2 acres—home to deer, raccoons and chipmunks. It is fairy-tale perfect with its heavy wood beams, cozy fireplace and so much more. It's a place where fantasies become reality for only $179,500.

Clyde Realty   476-8200

512

Insomniac Special

The fresh air surrounding this 3-bedroom home, set on 5 acres in a woodland glen only 45 minutes from the city, seems to have a remarkable effect on people without the side effects of those little red pills. Whether working in the garden, cutting firewood for the stone fireplace or just relaxing, your tensions will seem to vanish. This is a real sleeper at $114,500.

Clyde Realty   **476-8200**

If the newspaper doesn't have a separate heading for acreage homes, the above heading should instead read "Insomniac Special—5 Acres." Otherwise the ad might be overlooked by those seeking acreage.

513

"I Want To Be Alone"

If you really want to be alone, you'll do cartwheels when you see this end-of-the-road, 2BR, year-round log home set on 40 acres of the most desolate forest you have ever seen. Mrs. Simpkins from our office left last week to show the property, and we haven't seen her since. Actually, it's a super house with a huge native stone fireplace; large picture windows with woodland vistas; and warm, solid pine paneling. There's no doorbell, but it's priced for any hermit at $89,500.

Clyde Realty   **476-8200**

514

A Place To Hide

No one will find you in this 2BR, 2-bath Mountain Chalet set on 10 acres of the most beautiful land possible. Sit on the spectacular redwood deck and just relax. In winter, the gigantic wall of glass in the great room looks out over a wonderland while the massive fieldstone fireplace adds a feeling of cheer. For you alone, at $99,500.

Clyde Realty   **476-8200**

This ad sells a mood—an escape. Psychologists say that many people dream of escaping their lives.

515

Artists and Lovers

will love this 2-bedroom cottage secluded on 2 acres in a quiet valley just 30 minutes from the city. You'll be enthralled by nature's surroundings. There is a sun-streaked clearing perfect for your studio. Priced for you at only $89,500.

Clyde Realty   **476-8200**

This ad is aimed at artistic individuals rather than families.

516
Love Nature—
5 Acres

A morning stroll on a woodland path, a watchful deer, an eagle soars. . . . This can be yours as the owner of this 2BR and den, year-round cottage in the pines. You will love the solid cedar paneling, native rock fireplace and views from every room. A home that has it all awaits you at $269,500.

Clyde Realty   476-8200

517
You Can't Get There

This newer 3-bedroom Traditional on 4 wooded acres is so remote the homing pigeons need road maps. Your creditors and mother-in-law will never be able to find you. If privacy is what you want, there's plenty of that, yet surprisingly it's only 30 minutes from the city. This is a great place for hermits, children and dogs, and it's priced within reach at $147,500.

Clyde Realty   476-8200

518
Want To Be Alone?

If solitude is your thing, you'll have found your heaven on earth with this American Rustic, 3-bedroom home set on 4 lovely wooded acres off a quiet country lane. Your private forest is home to raccoons, fox, deer and at least one large owl. It's a private world for writer, artist or naturalist at $139,500.

Clyde Realty   476-8200

If the property offers a barn or room suitable for use as a studio, it should be emphasized.

519
A Curious Raccoon

watched as we put up the For Sale sign on this 3BR, 2-bath sprawling brick ranch home just 20 minutes from the city. The home features big-city conveniences; large, bright rooms; central air; a quiet den; and a rose brick fireplace with the added charm of rural America. Your children will love the miles of trails, trees, wild animals and friendly neighbors (both 2- and 4-legged). Set on 3 acres all your own, this is the chance to make all your labors worthwhile. $187,500.

Clyde Realty   476-8200

520

Where Hawks Soar High

and the air is free and clear, you'll find this 3-bedroom, 2-bath Arizona Contemporary set on 5 of the most beautiful acres this side of heaven. It is a home that will make all of your toil seem worthwhile. Located in a very private world that's only a short commute from town, this happy residence offers unparalleled vistas, a sense of spaciousness with its high ceilings and walls of glass, a private den or office, and indoor/outdoor entertaining areas that merge together in perfect harmony. More than a new home for you, at $179,500 this is a whole new outlook on life.

Clyde Realty   **476-8200**

521

Davy Crockett Special

You can have your own 2BR and loft, modern log cabin with deer your closest neighbors as the owner of this 4-season retreat on 10 end-of-the-road, wooded acres. A wall of glass brings nature right into your living room. For someone who wants a very special place, this is a must-see at $49,500.

Clyde Realty   **476-8200**

Modern *means inside plumbing.*

522

Wilderness Home— 10 Acres

This is a home as modern as the setting is rugged. The all-electric A-frame offers 2 bedrooms and a sleeping loft, a huge deck, central air and a 2-car garage. Built for year-round living, it is the ideal vacation or retirement home. While only 10 minutes to a golf course and Lake Kentucky, it's priced realistically at $69,500.

Clyde Realty   **476-8200**

This property ad is targeted at retirees or those seeking a vacation home.

523

Tall Trees

create a screen of privacy, and soft cascades of light and shade add a timelessness where today, tomorrow or next week need not mean urgency. In this very special place stands a home as solid as the trees that guard it. This 3BR, 2-bath American Traditional has an unassuming charm that complements the environment. Four acres of a very special love priced at $179,500.

Clyde Realty   **476-8200**

This ad is for an older home on a wooded parcel, and it effectively sells a mood.

The ad was taken with permission from an award-winning ad written by Gordon Wearing-Smith for Barry Plant Real Estate, Doncaster, Australia.

524

A Forgotten Valley

You could travel the world and find little to compare with this 3-bedroom, New England-style Colonial in a setting picturesque amidst 9 acres of oak-sprinkled fields with vistas that seem to reach out forever. The sparkling stream cascading through the property will fulfill a trout fisherman's fantasy or can be your quiet place to relax and enjoy. Escape from the world at $289,500.

Clyde Realty   **476-8200**

This ad appeals to retirees or escapists looking for weekend or vacation homes. Very little information is given about the home. If there were strong features, they should have been stated.

525

Perfect Away Spot— 10 Acres

Own a 2-bedroom modern cottage set in a wooded glen less than 2 hours from the city. With $5,000 down, it's not going to last long. Full price is $79,500.

Clyde Realty   **476-8200**

526

We Lost Charlie

He went to show this older 8-room Colonial on 2 lovely wooded acres last week, and we haven't seen him since. While the rooms are large, we should have found him by now. The office took up a collection, and we're offering a reward of $39. Oh, unless Charlie sold it, the house is still available at $89,500, but please return Charlie if you find him.

Clyde Realty   **476-8200**

The ad is of course a spoof to sell a large, older home at a low price. It is designed to prompt readers to call for more information about the house, not Charlie.

527

Live the Wild Life

in this 3BR, 2-bath, cedar and stone home that blends into a wooded hillside—home to deer, raccoon, chipmunks and porcupines. Glory in magnificent natural vistas from the huge deck. On almost 3 acres, this home includes a family room; a rock fireplace; and a dream tile, copper and brick kitchen. Priced at less than a city home at $189,500.

Clyde Realty   **476-8200**

528

Walk to Privy

Just follow the picturesque path to the privy behind this 7-room cottage virtually untouched by the twentieth century. While apparently solid in construction, its needs begin with the barest of necessities. In its favor, this property offers 3 acres of the most spectacular scenery you'll ever find. If you love working with your hands, then this is your opportunity to achieve pure rapture at only $47,000.

Clyde Realty   **476-8200**

The above ad heading draws attention to the fact that the home isn't modern, but the heading is nevertheless so unusual that it invites readers to peruse the entire ad. The ad will attract escapists as well as buyers of fixer-uppers.

529

The Birds and the Trees

Imagine a sun-drenched woodland glade, majestic oaks and wild flowers. Awake to the morning serenade of songbirds. If you long for the tranquility only nature can provide, you're bound to fall in love with this 3BR, 2½-bath Colonial with its huge screened summer porch and delightful dining patio. This 3-acre, private refuge is only a short commute from the city and can be your reality for $249,500.

Clyde Realty   **476-8200**

530

Forgotten Cabin— 20 Acres

Off of a little-traveled lane and nestled in a woodland glade is this picture-book cabin with its weatherboard siding and huge stone fireplace. The bath is at the end of the path, but there is a well and pump that supply sparkling pure water. Electricity is available but hasn't quite made it here. The cabin has 1 huge room and loft. It looks like the only occupants in the last few years have been squirrels and chipmunks. This ideal place to escape the world can be yours at $49,500.

Clyde Realty   **476-8200**

This ad paints a very desirable picture of a rather primitive cabin that will appeal strongly to many readers.

531

Amid the Apple Trees

Country living can be yours in this 3-bedroom American Traditional set on the most beautiful 2½ acres you have ever seen. It comes complete with a mouth-watering apple orchard of more than 50 trees. Also included is an ancient but solid barn framed with giant timbers that would make an ideal studio or? For a low-low down payment, we can put you up to your neck in apples. Full price only $89,500.

Clyde Realty   **476-8200**

532

A Quiet
Country Lane

leads to this carefully preserved, 4-acre bit of Americana. Set on a slight knoll sprinkled with hickory and sugar maple, this traditional Wisconsin farmhouse shows early Victorian influences. The 3-bedroom home features updated heating, electrical and plumbing systems. There is room for a harvest crew in the bright country kitchen, and the dining room has seen a century of Thanksgiving turkeys. The large barn is perfect for an artist's studio. With its large family garden and duck pond, this is about as idyllic as life can get, and it's all yours for only $92,500.

Clyde Realty   **476-8200**

Most older farmhouses have updated systems, a large kitchen and a dining room.

Many buyers of rural homes feel they have artistic talent, so pointing out that the barn is useful as a studio is a real plus.

If there are fish in the pond, the heading might say "Fish-filled Duck Pond."

533

Moo!

There's room for a contented cow, pigs, goats, horses and a gaggle of children on this 40-acre farm that's only a short commute from the city. There's plenty of life yet in the 2 ancient barns and this 4-bedroom home. Modernized around 1920 but like a worn shoe, it offers old-fashioned comfort for a happy family. It's not a showplace but a place for living. Available with excellent terms at $179,500.

Clyde Realty   **476-8200**

This ad is for a small, older farm. It will appeal to the fixer-upper buyer and to the family desiring escape from the city.

534

As the Crow Flies

This 3-bedroom American Traditional, with its little red barn and 5 acres, isn't very far from the city, but one look and you'll realize it's at least 50 years away. On a quiet, tree-canopied lane, the home features a huge, old-fashioned pantry; a claw-footed tub; high ceilings; and a rocking-chair front porch. It appears to have been carefully preserved in a time warp from a far gentler period. It's worth the extra drive to live a dream. Yours at $119,500.

Clyde Realty   **476-8200**

535 Farmhouse—5 Acres

Set among towering maples, this 9-room, 3BR American Traditional was built in 1910 to replace the original homestead log cabin. The home has been completely renovated with all new systems to satisfy the most demanding owner. You'll love the high ceilings and extensive use of rich woodwork. Features include 24′ × 48′ barn ideal for a studio, large garage, workshop that can be converted to a guest house, beautiful family garden area, fruit trees and fenced pasture. This is a place to enjoy living at $79,500.

Clyde Realty   476-8200

Adding a little history to an ad can heighten interest in a property (e.g., "originally homesteaded in 1858 by Ezra Smith . . ."). Historical information can be obtained from the abstract of title or your title insurance company.

536 For Country Folk

We have just a plain, white-clapboard, 7-room farmhouse that is neat as a pin. It has a small red barn, a large tool shed, a family orchard and garden, and 27 fenced acres. Country-priced at $79,500.

Clyde Realty   476-8200

This ad is likely to attract city folk.

537 1932 Farmhouse

You will be drawn to the warmth of this 2-story, clapboard farmhouse with its huge rocking-chair front porch. There are 3 large bedrooms; hardwood floors; a bright, airy kitchen; and a screened and glassed sun room that will make the perfect studio. It comes complete with 5 acres, a magnificent garden, a family orchard and a large red barn. Happily priced at $97,500.

Clyde Realty   476-8200

Including the year an older home was built in the ad heading is most effective, especially if the ad sells nostalgia.

538 Escape the Suburbs

Exurbia—the land beyond—offers this 3-bedroom Cape Cod on 3 acres with a century-old sugar maple ready for tapping. The huge barn will make an ideal studio, and the school bus stops at the driveway. What more could you want? And only $79,950.

Clyde Realty   476-8200

A school bus stops at the driveway of most rural homes.

539

Lost River Farm
20 Acres of Happiness

A gentle stream meanders through a quiet meadow. There's a natural pasture studded with ancient oaks and a wood lot that is home to raccoons and even deer. The 7-room traditional farm home sits amidst towering hickory trees on a gentle knoll. There is a red barn that has stood for nearly 100 years. It's an idyllic setting for weekends or forever at a very affordable $89,500.

Clyde Realty   **476-8200**

By giving a farm an attractive name, you make it that much more desirable.

540

Hog Heaven—
10 Acres

A former owner of this 3-bedroom traditional white-clapboard farmhouse kept pigs. Included are apple trees, a small red barn, a great place for a garden, several sheds, a wooded pasture (if you want to keep cows, sheep or goats), and a pond for ducks or pigs to wallow in. Priced less than a city home at $72,500.

Clyde Realty   **476-8200**

Most farms have had pigs at some time, so the above heading will surely attract attention.

If a house has strong features (such as a nice porch), the ad should mention them.

541

Keep a Cow

or a horse or 2 in the barn that comes with this 3-bedroom, authentic, white-clapboard American farmhouse on 3 large, fenced acres. You'll love this house with its wide, covered porch; country-sized kitchen; and exquisite woodwork. It has been completely and carefully modernized so as not to detract from its charm. Incidentally, there's a mouth-watering family orchard, a great garden, and it's priced for less than a city home at $89,500.

Clyde Realty   **476-8200**

542

Forgotten Farm

On 20 acres, this 3-bedroom classic brick farmhouse with sun porch that would make an ideal studio, old red barn, garage, family garden, orchard and land that has not seen a plow in many years is a great place to raise goats, horses, chickens or kids at $69,500.

Clyde Realty   **476-8200**

If location is a positive feature, it should be included. This farm is not being sold for economic purposes because of its size. It is sold as a home and will appeal to a retiree or person who can take work home with him or her (such as an artist).

543

Grow Your Own

children, vegetables and even a cow on this 5-acre minifarm just 45 minutes from the city. You'll love the 3BR traditional farm home with its white-clapboard siding, huge family kitchen and updated modern systems. There's a large red barn with room for a workshop, storage, a studio or a business as well as livestock. Less than the price of an ordinary city home at $89,500.

Clyde Realty   **476-8200**

544

Farm in the Dell

on 20 acres in a small secluded valley. There is an 8-room, 3BR, American-style, white-clapboard farmhouse with up-to-date systems. A traditional red barn, a poultry house, and even an equipment shed are all included. It's the idyllic retirement farm or the perfect place to raise a family. Country-priced at $89,500.

Clyde Realty   **476-8200**

545

The Old Homestead

This 9-room American Traditional stands on a slight knoll amidst a bright-green, tree-studded lawn. There's a large red barn that has seen better days, but it's ideal for an artist's studio or for restoring antique furniture. Only 5 acres are left of fields that once stretched to the ends of one's imagination. It is there, waiting for you, at $129,500.

Clyde Realty   **476-8200**

546

Opportunity of a Lifestyle

You can live in a 3-bedroom, American Gothic, white-frame farmhouse on almost 2 acres less than 2 hours from the city. There is a quaint barn that will make a delightful studio and a garden that makes most farmers envious. For weekends, weeks on end or forever, it's your chance to unwind and live life the way it was intended to be lived. Priced within easy reach at $79,500.

Clyde Realty   **476-8200**

547

Getaway Place

You can relax on almost 2 country acres off a quiet lane in a picture-book, 3BR, white-frame, American Gothic farm home. Your nearest neighbors will be the Holstein cows grazing across the road. Less than 2 hours from the city, it's the perfect weekend or retirement home, and it's priced at only $69,500.

Clyde Realty   **476-8200**

If a house has strong features—such as hardwood floors, beautiful woodwork, or porches—they should be mentioned in the ad.

548

Escape to Yesterday

A little wooded knoll, a white-clap-board farmhouse and an ancient barn can change your perspective on life. Offering peace and quiet in a pastoral setting, this is the ideal home for the writer, artist, craftsman or retiree. There is plenty of room for a garden, cow and horse on the 4 acres. The barn offers a multitude of possibilities. This home has 3 bed-rooms; a fruit cellar for your harvest; and modern heating, electrical and plumbing systems. It's your chance at a new direction for your life at an affordable $119,500.

Clyde Realty   **476-8200**

549

Barn—House— 5 Acres

The barn is great. You'll love the classic lines, and there's plenty of room for business, hobby, studio, storage or livestock. This 3-bedroom home needs restoration, as it has been vacant for several years. There's a fenced pasture, a garden area, a family orchard and lovely hardwood trees. Priced to sell at lit-tle more than land value at $49,500.

Clyde Realty   **476-8200**

By emphasizing the barn, readers will re-alize the house has little value.

550

Holsteins and Guernseys

will be your neighbors as owner of this 3-bedroom, American Gothic home set on 2 acres of pastoral splendor. There is a sun porch that is perfect for a studio and a huge garage/workroom waiting to be converted to a guest house. With a mouth-watering family orchard and a perfect garden spot, what more could you ask for? It's all yours at $89,500 with flexible owner financ-ing available.

Clyde Realty   **476-8200**

551

Lemonade Springs? Cigarette Tree?

No, it's not quite as idyllic as the big rock-candy mountain, but it comes close. Set on a full acre shaded by trees that were saplings during the Civil War, this house is the perfect escape from city drudgery. There's a great family garden, fruit trees, raspberry bushes, and a barn just waiting to become your private studio. The home has hardwood floors; an orchard stone fireplace; a sun porch; and light, bright rooms that convey an aura of happiness. All this and only 50 minutes from the city at an affordable $89,500.

Clyde Realty   **476-8200**

553

A Basic 40 Acres

Would you like a nice, traditional, 3BR farm home with a large red barn, an almost-new machine shed, a chicken house, a family orchard and a garden? For self-sufficiency or a beautiful lifestyle, you're unlikely to come close to this unique opportunity. It's priced for less than most vacation homes at $89,500.

Clyde Realty   **476-8200**

This ad is very simple, but effective, as it attracts buyers looking for a simpler lifestyle.

552

An Old Red Barn

comes with a lovely 3-bedroom American Traditional home set admist towering maples (ready for tapping) on 5 picturesque acres. There's even a family-sized garden and a mouth-watering orchard. Offering joy and tranquility for weekends or a lifetime at only $99,500.

Clyde Realty   **476-8200**

This ad paints the inviting image of a Norman Rockwell lifestyle.

12

Horse Property

To horse owners or buyers who want to own horses, where to stable their animals is every bit as important—and in some cases more important—than the homes they live in.

Ads for horse property can be written whenever a property has the proper room and zoning for horses, even though it may not presently have the facilities for them. The following ads were written to appeal to horse people. Note that the headings indicate that the ads are for horse property. Also note that another feature can be emphasized in a heading when a newspaper has a separate section for horse property.

554

A Horse of Course

should go in the 2-stall stable with tack room that comes with this 2½-acre ranch. The California-style, 3BR, 2-bath ranch home set beneath a giant oak seems to blend into the landscape. You'll love the bright family room with its native stone fireplace and rich wood paneling as well as the brick and tile kitchen with room for an entire roundup crew. Sparkling white board fences and an irrigated pasture make this the place where you'll want to hang your spurs. Better hurry at $198,500.

Clyde Realty   476-8200

555

Hold Your Horses

in this horse barn with 3 double stalls and a tack room that comes with this 2½-acre ranch. Fenced and cross-fenced, there is a corral and a picture-book Arizona-style, 3BR, 1½-bath ranch home with a brick and copper, family-sized kitchen; a family room; and a delightful patio where you can relax and gaze out over your spread. There's even a separate double garage and work-room. Blue-jean-priced at $97,500.

Clyde Realty   **476-8200**

556

Hold Your Horses

in the 3 corrals and quaint western-style barn with 6 stalls. This 20-acre ranch adjoins miles of riding trails and comes complete with a 3BR, 2½-bath ranch home that will delight any cowgirl. It has every modern convenience set in a down-home decor of rich wood paneling and antique rose brick. It's the life you deserve at $268,500.

Clyde Realty   **476-8200**

557

Cowboy—Cowgirl

If you love the smell of horses, you'll be ecstatic about this 3BR, 2-bath ranch home on 5 acres. Zoned for 10 horses, there's even a Dutch barn with 4 double stalls, a large tack room and 2 corrals. The whole package is tied together with white-board ranch fencing. A "mighty purty spread" for cowboys and cowgirls. Offered at less than the price of a city home, $239,500.

Clyde Realty   **476-8200**

For a more dramatic heading, see the following ad.

558

Horse Manure

not included with the 3-stall horse barn that comes with this Colorado-style, 3BR, 2½-bath ranch home set on 5 acres only 40 minutes from the city. The house has every conceivable built-in, a screened porch, a 2-car garage and central air. Fenced and cross-fenced, you'll want to put your brand on this spread at $219,500.

Clyde Realty   **476-8200**

This ad is specifically targeted at commuters.

559

Horse,
Cow or Camel

There's room for all in the 3 corrals; the 2 fenced, irrigated pastures; and the 6-stall barn that comes with a 3BR, 2½-bath ranch home right out of *Better Homes and Gardens.* This home features a family room paneled in limed oak, a huge ranch-house fireplace, a kitchen big enough for a whole crew of hands, as well as a full basement and attached double garage with a separate workroom. All this on 10 acres of deep, rich loam, and it's priced like a city home at $398,000.

Clyde Realty   476-8200

560

Get a Horse

You'll want several as the owner of this 8-acre ranch within commuting distance of town. The house has 3 bedrooms plus a den and family room to hold a gaggle of junior cowhands. The 4-stall barn has a huge loft that will make an ideal studio or? The entire property is fenced and cross-fenced. Trade your suit and wing tips for Levis and boots at $249,500.

Clyde Realty   476-8200

561

"Buy Me a Pony"

will be your children's cry when they see the red horse barn that comes with this 3BR, 2-bath California ranch home on 2 lovely acres in Waterbury Hills. With the white-board fencing, you'd think it a fine Kentucky estate rather than a family home priced at only $189,500.

Clyde Realty   476-8200

562

Appaloosas
Lived Here

The former owner of this 5-acre Westview ranch kept 4 horses in the large red barn that comes with this 3BR, 2-bath, Colorado-style ranch home. There is a delightful family room that looks out over your "spread." The ranch features a roundup sized ranch kitchen, warm wood paneling and a toe-warming fireplace. Of course, there is a 2-car garage and a corral. The property is fenced and cross-fenced with an irrigated pasture. A place any cowboy or cowgirl will love to call home at $189,500.

Clyde Realty   476-8200

The type of horse kept by a former owner can be used in the heading to attract attention to the ad.

13

Large Homes

Having more than 3 bedrooms is a definite plus for many buyers. When perusing a sea of ads, many readers looking for 4 bedrooms (or larger homes) will only look at the ad headings. Therefore, your headings should mention the number of bedrooms or indicate that a home is larger than normal.

Alternative ads for large homes can be found in other chapters of this book (e.g., chapter 2, Architectural Style, or chapter 17, Luxury Homes).

563

---

5 BR—2 Baths
$89,500

Attention kids! Imagine a room of your very own. There's even a full basement that will make an ideal playroom, a double garage with a workroom great for a clubhouse, and a whole forest of trees perfect for climbing. There are sidewalks for skating and lots of kids your age in the neighborhood. Hey, what more could you want? The last one to call is a loser.

Clyde Realty   476-8200

While a little on the cute side, this ad sells the home's benefits for children. Many homes are purchased by parents because of what they feel a home and neighborhood have to offer their children.

564
Bring the Gang—5BR

There's room for everyone, even cousin Mabel, in this 11-room, 2-bath American Traditional in a quiet West Side neighborhood. High ceilings; gleaming, solid-oak flooring; updated systems; a kitchen most restaurants would envy; a double garage; a full basement; and room for a garden are just a few of the special features. Best of all, it's priced at only $89,500.

Clyde Realty   **476-8200**

Because of the lower-than-expected price, the above heading could say "5 BR—$89,500."

565
Mother Goose—5BR

Leave your shoe forever. You'll have room for all the children and Grandma too with this huge American Traditional in an established West Side family neighborhood. There's a full basement, garage and walk-up attic for your storage; an eat-in kitchen to hold half the neighborhood; and a dining room big enough for a family reunion. Walking-close to schools and shopping, the best news is the price—only $79,500. Available with fairy-tale financing.

Clyde Realty   **476-8200**

566
Needs Children— 5BR

You can have a large white clapboard home on a tree-studded lot in a family neighborhood that is only a short walk to one of the best grade schools in the city.

$5,000 Down

and the owner will carry the balance at only 9 percent interest. Priced at only $98,500, we suggest you call immediately.

Clyde Realty   **476-8200**

The two main features—5 bedrooms and financing—are covered by the split-heading approach in the above ad.
If there is more than 1 bath, it should be stated in the ad copy.

567
Kids—Kids—6 BR

Forget planned parenthood. This brick American Traditional is for the old-fashioned, large family. It is reported that the original owner had 14 children. Set on a large lot close to everything, you'll see that an expansive home need not be expensive. Only $98,500.

Clyde Realty   **476-8200**

Facts about a former owner create special interest in a home. This ad, while short, has a similar approach as the following ad.

568

Kids—Kids—5BR

There's room for a large family plus assorted cousins in this 11-room, 2½-bath American Traditional built before anyone even considered birth control.

$8,000 per Room

It's the best bargain you can find in a home offering privacy, comfort and beauty. It has been a happy family home for many generations, but your chance for happiness depends on a quick call.

Clyde Realty   **476-8200**

When readers multiply $8,000 × 11, they'll discover the price is very low.

569

Room for Grandma— 4BR

There are 2 master suites in this split-plan, 2½-bath, Florida-style ranch that offers the ultimate in privacy. With its large fenced yard; great garden spot; and just minutes to schools, shopping, parks and bus line, it is truly a family home offering family comfort at a family price of $93,500.

Clyde Realty   **476-8200**

570

Mean Mother-in-law Special—5 Bedrooms

A separate Granny flat will provide privacy for you and your mother-in-law in this 11-room, brick American Traditional set on one-third of an acre in a quiet and friendly West Side neighborhood. There is a huge yard and garden as well as a large double garage. A lot of space for little money at only $89,500.

Clyde Realty   **476-8200**

Special thanks to Gordon-Wearing Smith and Barry Plant Real Estate Pty., Ltd., Doncaster, Australia.

571

Hoards of Kids

and a mean mother-in-law will all fit into this 11-room American classic on a quiet, tree-studded lot in Glenhaven. There are 5 bedrooms, and the sewing room could make it 6. The flexible floor plan will allow a completely separate suite for your mother-in-law. Loads of possibilities and a huge garage make this a rare opportunity at $97,500.

Clyde Realty   **476-8200**

Special thanks to Gordon-Wearing Smith and Barry Plant Real Estate Pty., Ltd, Doncaster, Australia.

572

Family Feud—4BR

Need more room? Getting in each other's way? This spacious 2½-bath home even includes a very private getaway den; a workroom in the oversized, double garage; and the perfect spot for a family garden in the huge backyard. At $169,500, you want to be the first family to call us, or the feud will go on.

Clyde Realty   476-8200

573

Being Squeezed— 4BR

You'll have room to stretch out with this West Side American Traditional that includes a lovely garden, mature landscaping and a double garage. The price is a relief at $89,500.

Clyde Realty   476-8200

If there is more than 1 bath, it should be stated.

If the house has other strong features, they should also be included in the copy.

574

Sleeps a Dozen

The 4BR and large enclosed porch plus family room in this West Side brick Traditional are perfect for the old-fashioned family. There's a tribe-sized kitchen and a garage that can hold 2 cars, a dozen bikes and a red wagon. All at a price you can love—$139,500.

Clyde Realty   476-8200

575

4 Huge Bedrooms

will hold your family in this 2-bath New England Colonial set on an estate-sized lot loaded with trees and squirrels in the friendly community of Newcastle. There's also a finished basement—the ideal rainy-day playroom; a 3-car garage to hold the bikes, trikes and wagons; and a tribe-sized kitchen that has room for a gathering of the clan. Built with traditional family values in mind, this is your home at $179,500.

Clyde Realty   476-8200

This ad conveys the image of a home for the all-American family.

This ad is for a large, older home. It was inspired by Ian Price of Surfer's Paradise, Australia.

This is an ad for a large, old home. The word "mansion" is not used because in some areas it bears the negative connotation of being old-fashioned and costly to maintain.

The split heading sells both price and size.

This ad forces the reader to compute the total price.

580

5BR—Southern Colonial

This 11-room, 2½-bath masterpiece with soaring columns is palatially ensconced upon a 2-acre knoll with all city services. Combining the charm of the early 1800s with the conveniences of today, it is a home to be loved at $249,500.

Clyde Realty   **476-8200**

Size can also be featured in ads such as this one, which emphasizes architectural style.

581

New England Colonial—4BR

White-clapboard siding; shutters that really work; 2 fireplaces; stately trees; 2½ baths; and an attached, oversized, double garage in a neighborhood you'll want as your own are awaiting you. Call.

Clyde Realty   **476-8200**

Both New England Colonial and 4BR are strong features, so they are combined in the above heading. The ad tells little about the house but in a few words provides a pleasant picture for the reader.

582

4 Bedrooms Plus Den—$89,500

Not a misprint, this West Side, brick American Traditional also includes a double garage, fireplace, completely updated kitchen, hardwood floors, friendly neighborhood and a great deal more. Better gather the clan and hurry over, as this one isn't going to be around long.

Clyde Realty   **476-8200**

A heading such as the one in this ad is really the best for a home aimed at a large family. It is less likely to be overlooked than anything more subtle. The ad includes the price on the second line, because it is also attractive.

583

4BR—$79,500

You can own a large, 9-room, brick American Traditional in a neighborhood of well-kept homes and quiet streets that's just a short walk to schools, park and bus line. You'll love the beautiful woodwork and light, bright rooms. A rare opportunity that will probably sell to the first caller.

Clyde Realty   **476-8200**

The 2 major features—size and price—were combined in the heading to reflect the home's extra large size and lower-than-normal price.

584

Big Home—
Small Town

It's the perfect combination for your family—a 10-room, 4BR, white-clapboard country Traditional with a full basement, walk-up attic and 2-car garage with storage loft on over a half-acre that includes a garden and apple trees. Best of all, there's only a short commute to town, and it's priced for your family at $89,500, with flexible owner financing.

Clyde Realty   **476-8200**

585

Get Lost—4BR

Lose yourself in the 11 rooms and 3½ baths of this impressive Pennsylvania Dutch Colonial on an estate setting in Westchester. With its authentic detailing, high ceilings and hardwood floors, it is a warm home for family living or entertaining on a grand scale. There is a hideaway den, a 3-car garage, a screened porch, a music or drawing room and even a separate sewing room in the master suite. Priced for the claustrophobic at $289,500.

Clyde Realty   **476-8200**

586

4 Bedrooms—
Who Needs Them

This Westport Colonial is too big for the present owners and probably too big for you. Besides the bedrooms, there's a separate den, a dining room, a full basement with recreation room and 2½ baths. Obviously no one wants this large a house surrounded by a huge lawn. Priced to unload at $184,500.

Clyde Realty   **476-8200**

The negative approach in the above ad will bring in calls from people who want this kind of property.

14

Location

It has often been said that the three most important factors in purchasing a home are location, location and location. Location is a primary determinant of value and appreciation. If a property is in a highly desirable area, this should be emphasized in an ad, preferably in its heading. If a newspaper categorizes property by location, don't repeat the location in your ad heading, as this serves no purpose.

You should also emphasize the proximity of a home to a hospital, mall or school. While there are many ads in other chapters of this book that feature location, the following ads specifically stress location.

588

Westlake

You can own a like-new, 3BR, 2½-bath Tennessee Colonial with all the fine detailing and craftsmanship you thought had been forgotten. A 2½-car garage, central air, a family room and a prestigious

WESTLAKE

address are yours for just $187,500.

Clyde Realty   **476-8200**

You can call attention to location by using a split heading, which is effective for a highly desirable area.

587

Southport under $100,000

Imagine owning a 2-bedroom bungalow in the most prestigious area on a huge lot at a price within your reach. Get ready to be envied if you call today.

Clyde Realty   **476-8200**

It isn't necessary to give the exact price. This ad emphasizes location.

160

589

A Bel Aire Address

At a down-to-earth price, this 3BR, 2½-bath Cape Cod is situated among exclusive estates. All the amenities for luxury living are included, such as 2½-car garage, family room, screened porch and central air. This is the lowest-priced home in Bel Aire at only $539,500.

Clyde Realty   **476-8200**

This ad has definite snob appeal.

For the heading, you can use a prestigious street (e.g., "Lake Drive" address) or a city or subdivision.

Always mention that a home has air conditioning when it is not a common extra. If most of the homes in an area have central air, it is not necessary to mention this.

590

Beverly Hills Address

and a 3BR, 2-bath American Colonial with family room and double garage are available but

Without the Price

That's right. The most impressive address imaginable at only $395,000.

Clyde Realty   **476-8200**

This ad sells the home's address, not the home itself. You can also use the name of a prestigious street or subdivision.

591

Malibu Address— $299,500

can be yours without a Malibu price. This 3BR, 2-bath Georgian town house offers a very private balcony and patio, a huge living room, and a kitchen with every convenience you will ever want. This fine residence deserves your immediate attention at a price you can afford.

Clyde Realty   **476-8200**

Note that the 2 strong points—price and location—are included in the heading.

592

Can't Afford Newport?

This stunning 3BR, 2½-bath Mediterranean with its tile roof and soaring marble entry compares with Newport's finest at half the cost. It's the home you dream of and only a half hour away at $219,000.

Clyde Realty   **476-8200**

This home is not in Newport, but Newport is used as an example of a highly desirable area. The home's location is not given, as it might limit the calls.

593

Newport—Almost

In a quiet family community adjoining Newport is the home you have dreamed about. Shaded by towering maples, this substantial brick Traditional offers 3 bedrooms, 1¾ baths, a separate den or office, a huge recreation room, and a gardener's wonderland of flowering trees and shrubs. You can live the lifestyle of Newport at only $99,500.

Clyde Realty   **476-8200**

Do not underestimate the effect of descriptions of trees and flowers. While often overlooked in ads, these descriptions create an extremely positive image in readers' minds.

594

Beverly Hills—Almost

This 3BR, 2½-bath, Italian Renaissance masterpiece is almost in Beverly Hills but is priced at half of comparable Beverly Hills property. On a fantastically landscaped estate lot with pool and cabana, the home has a large family room, den and a 3-car garage. It is priced to sell at only $695,000.

Clyde Realty   **476-8200**

Any time a home is close to a desirable area, but not actually in the area, this type of ad can be effectively used.

595

The Location

If you could choose the most prestigious block of the most prestigious street for your dream house, this would be your choice. Huge chestnut trees guard the private drive past well-manicured lawns and flowering bushes. The 3-bedroom Colonial with its separate den or private office, 3-car garage, family room and full basement is just what you always wanted in a home. The perfect combination can be yours at $395,000.

Clyde Realty   **476-8200**

Location can be stressed in an ad without revealing the exact area.

596

The Address

you only dream of having on the most prestigious street. This 3BR, 2½-bath, brick and frame Williamsburg Colonial will delight you with its spaciousness; gleaming woodwork; rich, new carpeting; work space in the oversized double garage; giant beech and walnut trees; and dream, brick and tile kitchen. Your dream is within reach at $169,500.

Clyde Realty   **476-8200**

597

Come Home to Saukville

You must see this 3BR, 1½-bath, double-garage, white Cape Cod sheltered by magnificent beech and maple trees on a quiet cul-de-sac that is only a short hop and a skip to grade and middle schools. You'll love the screened porch for summer living and the river-rock fireplace with its massive mantle. It's the place you'll proudly call home at $119,500.

Clyde Realty   **476-8200**

You can use the name of the town or subdivision in an ad's heading.

598

Westwood

—where we put the privileged few in their place. You can live in a community of quiet, tree-lined streets and truly fine homes on estate lots such as this 3BR, 2½-bath, classic brick English Tudor. The leaded glass, ivy vines and rich wood paneling in the drawing room seem to transport you to a proper English estate, where life centers on family and gracious living. Of course there's a rose garden, velvet lawns, carefully sculptured hedges and every amenity a civilized person wishes for. Proudly offered at $630,000.

Clyde Realty   **476-8200**

599

Middleton

with its quiet, tree-lined streets and old values, is the site of this 3-bedroom American Traditional that appears to be right out of a Norman Rockwell painting. Your children will love the softball-sized backyard with room to spare for a garden. There is plenty of room to tinker in the oversized garage and the basement makes a great rainy-day playroom. Invest in your family today at $98,000.

Clyde Realty   **476-8200**

The heading sells location, while much of the ad body sells the picture of an ideal family environment.

600

Be Among the First

to discover the pleasures of Westhaven, an exclusive community of fine homes only 30 minutes from the city. You will fall in love with this fine 3BR, 2½-bath French Colonial with its stone and brick exterior that seems as one with the naturally wooded half-acre site. Other features include a 3-car garage and clerestory-lighted studio. Offering the small-town ambiance of long ago with all the metropolitan conveniences, this can be your life of the future for $245,000.

Clyde Realty   **476-8200**

601

Meet the Neighbors

Ask them why they chose Clinton Hills. You'll realize you can't find a better place for your family than this 3BR, 2-bath, double-garage, split-level ranch set on a picture-perfect corner lot 2 short blocks to schools. The best description of all its great features is simply "perfect," and with one call we'll prove it to you. Incidentally, it's priced right at $149,500, and we can offer exceptional financing.

Clyde Realty   476-8200

602

Go West

to Livingston Estates and this 3BR, 2-bath Nantucket Colonial set amidst giant oaks in this premier community. You'll love the large recreation room, the double garage with room to spare for a workbench, and the feeling of spaciousness and quality. At $189,500, your future happiness is only a phone call away.

Clyde Realty   476-8200

603

Half-Price Sale

Adjoining Santa Monica but at half the price is this 3BR, 2-bath California Beach Contemporary with its over 2,400 sq. ft. of living space. The walls of glass and cedar and the soaring ceilings make it appear twice as large. It's everything you dream about in a home at only $199,500.

Clyde Realty   476-8200

604

Mt. Wilson Baptist Church

is just a short walk from this 2-bedroom, expandable Cape Cod in move-in condition. The home comes complete with finished basement, garage, central air, all appliances and a giant chestnut tree. Priced for your pocketbook at $89,500.

Clyde Realty   476-8200

Closeness to church or synagogue is a positive feature, especially if a home is apt to sell to an older purchaser who is more likely to attend regularly and might not wish, or be able, to drive.

605

Walk to the Train

from this 3BR, 1½-bath Dutch Colonial on a tree-shaded street in a family neighborhood. You'll love the well-tended landscape and the beautiful hardwood floors. Special features include central air, a workroom in the double garage, a completely new kitchen with Corian tops and every conceivable built-in. Priced to move at $179,500.

Clyde Realty   **476-8200**

Closeness to the train is a strong plus, especially in commuter areas. Buyers willingly pay thousands more for this asset, so it should be emphasized.

606

Walk to University

This is an exceptional 3-bedroom, brick bungalow located on a quiet street with a separate, paneled dining room; a living room built for entertaining; a picturesque front porch; and rose bushes that are the pride of the neighborhood. By renting 1 or 2 rooms to students, your payments can be practically made for you. It's an unusual opportunity at $89,500, with great terms.

Clyde Realty   **476-8200**

This ad stresses the benefit of living close to a university. It will appeal to people other than just students and employees because of its income possibilities.

607

Longdale Schools

You'll give your children the best education possible living in this 3BR, 2-bath, brick English Tudor. You'll love the landscaping with the manicured hedges, stately trees and colorful beds of flowers. This home has everything on your wish list. If there ever was a "must-see to appreciate," this is it. Priced at $179,500 with below-market, owner financing available.

Clyde Realty   **476-8200**

The idea of living in a particular school district is a strong motivator for many with children.

608

Feel Like a Chauffeur?

Have to drive your children everyplace? Then you'll love this 3BR, 2-bath, double-garage Cape Cod situated in a quiet family neighborhood skipping distance to park and schools, and best of all, it's only 1 block to a bus line. The house has it all, including a full basement, magnificent woodwork and a kitchen that will be the envy of your friends. Priced to sell quickly at $149,500.

Clyde Realty   **476-8200**

609

Had Enough

of wasting half your day commuting? Consider this charming 3-bedroom brick Traditional in an established neighborhood that will probably cut your commuting time by at least two thirds. There is an old-fashioned country garden resplendent with color in the private walled yard, an ideal spot to relax or entertain. You'll love the gleaming hardwood floors, intricate woodwork and wood-burning fireplace. Besides a garage, there's a place to park an RV or boat for those getaway weekends. You won't believe the price—only $89,500.

Clyde Realty   **476-8200**

This ad is for an older home located in the city or in an older, close-in suburb.
If a home has more than 1 bath, say so.
If a home has more than a 1-car garage, it should also be stated.

610

Walk

to schools, shops, churches and bus from this 3-bedroom Traditional in an established West Side neighborhood of impeccable lawns and fine homes. This home offers a double garage, hardwood floors, a sun-drenched family kitchen, and a delightful garden area for only $79,500.

Clyde Realty   **476-8200**

"Garden area" does not necessarily mean there is currently a garden.

611

Shopping Your Hobby?

Walk to West Side Plaza from this 3BR, 1½-bath Cape Cod set beneath a giant chestnut tree. The home offers a double garage, full basement, lovely screened porch, colorful landscaping, top-of-the-line appliances, and it's in move-in condition and decorated in soft, neutral tones. Sorry, but you won't need to buy a thing, other than the house, of course, at $129,500.

Clyde Realty   **476-8200**

612

Born To Shop?

Then you'll want this 3BR, 2-bath split-level on a large, wooded lot only 5 minutes from the new Westport Mall. It has a full basement, family room, Roman baths sheathed in marble and huge closets to hold all your purchases. Sale-priced at $189,500. (Sorry, we don't give green stamps.)

Clyde Realty   **476-8200**

Shopping is the No. 1 pastime in America, so proximity to malls is extremely important.

15

Lots

Like other ads, lot ads should include price. Other factors to consider for inclusion in lot ads are the following:

Access (Note the presence of a paved road if many other lots are not on paved roads.)

Utilities (only if other nearby lots don't have all utilities—sewer, water, electricity, gas, phone or cable TV)

Water Frontage (if applicable)

Highway Frontage (commercial)

View

Trees (Wooded lots are desirable.)

Slope (While lots with steep slopes are normally less expensive because of their greater construction costs, many buyers like lots where split-level or open-basement plans are possible.)

Zoning (if other than single-family residential)

Permits (If engineering, approval or building permits for a particular use have been obtained, say so in the ad.)

Size (This is very important for other than single-family residential lots. If a residential lot is larger than average, emphasize its size.)

Location (Location is the single most important feature of a lot.)

Terms (If a lot can be purchased with terms or if the owner will subordinate to a construction loan, point this out.)

When a lot ad is under the newspaper category "lots," don't mention the fact that you are advertising a lot in the ad.

613

Raspberries

are growing wild on this last wooded, estate-sized lot on a quiet, paved street in Westwood. Sewer and water are in and paid for. Ready for your dream home at $69,500.

Clyde Realty   476-8200

When a lot is the only one available on a street, block or subdivision, it should be mentioned in the ad, as it creates a sense of urgency and desirability.

The above heading is unusual and prompts people to continue reading. Variations on the heading are "Wild Flowers," "Blueberries," and so forth.

614

Last Chance

This is the last estate-sized lot available in the exclusive community of Brentwood Heights. Your neighbors will be doctors, lawyers and bankers. This fine location for your family's future is available at $79,500. Your prompt action is advised.

Clyde Realty   **476-8200**

The above ad heading draws attention to the fact that the lot is the last one available.

The ad body sells prestige by mentioning the neighbors' professions. While this appeals to most buyers, some will be turned off by the snobbery implied.

615

Ready To Build

A lot 100' by 180' with all utilities in and paid for, mature hardwood trees you can save, and a prime West Side location among quality homes make this exceptional at $44,500.

Clyde Realty   **476-8200**

This ad emphasizes that the lot is ready for building.

When a lot is larger than normal, include its size.

616

Question

Where can you buy a half-acre lot in an area of fine homes within a 45-minute drive of the city for less than $50,000?

Answer

In Rothmore Estates, we have estate lots priced from $48,000.

Clyde Realty   **476-8200**

The double heading question-and-answer practically ensures that readers will pay attention to the ad. This technique can be adjusted for any feature or any type of property.

617

Your Piece
of the Block

and a big one at that. Own a 100' by 140', estate-sized site with 2 apple trees in a delightful new West Side development of fine homes and friendly neighbors. It is ready for building and priced at only $37,500.

Clyde Realty   **476-8200**

618

Vertical Lot

Well almost. This 100' by 200' West-haven lot offers a fabulous view and an opportunity for imaginative architectural achievement. It's definitely not for the buyer who is satisfied with the ordinary. A rare opportunity if you act quickly at $69,500.

Clyde Realty   **476-8200**

This ad turns a negative feature—an extremely steep lot that is difficult to build on—into a positive one.

619

Mountain Goat Sanctuary?

What do we do with an oversized, practically perpendicular lot on McLeon Blvd.? Mrs. Smith of our office, who is afraid of heights, refuses to show it. Of course she doesn't like showing 2-story homes either. The view is spectacular, but it definitely is not for the buyer who walks in his or her sleep. The price, however, is not steep at $49,500.

Clyde Realty   **476-8200**

Like the previous ad, this one is for a steep lot and will stimulate the interest of readers. It uses humor to help create interest.

620

On the Ridgeline

Magnificent vistas will be yours as the owner of this 90' by 150' wooded parcel that seems to look down on the rest of the world. It's ready for your dream fulfillment at $69,500. Hurry, as once it's seen, this lot will be sold.

Clyde Realty   **476-8200**

Other possible headings for the same ad are "A Forever View," "Magnificent Vistas," and "On Top of the World."

621

A Lot and a Half

That's right. This is an oversized, wooded lot in prestigious Morning-side at the price of an ordinary lot, $39,900.

Clyde Realty   **476-8200**

The above heading can be used for any lot that's larger than normal. Other possible headings are "Wooded—Over 1/3 Acre" and "Huge Wooded Lot."

622

Explore

The possibilities offered by this 1/3-acre, wooded estate site in what is bound to become the most sought-after area of Northport. Situated on a quiet, winding lane, it will take only one look to know this is where you want your dream house. Unusual circumstances allow us to offer this exceptional opportunity at $57,500.

Clyde Realty   **476-8200**

623

To Appreciate

This oversized lot on a quiet, tree-lined street in prestigious Newberry Heights is bound to give added value to the home you build. This is a location you can appreciate as it appreciates in value. Ready for building at $39,800.

Clyde Realty   **476-8200**

This ad sells economics, as it is a fact that the best location results in the greatest appreciation in value.

624

Here Comes the Neighborhood

We have 32 huge residential lots in the nicest new West Side development. Some have mature trees. All the utilities are in, and one of these lots awaits your special home. Priced from only $37,500, call now for the first pick.

Clyde Realty   **476-8200**

This unusual heading invites people to read the entire ad. The idea of having first pick creates a sense of urgency.

625

Attention Builders

We have 32 estate-sized lots in a prime new West Side development with all utilities in. A number of lots have giant oak trees. Priced from $37,500, take one or all. Terms possible.

Clyde Realty   **476-8200**

This ad is for the same 32 lots as the previous ad, but rather than being targeted at individuals who want homes built, it's targeted at builders. The only new material is "terms possible," which is likely in a block sale.

626

Lots of Lots

We have 37 lots of all sizes in a number of choice areas ready for your special home. Some are wooded, some have spectacular views and some can be purchased with low down payments. Priced from $6,400 to $67,000, it's first come, first served.

Clyde Realty   **476-8200**

This general ad shows that the agent has many listings for lots and invites inquiry for a broad spectrum of needs.

627

Lots

Westhampton (3)	from $18,000
Truesdale Estates	$21,000
Weston Acres	$22,500
Clifton Heights	$31,400
Williamstown	$33,900
Plymouth Road	$37,500

Clyde Realty   **476-8200**

This is a simple way to show that you have many lots available at a range of prices.

628

Zoned for Mobile Homes

Almost a half-acre with county water and several ancient oak trees make this the perfect site for your family. It is in a semirural environment without park rules, restrictions or escalating rents. Great financing is available, and it's priced to sell at only $19,500.

Clyde Realty   **476-8200**

If zoning allows a use that has a greater demand than supply, mention it in the ad heading. While this ad was tailored for mobile home owners, it can easily be modified (e.g., "Zoned for Horses" or "Zoned for Junkyard").

629

Mobile Home Lot— $28,000

Don't be at the mercy of a park owner who constantly raises the rent. Not only can you be the owner of a triple-sized lot in a great location, we can finance the purchase with payments that are probably less than your current monthly rent.

Clyde Realty   **476-8200**

Unlike the previous ad, this ad is for a mobile-home park lot (possibly a condominium or cooperative). It appeals to readers who live in parks where the rent has recently been raised.

630

Mobile Home Owners: Never Pay Rent Again

as the owner of this huge 70' by 100' mobile home site in Brentwood Estates. It has all the amenities of a fine resort, but you are the owner. The full price is only $29,950. Call about our unbelievable financing.

Clyde Realty   **476-8200**

This ad is similar to the previous ad for a lot in a mobile home park.

631

100'—Lake Isabella

Here you'll find giant pine trees and a gentle slope to a lovely sand beach. You'll enjoy a sunset view over the tranquil water. It's the perfect site for your future at $39,500.

Clyde Realty   **476-8200**

The strong points of this ad are as follows:

water frontage 100'

sand beach

giant pine trees

sunset view

If a particular lake is highly desirable, its name should be incorporated in the heading. If not, you can use headings such as "100' of Lakefront," "On the Waterfront," or "On a Crystal-Clear Lake."

632

Miles of Beaches

for your morning walk, and the sound of the waves will lull you to sleep. This is a perfect site for your very special home just steps from the sand. A rare opportunity for you at $97,500.

Clyde Realty   **476-8200**

This is a lot near a beach, but it doesn't have water frontage. If a lot does have frontage, it should be clearly stated.

Other possible headings are "A Place on the Beach," "Buy the Sea," or "For Your Beach Retreat."

633

Fish-filled River

One hundred feet of frontage on the famous Brule River is the perfect site for your vacation or retirement home. It's a wooded wonderland, with oak, hickory and even sugar maple trees. For the Tom Sawyer in you, this is your opportunity at $29,500.

Clyde Realty   **476-8200**

Other possible headings are "Brule River Frontage," "Fish and Float River," and "At Water's Edge."

634

Zoned for 32 Units

This is a choice Westhaven location only 3 blocks from the new mall. There is a close-to-zero vacancy rate here. It's an exceptional opportunity at $400,000.

Clyde Realty   **476-8200**

The number of units possible for an apartment site is of prime interest, so be sure to include this information in the ad heading.

A new mall increases demand for housing, as does a hospital, college, new plant or office structure.

635

Plans and Approvals— 32 Units

in a choice Westhaven location only 3 blocks from the new mall. Ready for immediate construction at $450,000.

Clyde Realty   **476-8200**

The fact that plans have been approved will appeal to many builders, as the approval process can otherwise take months or, in some cases, years.

636

On Illinois Avenue

is a 120' by 240' choice commercial corner that is ideal for fast food or a mini-mall. This is an exceptional opportunity at $800,000.

Clyde Realty   **476-8200**

If a commercial street is highly desirable, the street should be mentioned in the heading. Suggesting uses for the site will make it more desirable.

637

Zoned M-3

A 110' by 240' choice West Side site on a high-traffic street that's priced to sell fast at $240,000.

Clyde Realty   **476-8200**

For commercial and industrial zoning, the exact type of zoning is important, as is size and location.

638

Industrial Park— Half-Acre

on a Westhaven site zoned for light manufacturing, assembly or warehouse use. All utilities are available. Priced to sell at $275,000.

Clyde Realty   **476-8200**

This ad is for a parcel of land within an industrial park.

A parcel's size is more important than its shape for most industrial users. In smaller communities, consider explaining the uses allowed by zoning, as zoning symbols are not universal.

16

Low-Priced Homes

While price is relative, these ads are written for the lower end of the market—many aimed at first-time buyers. The ads stress affordability.

Many of the ads in chapter 27 (Terms) and chapter 21 (Older Homes) can also be used effectively to market lower-cost homes.

639

$49,500—3BR

Not a misprint. This is a large brick and frame Traditional on a garden-sized lot with a garage, new furnace and roof in a well-established North Side neighborhood. Eligible for low-down FHA financing.

Clyde Realty   **476-8200**

This ad is for an older home in an established neighborhood.

640

Can't Afford

to buy? Then you haven't seen this 2-bedroom, expandable bungalow on a huge, wooded West Side lot. It's a dream home with separate garage; full basement; old-fashioned, rocking-chair front porch; child-safe, fenced yard; and the perfect spot for a garden. With flexible financing, it isn't going to last long at $59,500.

Clyde Realty   **476-8200**

The older home in this ad is presented in a very positive manner with an attention-getting heading.

641

Don't Be a Slave

to high house payments. You can have cash left each month as the owner of this 3-bedroom raised ranch with a price of only

$59,500

that includes a garage and a huge lot with large maple trees. And it's walking-close to schools and shopping. An unusual opportunity unlikely to be repeated.

Clyde Realty   **476-8200**

The split heading can be very effective.

642

$50,000

can still buy a 3-bedroom home in Westhaven with a full basement, garage, mature landscaping, delightful roses and only a short walk to schools. Sorry, there's only one home at this price.

Clyde Realty   **476-8200**

This is a short ad with an urgent message.

643

Giveaway! Almost!

Imagine a 3-bedroom home in a desirable West Side location with large, bright rooms; hardwood floors; a double garage; and 2 apple trees for $59,500 to the first buyer.

Clyde Realty   **476-8200**

A short, strong ad.

644

Tightwad

Do you squeeze the dollar until George Washington hollers "uncle"? If so, you'll be delighted with this 3BR, 1½-bath American Traditional in a fine West Side neighborhood. There's a double garage and separate workshop that will make a great studio, several huge oaks, and a garden included at a price any miser will love, $59,500.

Clyde Realty   **476-8200**

The above heading is a real attention getter. An alternative heading is simply "Miser."

The words "American Traditional" can be used to give desirability to almost any nondescript architecture.

645

Priced Right— $39,500

It's hard to believe, but you can buy this 3-bedroom brick home with a garage and lovely garden in an established neighborhood at a price any renter can afford. Flexible financing is available to meet your needs. This is the only home at this price, so hurry.

Clyde Realty   476-8200

If a home has positive features such as hardwood floors or a lazy-day front porch, they should be mentioned.

646

Starving Artist

This secluded, 2-bedroom bungalow in Waterbury Hills has an attic that makes you think you're in a garret on the Left Bank. The house has an ambiance of loving neglect. Best of all, it's priced for any pauper at $59,500.

Clyde Realty   476-8200

This ad was designed for a smaller home with an attic.

"An ambiance of loving neglect" turns the fact that the home is old and needs work into a positive feature.

647

Economically Yours

Own a 3-bedroom brick home with garage on a quarter-acre lot with room for a garden at less than the price of many new cars, $32,500.

Clyde Realty   476-8200

"Room for a garden" creates a positive image and adds desirability, even though most yards have room for a garden.

648

$69,000 Buys What?

Would you believe that there's a 3BR, 1½-bath brick home with full basement in a delightful family neighborhood? It's true, and you also get a 2-car garage, fenced yard, a beautiful oak tree and a brand new roof. Freshly painted, it's ready for the first caller.

Clyde Realty   476-8200

This ad shows prospective buyers that they will get a great deal for their money.

649

$69,500—4BR

We are serious. This redbrick American Traditional is really available. It is located in an established North Side neighborhood where owners take pride in their homes. Only a short walk to schools and parks, this home has a full basement, garage and a delightful garden spot. Best of all, it qualifies for

No-Down/Low-Down

VA or FHA financing. Please believe us when we say "You should call now, as this opportunity will not last."

Clyde Realty   476-8200

The home's strong features—its price and size—are combined for the first heading. The second heading sells the terms available.

650

A Basic 3BR Home

is available in a nice West Side location, with garage, full basement and a delightful garden. Excellent financing and a down-to-earth price, $49,500.

Clyde Realty   476-8200

The appeal of this ad is its simplicity.

651

Not a Fixer— $69,500

At last a 3-bedroom ranch with attached garage in desirable Westhaven at a price you can afford. This home, in immaculate condition, reflects the loving care of its owners. Loaded with extras and built-ins, it's a must-see now, as tomorrow might be too late.

Clyde Realty   476-8200

The above ad sells price and condition. Very little is mentioned about the house, but just enough to make readers want to know more.

652

Retirement Budget

Just about everyone can afford this 2-bedroom, West Side American Traditional with its large family-sized kitchen, full basement and garage. It has room for a garden, and it's priced at only $34,500. Ask us about the great terms available.

Clyde Realty   476-8200

Because many buyers looking for lower-cost housing have limited resources, mentioning the financing available is a strong plus.

653

The Affordable Dream

A 3-bedroom ranch with garage in Elmwood can be yours for

$79,500

with a low-low down payment. The best schools, close to park and great neighbors—this won't last.

Clyde Realty   476-8200

654

You Can Afford This

3-bedroom West Side ranch with garage in a family neighborhood. Down payment is flexible, and the full price is only $59,500. This is the only home with these terms, so be the first to call.

Clyde Realty   476-8200

The words "the only one" create a sense of urgency.

655

Ernie the Fish

plunks down more money for rent each month than it will take to buy this 3-bedroom split ranch with attached garage in a prime West Side location. With flexible financing and a full price of only $69,500, why doesn't Ernie wise up?

Clyde Realty   476-8200

This short ad has an attention-getting heading and a strong message. Possible variations are "Crazy Louie" or "Minnie the Mooch."

656

Don't Rent Your Dream

It can be yours to own. This 3BR, 2-bath, double-garage Colonial in a prestigious West Side location can be purchased with only

$5,000 Down

With a full price of only $129,500, it won't last long.

Clyde Realty   476-8200

Keep in mind that low cost is relative. A low-cost approach can be used for homes priced at several hundred thousand dollars when the price is low compared to most homes in the area.

657

Want To
Rent Forever?

If not, we have a 3BR West Side ranch with garage in a family neighborhood you can own with only

$2,000 Down—
$59,500 Full Price

if you hurry and call.

Clyde Realty   **476-8200**

The split heading will make this ad stand out from others.

658

Kiss Your Landlord

Good-bye. Why make your landlord's mortgage payments when you can buy your own home? We have a 3-bedroom split ranch with a garage and delightful fenced yard in a desirable family neighborhood that can be purchased with

No or Very Low
Down Payment

for qualified buyers with monthly payments like rent. The full price is only $79,500.

Clyde Realty   **476-8200**

In this price range, no-down VA loans are possible, as are low-down FHA loans in addition to conventional and owner financing.

659

Renter's Revenge—
$69,500

Your good taste and wallet will both agree you should be the owner of this 3-bedroom American Traditional set on a large lot in an established area of Oceanside. With flexible down payment and monthly payments that are probably less than you pay in rent, don't miss this opportunity to build equity, not rent receipts.

Clyde Realty   **476-8200**

660

Fire the Landlord

Own a 9-room, 3BR home for only $47,500 with payments less than the rent for a small apartment. With just $2,000 down, it's your opportunity to build equity, not save rent receipts. Call today, and give your notice tomorrow.

Clyde Realty   **476-8200**

Very little is said about the above home. This ad sells price and terms and is designed to make your phone ring.

661

Attention Landlords

We're not going to take it anymore. This is your official notice of a

Renter Revolt

because we found someone who can sell us a beautiful 3BR American Traditional with our own double garage and fenced yard on a great lot in Hillsville. FHA financing is available, the down payment is small and the total price is only $68,500. Because most of the monthly payments are tax-exempt, our actual cost is about the same as we were paying for rent. Oh! You want to know who to call? Why, it's

Clyde Realty   **476-8200**

Though a little cute, this ad is effective.

662

Cheaper Than Rent

This 3-bedroom American Traditional in a friendly West Side neighborhood has a garage and full basement. With $3,000 down, the payments will be less than $600/month. It isn't going to be around long at $54,500.

Clyde Realty   **476-8200**

The above heading sells low cost. The body of the ad emphasizes terms.

663

Have It All! Now!

No need to wait until your ship comes in. You can live in Northport in a 3-bedroom ranch with double garage and full basement right now with $5,000 down. Full price only $69,500.

Clyde Realty   **476-8200**

664

Not a Mistake

We have a 3-bedroom, West Side brick home with double garage available for only

$79,500

This home has a full basement, solid hardwood floors, and has been completely redecorated. The down payment is only

$5,000

With this kind of a deal, give ownership your immediate attention.

Clyde Realty   **476-8200**

The above is a unique ad with a triple heading.

665

There May Be Better

but we don't know of a better 3BR, 1½-bath, West Side Cape Cod that can be purchased with a low down payment and a full price of only $79,500.

Clyde Realty   **476-8200**

This ad sells price and terms.

666

Price Conscious?

Then you'll appreciate this 3-bedroom Cape Cod on a delightful West Side, tree-lined street. It's available for only

$69,500

and this includes a garage, lovely landscaping, full basement, and it's in move-in condition. This home won't last long, so call.

Clyde Realty   **476-8200**

667

Why Mortgage the Kids

when you can buy this 3BR, 1¾-bath American Traditional on the friendliest street in Golden Hills for only

$98,500

This home includes an oversized, double garage with built-in workbench and cabinets; a finished basement great for hobbies, parties or a home fitness center; and an absolute dream kitchen. This will go fast, so call.

Clyde Realty   **476-8200**

17

Luxury Homes

Luxury and *expensive* are relative terms. A home you consider middle-income might be considered luxury by a person at a lower economic level. Therefore, the language in luxury ads can be used effectively for homes over a wide spectrum of quality.

In luxury home ads, point out features that aren't often found in homes of lesser quality. Because many people buy expensive homes for the prestige they feel it gives them, this factor can be effectively used in your ads.

See chapter 2 (Architectural Style) for additional ads for luxury homes.

668

Reflect Your Success

Don't you deserve a home that mirrors your achievements? This brick and stone English Regency on an estate setting in Woodridge Heights combines architecture and craftsmanship into a home that whispers, "success." With its high ceilings, massive beams and gleaming hardwoods, this spacious 3BR and den, 2½-bath home provides over 3,000 sq. ft. for gracious living. You'll love the rock-scaped pool, your own championship tennis court and the impeccably maintained grounds that provide an ambiance of quality living. For a very special few at $890,000.

Clyde Realty   **476-8200**

669

A Home
You Deserve

You have worked hard for your family, and this 3BR, 3½-bath French Regency reflects your success. With its walnut-paneled den; leaded glass; French doors; 40-foot living room; and of course pool, spa and cabana, this is the ultimate in material things life has to offer. An enviable estate at $1,200,000.

Clyde Realty   **476-8200**

670

Millionaire's Home

Fickle multi-millionaire wants something different, so it's time to change houses again. This dramatic 9-room Dutch Colonial is set amidst 2 acres of trees and lawns in the estate area of River Hills. Offering all the amenities money can buy, it has been tastefully decorated by Claude Lewis—and the luxurious but comfortable furnishings stay. The home has 3 bedrooms, 3½ baths, a family room and a den in the 3,500+ sq. ft. of living area. A truly exceptional opportunity at $450,000.

Clyde Realty   **476-8200**

The fact that a multi-millionaire owned this home gives it prestige. It also implies that a bargain is possible.

Don't indicate that an owner is a millionaire or is fickle without express permission.

671

The ? Home

The celebrity owner of this delightful 3BR, 2½-bath California Regency in the estate section of Southport must, because of unusual circumstances, sell his dream home. Built to exacting specifications with almost no regard to cost, the home features a huge game room for informal gatherings; a masculine, paneled den; a breakfast patio overlooking the pool and gardens; and all the other amenities one can wish for. The impeccable taste of this owner is yours at $675,000.

Clyde Realty   **476-8200**

Without revealing his or her name, the ad indicates that the home has a famous owner. This adds prestige to the house. You could also refer to the owner as world-renowned or well-known.

672

For a
Special Family

This magnificent family home makes a statement as individual as yourself. Superbly appointed and majestically proportioned, this 3BR, 2½-bath residence offers marble-sheathed baths, private music room, flowing floor plan, 3-car+ garage and address to be envied. Available for the first time at $650,000.

Clyde Realty   **476-8200**

This ad is aimed at the upper end of the price spectrum.

673

If You
Didn't Care

what it cost and simply wanted the finest home possible, you would probably duplicate this 3BR, 3½-bath, 4-car-garage Carolina Contemporary set on over 2 acres of manicured grounds in Westbrook Heights. The home features lavish marble baths (larger than most bedrooms); closets you can get lost in; a great room you can barely see across; a richly paneled den; a music room with built-in stereo system; a kitchen that makes all others plain by comparison; a heated greenhouse, tennis court, pool and spa; and all the usual and most of the unusual luxuries. To duplicate it would cost far more than the owners are asking—$1,200,000.

Clyde Realty   **476-8200**

674

Cloistered

Set among giant oaks in an exclusive community of fine estates, this 3BR and den, 2-bath French Regency offers a double garage, family room and central air. The understated elegance seems to whisper, "quality." Offered to the family accustomed to the very best at $249,500.

Clyde Realty   **476-8200**

This ad has an unusual heading to pique the interest of readers. It is for a better-quality, family home. Very little is said about the home—hopefully just enough to prompt a telephone call.

675

Renfrew
Family Estate

This is one of the truly fine homes in Akron. It has 14 rooms, 6 baths plus the servants' quarters over the 4-car carriage house. English Baronial in style, this home has been built and modernized with quality taking precedence over costs. Set on almost 2 impeccably landscaped acres, it's a home that demands respect. Proudly offered to qualified buyers at $1,200,000.

Clyde Realty   **476-8200**

This ad appeals to the newly rich with the phrase "a home that demands respect."

If a home once belonged to a well-known and respected local family, the family name can be effective in the heading.

676

There's Room
for the Bentley

the Rolls, the Jaguar and the station wagon in the 4-car carriage house on this English country estate in fashionable Southport. The manor house has 14 copious rooms, including 5 bedrooms and an estate office. Of course, there is rich detailing, warm paneling, redbrick, leaded glass and a formal rose garden. The servants' quarters over the carriage house are currently used as a studio for the artistic owner. An estate for the civilized family at $1,600,000.

Clyde Realty   **476-8200**

677

Darn Expensive

but well worth every penny. This 3BR, 2½-bath, brick English Tudor is set behind a stone wall on an estate-sized site in the best area of Wilmington. You'll love the paneled den, impressively proportioned rooms, completely updated kitchen and baths as well as the fabulous craftsmanship evident in the intricate cut glass and carved woodwork. Other amenities include pool and championship tennis court. Offered to the person who doesn't know the meaning of compromise at $319,500.

Clyde Realty   **476-8200**

This ad has an unusual heading to get the reader's attention.

678

Once in a Blue Moon

do we have the opportunity to present a truly world-class residence. This 12-room Mediterranean is positively magnificent in scope and set on the finest 3 acres in Bel Air. With its cobblestone drive, 5-car garage, separate servants' and guests' quarters, pool, court, greenhouse and superlative grounds, it represents what others can only strive for.

Offered at $9,500,000

Shown by appointment to qualified applicants.

Clyde Realty   **476-8200**

679

Five Oaks

We are proud to offer this outstanding English Tudor Estate in the hills of Mequon. Lush lawns, manicured hedges, ancient oaks, a picturesque rose garden, colorful plantings and a sparkling pool and cabana are but a prelude to what truly gracious living has to offer. The brick and stone home features 3 master suites, plus powder rooms; a walnut-paneled den; massive fireplaces; a great room suitable for entertaining on a grand scale; a kitchen to delight any chef; and French doors opening onto a dining terrace and gardens. Of course, there is a 4-car garage. Available for the first time at $725,000.

Clyde Realty   **476-8200**

Giving an estate a name increases its desirability. You might even consider putting the name on a signpost.

680

Rich Wino

This is an estate a wealthy wino will love. The cavernous wine cellar has room for literally thousands of bottles of vintage wines. The cellar comes with a 14-room English Manor House in a premier West Side estate setting, a 4-car garage and all the amenities one can wish for. Offered for the few who have impeccable taste in all things at $1,600,000.

Clyde Realty   **476-8200**

As crude as the heading is, it will attract attention and cause the ad to be read.

681

Who Used the Tub?

We suspect Mr. Buckley of our office has been bathing in the Italian marble tub in the sumptuous master bath of this 3BR, 2½-bath Italian Renaissance estate in Westhaven. Every afternoon he visits the house and takes along a towel. When he returns, he's singing Italian arias. When you see the tantalizing Roman baths, you'll want to join him. The estate has an aura of elegance that makes you want to pamper yourself. With more than 3,500 sq. ft. of sheer luxury and almost a half-acre of grounds, this is your chance to be good to yourself for $349,500. After all, who deserves it more?

Clyde Realty   **476-8200**

The above heading is a real attention getter.

682

Don't Envy— Be Envied

as the owner of this 9-room, stone and glass, 3BR and den Colorado Contemporary with its 2½ baths and 3-car garage in a premier setting. The flowing floor plan, walls of glass and cantilevered decks make this the home for grand entertaining or simple family relaxation. It looks far more expensive than $395,000.

Clyde Realty   **476-8200**

The last sentence will appeal to people who want to impress others but don't have the wealth they want others to believe they have.

683

Behind the Gates

in Elmwood Heights and down a quiet, tree-lined street you'll find this truly outstanding example of Italian Renaissance architecture with its generous use of tile and graceful arches. There are 3 bedrooms, 3½ baths, a conservatory that is ideal for an artist's studio, and a separate study. The 3-car garage includes a built-in workbench. For a life of quiet dignity, you'll want to call this your home. Conservatively priced at $289,500.

Clyde Realty   **476-8200**

The above heading is for a home in a gated community that provides privacy, a measure of safety and some degree of snob appeal.

684

Not a Steal

No, you can't buy this almost-new, Holloway Hills, 3BR, 2½-bath Southern Colonial estate for pennies on the dollar. Nor is it a fixer-upper. It is, however, one of the most impressive fine homes we have had the pleasure to offer. You'll love the soaring, fluted columns; high ceilings; and authentic period detailing that have been reproduced with loving care. Other features include a richly paneled billiard room, pool and hot spa as well as landscaping that makes everything else look ordinary. Fairly priced at $479,500.

Clyde Realty   **476-8200**

685

A Shade Better

than anything you or your friends have ever seen describes this Italianate masterpiece by the internationally known architect Phillipe Rodman. There are 3 bedrooms, 3½ baths, a heavily paneled den with a rose brick fireplace, a great room of baronial proportions, a 3-car garage and a host of desirable amenities set on the most desirable site in Westhaven. Imagine the very best and you will still be pleasantly surprised. Proudly offered at $489,000. For your private showing, contact

Clyde Realty   476-8200

Even when readers aren't familiar with an architect, mentioning him or her by name adds a great deal of desirability to a home.

686

A Robber Baron

is reputed to have built this 14-room, brick masterpiece, which he patterned after one of the great homes of England. No expense was spared, and nothing was compromised in its construction. Impeccably maintained and skillfully updated, you can expect to be envied as the owner of this premier estate in its richly landscaped setting. Proudly offered at $1,200,000.

Clyde Realty   476-8200

This is an ad for an older estate home. Other possible headings are "A Beer Baron," "A Lumber Baron," or "A Railroad Magnate."

687

Doctors' Row

A block party in this Pinewood Cove community will seem like a medical convention. This 3BR, 2½-bath English Tudor estate is the perfect home for a hypochondriac. When not providing the neighbors with your symptoms, there's a heated pool and spa for therapy and a fantastic garden guaranteed to lower your blood pressure. This home has all you expect and more with its fine French doors; leaded-crystal, cut windows; exquisite woodwork; a kitchen that will make you want to eat at home; and a richly paneled library. Hurry, or a doctor will beat you to it at $469,500.

Clyde Realty   476-8200

This ad treats the home's quality neighbors in a very light manner.

688

The Thomas Estate

We are proud to offer the family estate of Mr. Henry Thomas. Magnificent in design and scale, this is undoubtedly the finest home in Southport. If you're one of the very few who can afford a truly spectacular residence, you owe it to yourself to view this 14-room masterpiece in its formal garden setting. A truly enviable estate at $1,600,000.

Clyde Realty   476-8200

This ad sells an ambiance of the finest. Note that its amenities are not listed.

689

The Standard of Excellence

from which all other fine homes will be measured. This masterfully designed French manor house located in a semirural neighborhood of outstanding estates offers 3 bedrooms, a delightful music room, French doors, leaded glass, a gourmet kitchen, a slate roof, an extraordinary sense of light and space and a dizzying array of exquisite features to delight your senses. An exceptional opportunity for one fortunate family at $398,000.

Clyde Realty   **476-8200**

690

World-Class Residence

Once in a rare while will a truly magnificent home such as this be available. Built without compromise, the home reflects only the very best. This 17-room American classic has baths sheathed in Grecian marble; woodwork of American walnut; leaded-crystal, glass windows; a slate roof; and all the amenities present on your wish list including a lighted championship tennis court and heated Olympic pool. Set on 12 rolling acres, it is what success is all about. If you promised yourself the best in life, you can keep that promise at $2,600,000.

Clyde Realty   **476-8200**

691

Palatial Estate

This turreted French Norman estate offers a charismatic blending of regal splendor and delicate charm. Fourteen magnificently proportioned rooms resplendent with elaborate details provide the epitome of elegant living with all the amenities one would demand of a home of this stature. Set amid lush, landscaped grounds bound to be envied, this estate may be copied but will never be equaled. It's the ultimate statement of your success at $2,900,000.

Clyde Realty   **476-8200**

This ad really tells very little about the house other than that it is large and of high quality.

692

Superlatives Fail Us

We could use words like "magnificent in concept and proportion," "a world-class residence," and "a home to be envied," but words alone don't do justice to this exceptional residence. If you're one of the very fortunate few, we offer everything on your wish list at $1,650,000. Call today for a private showing of the indescribable.

Clyde Realty   **476-8200**

The price limits calls to qualified buyers. The fact that absolutely nothing is said about the house will entice readers.

693

To the Manor Born

This proper English residence is a product of the golden age of architecture when cost ran a distant second to beauty. Set on an estate lot in Westbury Heights, the home offers 3 bedrooms, 2½ baths, a paneled estate office, a baronial-sized dining room and so much more. The home clearly shows the love craftsmen had for their art. This is a home as distinctive as yourself set amidst landscaping second only to Hampton Gardens. It's offered for your family and your family's family at $439,000.

Clyde Realty   **476-8200**

This heading was, of course, the title of an English television series that was set on a fine English estate.

694

Ancient Brick

hewn timbers and leaded glass were combined by skilled artisans to produce one of the finest estate homes we've been privileged to offer. This newer, 3BR, 2½-bath Georgian Colonial on almost a full acre in Holiday Hills is impressive in scale and detailing. Its features include a 3-car garage, 11' ceilings, extensive hardwood trim, fireplaces, paneled study, family room and professional decorating to make this home a delight to behold. At $315,500, it's truly incomparable.

Clyde Realty   **476-8200**

Unusual or prestige features or materials can be used in a heading to attract attention.

695

A House To Hate

If you want a home everyone can see so they'll know how rich you are, you will hate this 12-room English brick Tudor, which can't even be seen from the street. The owners and their guests will be the only ones to know about the imported cobblestone driveway, slate roof and leaded glass of this elegant residence. People won't even know about the private championship tennis court. This home has none of the glitz a rock star would love. It is more the home of the rock star's banker. There are no mirrored walls, flocked-purple wallpaper or plastic accents. It's not a house that shouts, "money," it's one that softly whispers, "quality." While you will pay $1,200,000 for this home, no one will know.

Clyde Realty   **476-8200**

696

Quiet Elegance

Designed by a world-renowned architect and crafted by one of the most respected builders, this 3BR, 2½-bath Colonial estate reflects all that is good from the dramatic 2-story foyer to the intricately carved, gently curving staircase. Set on over 1 acre of manicured lawns and stately trees, this can be your dynasty at $385,000.

Clyde Realty   **476-8200**

697

The Taj Mahal

of East Hampton. Truly the most spectacular residence in the city, this 12-room masterpiece has been featured in national publications as one of the finest examples of contemporary architecture. The open-space concept provides an ambiance of luxury so seldom achieved in lesser homes. This exceptional residence is priced at $1,200,000 and will be shown to qualified applicants.

Clyde Realty   **476-8200**

698

The Ultimate Residence

Magnificently alive with elaborate craftsmanship, this 14-room French Regency echoes achievement. The awesome list of amenities includes rooms of baronial proportion; rich, solid walnut paneling and trim; Roman baths sheathed in marble; a secluded pool and cabana; a championship tennis court; and a premier setting amidst 3 magnificently landscaped acres. Offering a new dimension in luxury living at $1,600,000.

Clyde Realty   **476-8200**

699

Life Is Full of Compromises

but you need compromise no more. This 10-room, Italian Renaissance residence has been thoughtfully planned to provide the ultimate lifestyle for those accustomed to the very best. From the magnificent public rooms to Roman baths sheathed in marble and the library with its solid walnut wainscoting, you'll immediately appreciate the superior appointments. Set on breathtaking grounds, the description "magnificent" seems like an understatement. Proudly offered to the very few at $870,000.

Clyde Realty   **476-8200**

700

Dom Perignon

of fine estates. This 9-room, 3BR French Regency is a home that truly mirrors your achievements. Featuring rooms of baronial proportions, a richly paneled music room, a chandeliered dining room, a glassed conservatory and a 4-car garage, this exceptional residence is located behind the walls on almost 2 acres. This is truly the epitome of elegant living for the buyer who doesn't know the meaning of compromise at $850,000.

Clyde Realty   **476-8200**

701

A Private World

Ancient oaks create a screen of privacy and gently filter morning light on this 3-bedroom brick English Traditional set back from a quiet street on an estate-sized lot. You'll be delighted with its rich wood detailing, leaded glass, quiet study that looks out upon the rose garden and the 3-car carriage house with a room just perfect for a studio. This can be your sanctuary at $398,500.

Clyde Realty   **476-8200**

702

A Bubbling Fountain

in the cobblestoned, flower-bedecked courtyard is just a prelude to the delights awaiting you in this 3BR, 2½-bath Spanish Colonial with its massive arched veranda, huge beams and soft red tile roof. The home is bright and has a happy, comfortable ambiance. For entertaining or family living, this is a home that will afford you and your family great pleasure. A whole new lifestyle can be yours at $249,500.

Clyde Realty   **476-8200**

The above ad heading could read "Hand-carved Doors" or use other entry features.

703

More
Than a Home

This 11-room, brick, English Tudor residence on 5 acres in River Hills is the estate you'll want to pass on to future family generations. With its cut stone, massive beams and intricate woodwork, it reflects craftsmanship that is becoming a lost art. The numerous amenities include a championship tennis court, landscaping to please the most fastidious, heated greenhouse, indoor pool and a 3-car garage. Start your dynasty for $850,000.

Clyde Realty   **476-8200**

704

$1,000,000

If you are one of the few who can get past the price, you'll want to know about this 3BR, 3½-bath, Italian Renaissance estate set on 2½ acres in Holiday Hills. You'll delight over the feeling of gracious spaciousness, the quality accouterments, the lovely rose garden and entertaining patio, the championship tennis court and the Olympic-sized pool. If you're one of the very few within reach of such a residence, call.

Clyde Realty   **476-8200**

705

It's Expensive

but we're proud to offer this 3BR, 3½-bath Lincoln Park Colonial on 2 rolling acres because

It's Worth It

Amenities include 4-car garage; cobblestone driveway; championship, lighted tennis court, pool and spa; golf-course-quality putting green; and a greenhouse where the previous owner raised orchids. The home offers a paneled, lion-sized den with its own entrance; soaring ceilings; closets the size of bedrooms; and marble baths of Roman proportions. Not the least bit ordinary in size, quality or price— $1,300,000.

Clyde Realty   **476-8200**

This ad makes a virtue of the home's high price.

706

Presidents

of corporations will be your neighbors as the owner of this West Side, 3BR, 2½-bath American Traditional in an estate setting midst ancient trees and carefully nurtured, colorful plantings. Professionally decorated in muted tones, you'll marvel at the feeling of bright spaciousness, the flowing floor plan, the state-of-the-art kitchen and the many little amenities providing for the lifestyle you deserve. Presently available at $595,000.

Clyde Realty   **476-8200**

This ad is really aimed at the recently wealthy buyer. The features listed fit most better homes.

18

Mobile Homes

Mobile homes differ from other housing in that a mobile home is often on leased land located in a park. The desirability of a particular park, its amenities and its rent are important factors for the purchaser. Woodall has developed a rating system for mobile home parks with 5-star being the highest rating. If a mobile home is sold with land, it is a very positive factor that must be emphasized when advertising.

Certain brands of mobile homes have a quality image and are important to purchasers familiar with mobile homes. However, the brand of mobile home has much less significance for first-time buyers.

The size of a mobile home is often given in an ad, and this is of importance to many buyers. If a unit is a double- or triple-wide unit, it is much more desirable than a narrower, single-wide unit, so this should also be mentioned in an ad.

Mobile home ads are generally found under a separate category. If not, be sure to state clearly that you are advertising a mobile home. The ads in this chapter have been designed specifically for mobile homes.

707

Here Comes the Neighborhood

You can own a brand new 24' × 60' Spartan with 3 bedrooms, 2 baths, a screened lanai, a double carport and central air in the family section of a brand new West Side Park for only $47,500.

Clyde Realty   476-8200

Many parks have adult and family sections. If so, consider mentioning this feature in your ads.

If the park has a high Woodall rating, it should be stated in the ad.

708

24 × 60 + Garage

This is a huge 2BR, 2-bath Coachman Model with central air and a screened and glassed porch in a choice West Side, 5-star park that has all the amenities of a fine resort. It's an exceptional opportunity that won't last at $69,500.

Clyde Realty   **476-8200**

Other features can be emphasized with headings such as "24 × 60—5-Star Park" or "24 × 60—Hacienda Estates."

709

24' × 60' + Lot

You own the land with this 2-year-old, 3BR, 2-bath Coachman model in a great location with landscaping you only dream of. There is a huge screened and glassed lanai, a double carport and central air. It can all be yours at only $79,900.

Clyde Realty   **476-8200**

710

Own Your Own Lot

behind guarded gates with this triple-wide, 1,950 sq. ft., 3BR, 2½-bath, exquisitely furnished home in Palm Greens. Features include double carport, oversized storage building and huge screened veranda for relaxation or entertaining. On a quiet cul-de-sac (yet only a short walk from the clubhouse), it is a better-than-new opportunity not to be missed at $87,500.

Clyde Realty   **476-8200**

711

No Park Rent

You own the oversized lot with this 3BR, 2-bath, double-wide Great Lakes model in a 5-star park that has everything. Great financing and a price of only $69,500.

Clyde Realty   **476-8200**

712

Children Welcome—
$26,000

This 3BR, 1½-bath double-wide in the friendliest family park has everything except a high price. It is available with all appliances for $4,000 down.

Clyde Realty   **476-8200**

This ad sells the fact that families are welcome and the price is low.

713

NADA Value $32,500
Sale Price $28,000

A 1985, 28' × 60' Rollahome set on the nicest lot in Ocean View with a 2-car carport can be yours with great financing. Call now for details, as this one won't last.

Clyde Realty   **476-8200**

Because a mobile home has a blue-book price much like an automobile, a two-line heading can be very effective when the price is less than the blue-book value.

714

Rent Stopper

You can own your own 3BR, 1½-bath home in the family section of Weston Mobile Estates for only

$19,500

and that includes refrigerator, built-in range, dishwasher and a washer and dryer. But hurry, as this one won't last.

Clyde Realty   **476-8200**

This ad sells price. By listing appliances separately, the reader will think he or she is getting much more for the money.

The above ad is probably for a single-wide unit. By not stating this directly, you increase your calls. This provides the opportunity to switch callers to property that might better meet their needs.

715

$2,000 Down

makes you a homeowner. This lovely 14' × 60', 3BR, 1½-bath Spartan home has much more space than the average apartment and has payments that are probably less than you currently pay in rent. The home comes complete with all appliances, carport and storage shed at only $16,900.

Clyde Realty   **476-8200**

See the next ad for a different way of advertising the same unit.

716

Your First Home?

This 14′ × 60′, 3BR, 1½-bath Spartan is much larger than most apartments and will probably cost you less. In the family section of a lovely West Side park, the home includes a carport and storage shed. Available with $2,000 down and a full price of only $16,900—and this includes all appliances.

Clyde Realty   476-8200

717

$150 Per Month

is your total rent in this quiet family park in Westwood. The 24′ × 60′ home features 2 full baths, a family room and 2 oversized bedrooms. It comes with all appliances, some furnishings and great financing at $29,500.

Clyde Realty   476-8200

718

Repo 24′ × 50′

In a choice West Side park, this newer unit offers 3 bedrooms and 2 full baths, upgraded appliances (including washer and dryer), a large screened lanai and a 2-car carport. Act quickly, $39,500 and only $5,000 down for qualified purchaser.

Clyde Realty   476-8200

Because mobile homes are often sold with low down payments to younger families, there are many repossessions available. By advertising a mobile home as a repossession, it gives the impression that the home is a bargain.

719

Low Park Rent

and a 5-year lease are yours as the owner of this 2BR, 2-bath, almost-new double-wide with central air, a huge covered porch and a carport in a choice West Side location. With a full price of only $37,500, you'll be sorry you delayed.

Clyde Realty   476-8200

If an exceptional lease is available, it should be mentioned in the ad, as many buyers fear rents will increase shortly after they buy. New parks often give long-term leases to fill themselves and/or sell units.

720

Low Space Rent

You'll have only $135/month total rental in delightful Woodacres, a park with everything. You will love this 24′ X 42′, late-model, 1½-bath unit with its central air, huge screened lanai and double carport. Priced for you at $44,500.

Clyde Realty   476-8200

If exceptional financing is available, it should be stated in the ad.

721

Not a Trailer

This 24′ X 50′, 2BR, 2-bath double-wide is a "manufactured home" built in a factory to rigid specifications that are every bit as demanding as those of local builders. The difference is the significant cost savings of assembly line production. You can own this like-new home with masonite siding, 2″ X 6″ sidewall construction and roofing of asphalt shingles with quality appliances set up in Northport Mobile Estates with a double carport, huge screened porch for relaxation or entertaining and a storage building for only $49,500.

Clyde Realty   476-8200

This ad attacks the objections to mobile homes and sells the price advantage.

722

Great Vacation Place

A hillside acre overlooking Lake Matthews and a low-maintenance, 24′ X 50′, 2BR, 2-bath manufactured home is the perfect spot for weekends, vacations or a lifetime. There is a 2-car garage with workspace, beautiful trees and plantings, and the like-new home features every conceivable built-in. Best of all, it's priced at only $69,500.

Clyde Realty   476-8200

Many mobile homes have become vacation homes on acreage sites.

723

Weekender—$12,500

Vacation very weekend in this 2-bedroom unit with carport and central air in a quiet, low-rent Palm Springs park. The home has been meticulously maintained and provides a haven close to everything at far less cost than motel rent. Hurry, as this one isn't going to last.

Clyde Realty   476-8200

Mobile homes are often used as vacation homes. The above home is probably an older single-wide with 1 bath, or the ad would indicate otherwise. It is likely to be located in an older park as well.

724

Retired But Not Tired

You'll love this 2BR and den, 2-bath, triple-wide Regency Model on an oversized lot in a country club setting. Your monthly rent entitles you to unlimited golf, tennis and use of the fitness center. The home has a huge screened lanai perfect for entertaining, a carport and a storage building. It can't be duplicated at $79,500.

Clyde Realty   **476-8200**

725

Retirement Home

Own a 24' × 52', 2BR, 1½-bath former display model with every conceivable upgrade on a large, landscaped lot in a lovely senior park. There is a huge screened and glassed lanai as well as a large carport. It's walking-close to the clubhouse, pools, shuffleboard and horseshoe pits. There are quiet streets for evening strolls, a well-equipped craft shop and activities of all types. This perfect lifestyle for the young at heart can be yours at $39,900.

Clyde Realty   **476-8200**

19

Negative Ads

Fixer-upper ads are the most common of the negative ads. (See chapter 7 for fixer-uppers.) This chapter deals with negative ads that advise readers not to do something or that tell them what is wrong with a particular property. Like fixer-upper ads, they appeal to many perverse readers. As a word of caution, never criticize or make fun of a property without the owner's prior permission.

726

727

Wrecking-Ball Special

The lot is worth at least as much as we're asking for the house and lot as it stands. The small, older, 3-bedroom home doesn't fit the area of fine, large homes, and we haven't been able to figure out what to do with it short of demolition. Mrs. Hopkins of our office thinks the home is "darling," but who wants to pay $89,500 to live in a quaint bungalow in an area of $300,000 to $500,000 homes?

Clyde Realty   **476-8200**

The final question will be answered by a ringing phone.

728

Don't Call

as you probably are too late anyway. This 3BR, 2-bath Pennsylvania Dutch Colonial on its large wooded lot in Westhaven is bound to be sold to the first family who sees it. Not only does it have the most beautiful fieldstone fireplace you have ever seen, the woodwork gleams and the tile sparkles in this Quaker charmer. There is a full furnished basement, a double garage and a family room big enough for reunions. It's a home Currier would have traded Ives for, and it's priced at only $179,900.

Clyde Realty   **476-8200**

729

Not Trendy

but it's a darn comfortable 3-bedroom home in a truly fine neighborhood. No, it doesn't have Carrera marble in the baths, nor does it have electronic security, walls of glass or cutesy conversation pits. It does have white-clapboard cedar siding, shutters that actually work, solid oak flooring and trim that came from trees (not a plastic factory), a fireplace that actually burns real wood and bookshelves rather than a TV nook. If you're secure so that substance is more important than flash, this is you home at $89,500.

Clyde Realty   **476-8200**

This ad makes a virtue out of a plain, older home, and this will appeal to many readers.

730

Gaudy

Poor taste abounds in this 3BR, 2½-bath French Provincial in Hillcrest. Actually, it looks rather nice from the outside with its manicured lawns and stately trees, but once you step through the double doors you'll see why we haven't been able to unload it. It's quite obvious the decorator was color-blind. It's perfect for the buyer with bad taste or for one who can imagine what redecorating will accomplish. Priced to reflect its unique qualities at $237,500.

Clyde Realty   **476-8200**

731

Are You Eccentric?

If so, you'll love this tasteless, 3BR, 2-bath West Side Colonial. While Miss Jones of our office thinks it's cute, one of our buyers described it as "early brothel" with the bright reds accented by pinks and mauve. The house looks great on the outside; apparently the decorator didn't get around to that yet. The house does have central air, a full basement, a 2-car garage and a beautiful natural stone fireplace. If you're color-blind, it's a fabulous find at $219,500.

Clyde Realty   476-8200

The decorating is the only problem with this home. It will attract fixer-upper buyers who can visualize how to improve the property.

732

Decorator's Nightmare

Leprous yellow walls, jarring purple accents and blood-red tile are just a few of the features in this 3-bedroom Dutch Colonial that prove money and good taste aren't synonymous. This home appears structurally sound, and it does offer an excellent West Side location as well as an attractive exterior and landscaping. The price reflects the poor taste of the decorator—$169,500.

Clyde Realty   476-8200

This ad is a variation on the fixer-upper ad. Be certain you have the owner's permission before you comment negatively on the decorating.

733

Bad Taste Abounds

in this 9-room, 3BR, 3½-bath residence in the most fashionable area of Southport. The architecture appears to have been copied from the worst of defunct civilizations. If you want to impress your friends, you can say it's a "Romanesque baroque home with definite Greek and Assyrian influences." This home does have a lovely garden (obviously a different designer), and the rooms are huge. It's the ideal home for the pickle magnate who's firm has just gone public. Would you believe $495,000?

Clyde Realty   476-8200

If you make the home sound worse than it is, the buyer will have a positive reaction, rather than a negative one, upon viewing the property. The next few ads are quite similar.

734

Yellow Monster—5BR

It's big and ugly, although Mrs. Jones in our office thinks it has genuine character, but her taste has always been a little different. Set on an estate-sized lot in Clinton Hills, it offers a lot of space for $89,500.

Clyde Realty   476-8200

This ad says very little about the house. Its purpose is to arouse the reader's curiosity. Because the home has more than 3 bedrooms, this feature was added to the heading.

735

A Monument to Bad Taste

If you have more money than taste, you'll love this gaudy French Provincial with Italianate influence, finished to excess in a sort of baroque style. There are 11 huge rooms, all equally ugly. It does command a premier West Hills location, offering every conceivable amenity; but while you might like to visit, you wouldn't want to live here. Mr. Clements of our office, a former Edsel owner, thinks it's beautiful—just the way he imagines a movie star's home to be. It's priced far below reproduction costs at $289,000, but then who would want to reproduce it?

Clyde Realty   **476-8200**

As strange as it may seem, this ad will bring in calls from qualified buyers.

736

Don't Do It

You could neglect to call on this 3BR, 2-bath Hacienda Heights Spanish villa with tile roof, graceful arches, bubbling fountain, 2-car garage, massive beams and cathedral ceilings. Of course for the rest of your life you'll be telling of the terrific home you could have purchased for only $179,500.

Clyde Realty   **476-8200**

737

Don't Buy This Home

Mrs. Kelly of our office has fallen in love with this 3BR, 2-bath, Morningside Heights Colonial. She says this home has "an ambiance of happiness because of its brightness and spaciousness." (Mrs. Kelly talks this way.) The home has a double garage, family room, central air, greenhouse kitchen and 4 apple trees. Mrs. Kelly hopes no one looks at it until she talks Mr. Kelly into moving. At $189,500, she claims it's a real bargain, and she's a professional.

Clyde Realty   **476-8200**

This simple heading will practically force a reader to look at the entire ad. Its humor makes this ad stand out.

738

So What!

if you miss buying this Newport Hills, 3BR, 1¾-bath Cape Cod with large screened breezeway, double garage and full basement on an estate-sized wooded lot. Sure you would have loved the rose brick fireplace with its massive mantle and the bright and spacious feeling pervading this fine dwelling. Keep looking, and who knows, in 4 or 5 years you might find a home you like as well as this one. Of course, you'll probably pay a great deal more than $98,500.

Clyde Realty   **476-8200**

739

Is Ugly Your "Thing"?

Then you'll love this 9-room, 3BR, 2½-bath, brick, fortresslike structure in a community of otherwise fine homes. The neighbors would love to see you tear it down. It's going to take a great deal more than paint and shutters to make this place appear presentable. While only 7 years old, it's permanent proof of the axiom "money and good taste are not synonymous." Certainly it's a lot of house for the money, but do you have the guts to show your friends what you purchased at $189,500?

Clyde Realty **476-8200**

This ad teases the imagination. It will attract artistic people and those who positively react to fixer-upper ads.

740

Monotonous

The trouble with this 3BR, 2-bath Cape Cod is it's just like every other house on the quiet, tree-lined block. No one ever accused the builder of originality. However, it's a sturdy, attractive residence with a large yard that can't be duplicated at $79,500.

Clyde Realty **476-8200**

741

For the Conformist

Remember the tract homes of the 1950s, standing like soldiers in rows—all the same? Well, this is your chance to own a West Side suburban, 3BR, 1½-bath Cape Cod that looks like every other house on the block. If you always wanted to "belong," this is your chance. Ownership requires you join your neighbors and mow your lawn on Saturday mornings and dress your children in Reeboks and Levis. Close to schools, park and freeway, you'll find living here is a very comfortable rut to be in. Your entrance fee is $114,500, with low-down FHA financing.

Clyde Realty **476-8200**

This ad appears to make fun of the conformist, but it does sell a pleasant lifestyle.

742

Yuppie's Paradise

Live in a neighborhood where hardly anyone can afford their mortgage payment and the round of cocktail parties echoes with talk of big deals and new BMWs. This 3BR, 2½-bath Colonial is perfect for the area, as it looks far more expensive than it costs. It has all the "in" requirements, such as Berber carpeting and Euro-cabinets. You can join the neighborhood for $219,000.

Clyde Realty **476-8200**

While making fun of yuppies, the ad will actually attract people who don't consider themselves yuppies.

743

4BR Nondescript

If it had any less class, we'd raise the price and call it a classic. There are 9 nondescript rooms in this rather nondescript brick residence located in one of the most desirable areas of Westhaven. "Unimpressive" is a word that fits the landscaping. It's the perfect home for the nondescript family at only $89,500.

Clyde Realty   **476-8200**

744

A Rotten Floor Plan

is why this 3BR, 2-bath, double-garage executive ranch in Brookfield Heights has not been sold. The living room is too small—more like a sitting room. The space was used to make a huge family room off the kitchen-dining area. You'll see the home was designed more for family living than for entertaining or impressing others. On the positive side, there's a huge fenced yard with several magnificent maples and a perfect spot for a vegetable garden. This home priced to overcome its problems at $149,500.

Clyde Realty   **476-8200**

A heading like this demands that readers check the entire ad.

The body of the ad shows that the floor plan really isn't rotten; in fact it's quite practical and is apt to appeal to readers.

745

Contrarian Special

The area hasn't been discovered by the yuppies, and this 3BR, 2-bath home doesn't have soaring ceilings, clerestory windows or fabulous built-ins. In fact, aside from a roof and walls, it has very little in common with most of the clone homes your friends are buying. What it does have is plenty of space; old-fashioned brick, plaster and hardwood; a private garden; a garage; a location only 20 minutes from the civic center; and a price tag so low you'll be ashamed to tell your friends. $69,500.

Clyde Realty   **476-8200**

This ad actually sells the virtues of an older home in an older central area.

746

Truth in Advertising

This 3-bedroom home isn't much. It's plain, fairly clean, fair-sized, but not what you would call huge. There's no wet bar, soaring ceilings or breathtaking view. It didn't appear on the cover of *House Beautiful,* and it never will. It is, however, the lowest-priced home in the Edgewood School District, and you won't need to sell your kids to raise the down payment. Call today on this plain-wrapper home priced at a plain $89,500.

Clyde Realty   **476-8200**

The next ad takes a similar approach.

747

It Ain't Much

but it does have 3 bedrooms, 2 baths and a double garage, and it's located in Willow Creek. It doesn't have soaring ceilings, clerestory windows or the exotically carved woodwork you'll probably insist upon, but what do you expect for

$89,500?

If you can get by with just a nice plain home without all the frills in a darn good neighborhood, call

Clyde Realty   **476-8200**

749

Tear It Down

and your neighbors will love you. This 3BR, 2-bath Colonial in Malibu is available for the price of the lot alone. While you'll have a Malibu address, the home is unpretentious; you might even say modest. Solid and comfortable, it has no real flash. Of course, you can live in the house as it is, but wouldn't it bother you to be living in the least-expensive home in Malibu? Priced to be demolished at $345,000.

Clyde Realty   **476-8200**

748

What Did
You Expect?

It has 4 walls, a roof that doesn't leak, 3 bedrooms, 1½ baths, a garage and is located in the Kimball School District. It's not a mansion, but you're only paying

$69,500

and we can arrange financing for almost anyone.

Clyde Realty   **476-8200**

750

Looks Like
Old Money

is what your guests will say about this dingy monstrosity that skillfully blends the ugly with the vulgar. The 11 rooms on a rather tasteless street of similar residences (considered by many to be fashionable) show a patrician disdain for beauty in favor of gauche. It's the perfect home for the social climber who wants to appear to have arrived at $280,000.

Clyde Realty   **476-8200**

This ad sells price and location but asks buyers to be realistic.

This ad is for a large, older home in an area of people with old money. It makes fun of buyers who want this type of home, although the ad will attract them.

751

Social Climber

People will think you have class living in this 3BR, 2½-bath, older Georgian Colonial. This very fine residence is in an area where the same families have lived for generations, intermarrying and producing clone offspring with names like Buffy and Scott. There's an old carriage house with a large, bright studio above— perfect if you are an artist, even if only in your own mind. When you move in, make certain the neighbors see your polo mallets. Positive snob appeal at a surprisingly reasonable $385,000.

Clyde Realty **476-8200**

752

High Society

This 11-room brick Traditional bears an atmosphere of gentle age and quality that seems to whisper "old money." The intricately carved woodwork and flamboyant floating staircase eloquently express the fact that no expense was spared to pamper its owners. The feeling of being filthy rich can be yours at a conservative $249,500.

Clyde Realty **476-8200**

This ad also makes fun of old money but will attract people who have social aspirations.

20

New Homes

While display ads are often used to advertise new homes, classifieds are very effective, as many readers pass over display ads. The smaller classified ads have a significant price advantage over display ads.

Ads for particular features or types of homes found in other chapters in this book can also be readily tailored for new homes, as can open house ads (chapter 22).

A Brand-New Classic

In the rural suburb of Westmont, Preeble Builders have constructed an ageless home of baronial proportions with sandstone, slate and huge timbers. Filled with life and comfort, this 3BR, 2½-bath residence offers a sparkling pool, a tantalizing hot spa, sweeping lawns and a garden ablaze with color. The glass walls of the magnificent family room look over a changing panorama of nature. This is a home where dreams come true, and it's proudly offered at $295,000.

Clyde Realty   476-8200

The name of the builder adds desirability even when the builder is not well known.

Special thanks to Ian Price of Surfers Paradise, Australia.

754

Just Finished Hammering

Designed by Kermit Kingston and built by Dawn Builders, this sensational residence offers 3 bedrooms, 2½ baths and a separate family room on its pool-sized lot in Hacienda Highlands, a community of fine designer homes. There's still time to decorate to your individual taste. Call today, as the builder will only guarantee the price of $219,000 for 30 days.

Clyde Realty   **476-8200**

Including the names of designers and builders adds prestige to a home—even when they aren't well known.

The fact that builders won't guarantee price provides an element of urgency and gives the impression that the price will increase.

"Pool-sized" indicates that there is room for a pool in the future.

755

New But No Squeaks

This builder-fresh 3BR, 2-bath, double-garage split ranch in prestigious Hacienda Highlands offers a huge family room, a perfect garden spot and all the amenities you dream of, just waiting for your family at $129,500.

Clyde Realty   **476-8200**

756

The Paint Isn't Dry

on this brand-new 3BR, 2-bath, Victorian-style residence in Westwood. You'll love the authentic detailing, soaring ceilings, huge multi-paned windows that provide a feeling of bright spaciousness and the warmth of natural woodwork. Of course, there is a 2-car garage and every conceivable built-in in the huge country kitchen. If ever there was a must-see, this is it at $139,500.

Clyde Realty   **476-8200**

757

Why Settle For Hand-Me-Downs

when the same money can make you the owner of this brand-new, energy-efficient, 3BR, 2-bath, double-garage, California-style ranch home on an estate-sized lot in Weston Hills? Huge rooms, the latest in quality built-ins, a family room, a delightful patio, a rose brick fireplace, central air, a builder's warranty and a great deal more is included at $167,500. This is an opportunity that won't wait.

Clyde Realty   **476-8200**

758

Undressed

This brand-new, 3BR, 2-bath, double-garage Colonial is awaiting your individual touch. There's still time to choose the colors. You'll love the high ceilings, authentic moldings and the feeling of bright spaciousness. Set on an estate-sized lot on the most desirable street, this is an opportunity that won't last long at $179,500.

Clyde Realty   **476-8200**

The above heading will ensure that the ad is read. A more racy heading would be "Undressed and Waiting."

759

Nobody Slept Here

unless it was Hank the plumber, who seems to have put in quite a few extra hours on the job. This 3BR, 2-bath Dutch Colonial in a quiet, village-like setting in New Glares offers solid hardwood floors; a full basement; an oversized double garage with automatic opener; a positively dream kitchen loaded with copper, tile and brick; a recreation room big enough for a family reunion; walk-in closets; and darn near everything you can think of. This home will have the Jones family trying to keep up with you. Don't tell them you only paid $249,500.

Clyde Realty   **476-8200**

760

Ralph Washington Slept Here

It is reputed that Ralph, no relation to George, spent at least 1 night in this new, 3BR, 2-bath Colonial while it was under construction. Despite Ralph's brief occupancy, the home turned out extremely well. The wood floors and trim; used-brick fireplace with a mantle made from an ancient beam; and brick, copper and tile family kitchen all add a feeling of gentle warmth. You'll love the bay windows and the family room that opens onto your own wooded grove. Of course, all the amenities are present, such as air conditioning, a 2½-car garage, and a full basement awaiting your finishing touches. After Ralph, you can be the second person to sleep here for $197,500. This moment in history is brought to you by

Clyde Realty   **476-8200**

This ad is a takeoff on ads used by some brokers on historic homes.

761

Why Buy Used

No one has ever slept in this 3BR, 2-bath Cape Cod set on almost a quarter-acre in the nicest West Side location you can find. You'll be delighted with the sparkling country kitchen and tile-sheathed baths. The home even has the smell of newness. We guarantee it will be love at first sight, and it's priced at no more than you expect to pay for a used home—$189,500.

Clyde Realty   **476-8200**

762

Precompletion Special

If you buy this 3BR, 2-bath, Colorado-style ranch home on its oversized, wooded lot in Weston Estates before it is completed, the builder will give you an additional

$5,000 Credit

to apply to upgraded carpets, tile, fixtures, landscaping and appliances. The home features a full basement, 2++-car garage, huge country kitchen, family room, fireplace and covered patio. It's an exceptional opportunity at $184,500.

Clyde Realty   476-8200

Builders of homes for speculation will often provide discounts for purchases made prior to completion because this reduces financing costs.

Discounts given as upgrades can mean more to a buyer than a lower price, as they get extras they might otherwise decline.

763

New Is Better—4BR

Everything is guaranteed by the builder for at least 1 year in this sparkling-new French Provincial in highly coveted Newton Hills. Everything you've seen in *House and Garden* can be yours including soaring ceilings, French doors, greenhouse kitchen of tile and copper, formal dining room and classic fireplace. The best news: it's priced like an ordinary home at $169,500.

Clyde Realty   476-8200

764

Trade-In

The builder says he'll accept almost anything of value that he doesn't have to feed as down payment for this new 3BR, 2-bath French Regency set on a hillside lot overlooking the city. It's one of the finest homes we've seen, with all the amenities you can want including a huge country kitchen, a dining terrace and closets you'll get lost in. Full price: $219,500.

Clyde Realty   476-8200

765

Get in Line

with your money in hand if you want to become the owner of 1 of these last 4 brick, 3BR, 2½-bath town houses in Clydewood Estates. When these are gone, there won't be any more. Each unit has a huge 2-car garage (with room for a hobby shop), all appliances, ceramic-tiled kitchen floor, baths sheathed in marble, Jacuzzi tub in the master suite and all the model home features you dream of. They should sell out quickly at $164,500.

Clyde Realty   476-8200

A classified ad can be effectively used for entire subdivision sales.

766

Builder S.O.S.

We must sell 7 brand-new 3BR, 2-bath ranch homes on estate-sized lots in prestigious Westwood Hills by this weekend. All homes have full basements; 2-car, attached garages; quality carpets; hardwood trim; Eurostyle kitchens; covered rear patios; and front yard landscaping. Save thousands. It is first come, first served at $124,500.

Clyde Realty   476-8200

The above ad indicates that the price is a bargain. (See chapter 4, Bargain Homes, for other ideas.)

767

Builder in Trouble

Too many homes and too little cash. This is once-in-a-lifetime opportunity to beat the bankruptcy court. You can be the owner of a brand-new 3BR, 2½-bath Mediterranean Colonial in the most desirable area with amenities that don't seem possible.

Don't Pay $300,000

Available to the first buyer at $219,500.

Clyde Realty   476-8200

Obtain the owner's permission in writing when using an ad such as the above. This ad will be highly effective, as everyone loves a bargain. Expect the phones to ring.

The two separate headings will be very effective. Consider placing a slug (line of blank type) above and below "Don't Pay $300,000."

While the ad doesn't say the price was reduced, it does give that impression.

21

Older Homes

Older homes have received increased interest over the past few years because of their architectural detailing, size, workmanship and material. Instead of thinking newer is better, many people opt for older homes out of choice.

Ads for older homes appeal to quality, size, beauty, value and to the buyer's desire for a gracious way of life. They even offer historical appeal for many.

Some ads suitable for older homes are also found in other chapters in this book such as "Architectural Style" (chapter 2).

768

Time Forgot

about this 3-bedroom remnant of a gentler past embraced by its wraparound, covered porch. You'll fall in love with the polished oak paneling; dramatic staircase; high ceilings; light, bright rooms; double garage; and country garden in its quiet community of fine homes, towering trees and friendly neighbors. This is a home your family deserves at the old-fashioned price of $89,500.

Clyde Realty   **476-8200**

769

Old-Fashioned?

It certainly is. This 3-bedroom home has a large rocking-chair front porch, a claw-footed tub in the bath, solid maple flooring, gleaming woodwork and built-in cabinet work that has been cared for and polished for generations. Not quite good-as-new (but darn near), it's available in an old-fashioned neighborhood at the old-fashioned price of $79,500.

Clyde Realty   **476-8200**

770

Why Buy New?

when you can buy a fine English brick Tudor residence built for the centuries and not just for today. Offering an elegance unobtainable in today's homes, this 3BR, 2½-bath home features massive pegged beams, solid-black walnut wainscoting, a den lined with shelves for your books and mementos, leaded glass and intricate French doors. Every room is filled with classic appointments that reflect memories of workmanship and pride. For the special buyer who will not accept style as a substitute for quality, we proudly offer this estate at $289,500.

Clyde Realty   **476-8200**

This ad sells the quality of an older home.

771

Watch the Joggers

from the old-fashioned, lazy-day front porch of this 3-bedroom American Traditional on the nicest street in Westhaven. This is a home built for comfort and enduring beauty that can ensure your future at a very affordable $79,500.

Clyde Realty   **476-8200**

The above ad sells an ambiance of comfort and relaxation without giving details about the house.

772

Country Modern?

If modern means inside plumbing, then this 3-bedroom American Traditional with its claw-footed tub is modern. Actually, the house is a great place for an antique collection with its polished woodwork and nooks and crannies. There is a full basement and a walk-up attic to provide a lifetime of storage, and there's room for a garden on the huge half-acre lot. The garage is slightly tilted, but it's serviceable. Go modern for $69,500.

Clyde Realty   **476-8200**

In some rural areas the word "modern" means inside plumbing.

773

Once Upon a Time

in a land not very far away, a man carefully crafted a home for his family to endure for generations and bring joy to all who live there. He succeeded, and this American Traditional with its 3 bedrooms, 1½ baths, paneled music room, front parlor and great room is magnificent in proportion and concept to bring joy to your family. Proudly offered at $97,500.

Clyde Realty   **476-8200**

774

Remember Grandmother's House

with the gleaming hardwood floors, rich wood paneling, corn-popping fireplace and old-fashioned bay window with a window box full of treasures? Well, it has been carefully preserved for you in this 3-bedroom American Traditional that combines the best of the past with modern conveniences of today. Don't look for reproductions when the real thing is available for only $89,500.

Clyde Realty   476-8200

775

Built Like a Fortress

This 3-bedroom European Traditional reflects the finest in craftsmanship inside and out. Constructed of native stone and brick with gleaming hardwoods, this home was built to last for generations. There's a feeling of spaciousness in the large, bright rooms with their high ceilings. There is also a separate 2-car garage, full basement and walk-up attic. For the buyer who refuses to accept compromise as to quality, this fine residence is available at less than the cost of an ordinary home, $119,500.

Clyde Realty   476-8200

If there is more than 1 bath or if the location is desirable, it should be stated in the ad.

776

Romantic Wanted

to appreciate the 200 years of living that has given this 3BR, 2-bath Virginia Colonial its unique charm and warmth. Set back from a quiet street amidst ancient hardwoods, this home seems to echo centuries of laughter and happiness. You'll love the floating staircase and museum-quality woodwork. Proudly offered for your future at $179,500.

Clyde Realty   476-8200

If a house has been extensively renovated, it should be stated.

777

Fiddler on the Roof

This house has tradition. Built in 1870, this 8-room, 3-bedroom Edwardian masterpiece has seen America grow from the days of horse-drawn carriages to modern times. It has been home to suffragettes and Civil War veterans. The long covered porch has heard tales of the days when the country was new, and the front parlor held many nervous young beaus who came courting. This happy home of the past has much happiness to give for your family's future. A rare bit of Americana can be yours for only $89,500.

Clyde Realty   476-8200

This ad sells a mood to make the home desirable.

778

Tradition

You can own a white-clapboard, 3-bedroom American Traditional bungalow with a full-width, covered front porch; impeccable woodwork; full basement; and double garage in a neighborhood that retains the best of the past. Available for many to-morrows at $89,500.

Clyde Realty   **476-8200**

779

Built for the Ages

This 3-bedroom, redbrick and stone American Traditional was built when craftsmen showed pride in their work. No corners were cut in making this one of the finest-constructed homes we have seen. The hardwood floors are as true today as the day they were laid, and we expect them to be the same way for future gener-ations. The oak woodwork was carefully matched as to grain and was fitted with meticulous precision. In a stable family neighborhood, this is indeed a home for your family and their families and their families. Priced less than an ordinary home at $99,800.

Clyde Realty   **476-8200**

This is an excellent ad for a brick, city home built in the period 1880–1940. The details will fit many homes built during that time.

If there is more than 1 bath, it should be pointed out in the ad.

780

Norman Rockwell Traditional

Own a white-clapboard, 3-bed-room, country-style home with a large covered porch, an apple tree, a large garage and a myriad of flowering plants and shrubs. Idyllic living for $79,900.

Clyde Realty   **476-8200**

This ad paints a pleasant picture of a wood-frame, 1-bath home without providing much detail.

781

Like Them Mature?

While not sparkling new, this 3BR, 2-bath, brick English Traditional on its estate-sized lot in Westhaven still has plenty of class and an ambiance of gracious living seldom found in newer homes. Amenities include a basement pub room, a paneled den, French doors opening into the well-cared-for garden, a delightful patio and a 3-car garage. Set amidst stately beech and maple, it will probably endure for many more generations. A rare find at $169,500.

Clyde Realty   **476-8200**

782

A Home and Love

This immaculate 3-bedroom brick Traditional reflects the love of many generations. It has been updated to satisfy the family of tomorrow but retains all the charm of a glowing past. The home includes a large garage, and you'll love the intricate woodwork and feeling of spaciousness so seldom felt in newer homes. This is your opportunity to continue a legacy of love for $79,500.

Clyde Realty   **476-8200**

783

Haunted House—4BR

This circa 1880, brick Traditional is haunted by over 100 years of happy living. No restoration is needed because it has never been abused. It has, however, been thoughtfully updated to combine modern amenities with the best of the old. Like previous generations, you'll be smitten with the beauty of the gleaming woodwork and the simple grace of the design. Situated in a parklike setting, it presents an experience to be lived at $87,500.

Clyde Realty   **476-8200**

The above ad has an attention-getting heading.

784

Ghost Wanted

This large 3-bedroom Victorian, set on a massive corner lot behind an old-fashioned iron fence, looks as if it should be haunted. There is a cavernous basement that might have been a dungeon. The landscaping is overgrown, and it will make a great location for a Halloween party or the set for a horror movie. The price won't spook you at $87,500.

Clyde Realty   **476-8200**

This rather perverse ad might turn off some readers, but it will attract perverse types such as fixer-upper buyers (although the home is not advertised as a fixer-upper).

785

Step Back 60 Years

You can live on a quiet street with huge maple and chestnut trees, large homes that show their owners' love and neighbors who care. You'll take a giant step back in time as the owner of this 3BR, white-clapboard Traditional with its tribe-sized kitchen, formal dining room, old-fashioned front parlor, high ceilings and bright sense of spaciousness. There's an old-fashioned garden with sweet peas and hollyhocks. Your escape from today at $79,500.

Clyde Realty   **476-8200**

This ad sells nostalgia and makes an older home very desirable.

786

American Gothic

This is a 3-bedroom farmhouse Andrew Wyeth would have loved to paint. Set on an idyllic, tree-shaded knoll, it's perfect just the way it is. Forget restoration, although you might want to convert the garage loft to a studio. Have a home and way of life that's bound to be envied at $89,500.

Clyde Realty   **476-8200**

This ad appeals to artistic city people and sells an image. If acreage is included, it should be mentioned in the ad.

787

Back to the Future

Turn back the clock with this Southern Colonial estate that was new when your great grandparents were young. There are 9 rooms, 3 bedrooms, 2 baths and detailing that's the envy of a master craftsman. On a large, wooded lot in a premier location, this can be your gracious future at $169,500.

Clyde Realty   **476-8200**

788

100 Years Young

This solid, 8-room American Traditional has been barely broken in and should be fit for many more generations of joyful living. Solid oak floors and gleaming hardwood trim reflect a time when craftsmen took pride in their work and compromise was not in their vocabulary. The mature landscaping and emerald lawn provide a setting not to be duplicated today. For less than the price of a house, you can own a real home—$79,500.

Clyde Realty   **476-8200**

An older home of nondescript architecture can be made more desirable with the description American Traditional.

789

A Century Old—4BR

This home has all of the charm you expect from a 9-room home of this vintage. Carefully integrated modern systems, gleaming woodwork, leaded-glass entry, high ceilings and am ambiance of gracious living can be yours, complete with a magnificent rose garden, garden shed and garage in a prestigious neighborhood for $89,500.

Clyde Realty   **476-8200**

If a home has more than 1 bath, it should be pointed out in the ad.

790

A New Century

began with this 8-room, 3BR American Gothic home. On a tree-shaded lot in a quiet, family neighborhood, it has been skillfully modernized without sacrificing charm. There is a large garage with a separate workroom; a full basement; and even an old-fashioned, walk-up attic. It's the ideal place for your future at $79,500.

Clyde Realty   **476-8200**

791

A Relic—4BR

of a glorious past. This 9-room, 2-bath Greek Revival Colonial is nearly 200 years old, and we believe it's better than new. You'll love the careful attention to detail. Modern systems don't detract from the architectural charm. A rare find at $198,500.

Clyde Realty   **476-8200**

Since having 4 bedrooms is an important feature, it is included in the heading. "Relic" is a little misleading, but the word is an attention getter.

792

Yearning for Yesterday?

This 3-bedroom American Traditional with its wide, rocking-chair front porch is a product of an era when homes were built for gracious living. You'll fall in love with the quiet, friendly neighborhood; hardwood floors; carefully polished woodwork; country-sized kitchen; and large, bright rooms. Waiting for you at an affordable $69,500.

Clyde Realty   **476-8200**

793

It Takes a Special Person

to appreciate the old-world craftsmanship that went into building this 10-room, one-of-kind masterpiece. Beveled glass, intricately carved banisters, a floating staircase, nooks and crannies for those special keepsakes and hand-cut stone combine to make this home a premier example of the builder's skill.

If

you think you are that person, you have the opportunity to live amidst splendor. Priced less than most ordinary homes at $97,500.

Clyde Realty   **476-8200**

This unusual way of describing an older home is designed to elicit positive responses from people who consider themselves cultured and/or artistic.

794

A Call from the Past

Want to live in a quiet, friendly neighborhood with children roaming freely, old-fashioned front porches, pride in one's home and respect for one's neighbors? You can have it all today with this 3-bedroom American bungalow with its full basement, storage attic, garage and very special garden at a price truly old-fashioned, $69,500.

Clyde Realty   **476-8200**

795

1896

Civil War veterans led the July 4th parade, horsepower still referred to horses and a man's home was truly his castle when this turreted, 10-room Victorian, with its lavish wood trim and high ceilings, was built for gracious living. If you desire to recapture the joy of a gentler time, call today for a private showing. Offered at $179,500.

Clyde Realty   **476-8200**

The year an older home was built can make an effective heading. The ad body above creates a pleasant, nostalgic image.

796

1926—A Classic Year

Homes back then were built of brick and stone with intricate hardwood detailing. This Gatsby-era masterpiece reflects the best of the time. On a magnificent site with lawns and hedges that took 60 years to perfect, all systems of this 10-room residence have been carefully updated to provide the utmost in amenities. Nooks and crannies abound for your precious collectibles. You can own the very finest for a very modest $149,500.

Clyde Realty   **476-8200**

The year of construction can be effectively used as a heading.

797

A Fallen Woman

Once she was stately and acceptable by the best of society; today she stands empty and worn. This 9-room, 3BR, turreted Victorian in the desirable Newhall area offers limitless possibilities and a challenge to the bold. With the curved wraparound front porch, intricate detailing and hardwood floors, this can be a home that knows no equal. Control her destiny for $89,500.

Clyde Realty   **476-8200**

This ad is really for an older, fixer-upper home.

798

The Age of Innocence

Built in 1912, when one's life centered on home and family, this 3-bedroom American Traditional reflects that uncomplicated time. The large living room with the intimate sitting room alcove has entertained generations of friends and neighbors. Guests must have marveled at the impressive built-in, hand-carved dining room buffet. Herculean-sized rooms, a full basement, a walk-up storage attic, and one of the nicest gardens you'll ever see are just a few of the features of this friendly home. While all of the charm remains, all systems have been updated for your comfort. It's your chance to set the clock back to a far gentler period for only $89,500.

Clyde Realty   **476-8200**

This ad sells a mood and makes older seem better. It can easily be adapted for almost any older home.

799

$3,000,000 Brownstone

Well, it would be worth $3 million if it were moved to Manhattan. Because of a slight deviation in geography, this 9-room, 3BR, 2-bath luxury residence can be yours in Milwaukee for

$79,500

This is truly your chance to live like a millionaire.

Clyde Realty   **476-8200**

800

Built by a Hero

Buford Jones, a colonel in the Confederate cavalry, built this 3-bedroom American Traditional for his family. This home reflects his attention to detail and quality. You'll delight in the high ceilings; museum-quality, gleaming woodwork; lazy-day front porch; and stately walnut and pecan trees he lovingly planted so long ago. The home has been updated to offer all the conveniences of today without detracting from the charm of long ago. This is your chance to own a piece of history at $119,500.

Clyde Realty   **476-8200**

Homes built from the late 1860s to the 1890s were probably built or occupied by veterans of the Civil War. If you obtain information on a home's former occupants from its abstract of title or from checking with your local historical society, you will have ammunition that will greatly increase the desirability of the home.

801

Restoration-Ready

This 10-room, Pennsylvania Dutch Colonial shows 200 years of wear. You'll fall in love with the classic lines and the neighborhood of stately homes with giant trees separated by impeccable lawns. This is truly a home that needs and deserves your love and dedication. The price is not a misprint at $89,500.

Clyde Realty   **476-8200**

802

Do I Have the Girl for You

Of course she's a bit old-fashioned. I guess you would say she's Victorian. She will never see 30 again, or 60 or even 90. Nevertheless, she's as good as she ever was, standing like a bride in her new coat of white paint. She has classic lines with her gently curved, wraparound porch; twin turrets; and fine detailing. You could even say she's magnificent. Inside, she has been carefully updated yet retains all that is gracious. Her 10 rooms will suit even the largest family, and she has been known to entertain dozens at a time. This is a home you'll want to bring mother home to, available now at $187,500.

Clyde Realty   **476-8200**

While an allegorical ad such as this is difficult to write without being overly cute, this one comes off well, even with its feminine references.

803

Class of 1936

This 3BR, 1½-bath American Traditional was built with brick and plaster at a time when workmen were proud of what they built and before the days of construction shortcuts. While only minutes from everything, the home offers a very private, walled garden; large, bright rooms; woodwork that is nearly impossible to duplicate today; and an ambiance of strength and stability in a neighborhood where old values are still respected. Strange as it seems, the best really costs less at only $79,500.

Clyde Realty   **476-8200**

This is an ad for an older home in an older, close-in neighborhood.

804

Remember When

you could buy a hamburger for a dime and a phone call cost a nickel? That's when this 3-bedroom stone Colonial was built on its double-sized lot in Westbrook. You got a lot for your money then, and this house has it all—cut-stone fireplace; French doors to the patio; a lion-sized den; a full basement; large, bright rooms; a double garage; and even a greenhouse. Far better than new, this home is available at a fraction of the reproduction cost at $239,500.

Clyde Realty   **476-8200**

This ad emphasizes the value of older homes as well as their workmanship.

805

A Lady with a Past

This stately Victorian with its intricate detailing and wraparound, rocking-chair veranda reflects a glorious era when one's life centered around the family and gracious living. Her 10-foot ceilings, front parlor, window seats, summer room or studio, formal dining room and bright living areas have all been carefully preserved for you. There is even a walk-up attic with room to store the memories of a lifetime. If you desire a home that will return the love you have to offer, this is an opportunity unlikely to be duplicated at $179,500.

Clyde Realty   **476-8200**

This ad sells a mood but also includes the home's details.

806

Circa 1840

This 3BR, 2-bath Colonial has stood the test of time and has been updated to provide the most modern conveniences without detracting from its charm. Set on a huge estate-sized lot sheltered by magnificent beech and chestnut trees, this beauty of the past has been preserved just for your future. Happily offered at $149,500.

Clyde Realty   **476-8200**

The above heading indicates that the exact date of construction is not known.

807

William Howard Taft Would Love the Bath

Of course back then he would have taken a huge, claw-footed, cast-iron tub and sparkling brass for granted. But what would he think about the copper, brick and oak kitchen with its microwave and built-in conveniences? This would be a wonder of wonders. This 3-bedroom period piece has been preserved and thoughtfully updated for the family who is tired of plastic. A far better way at $113,500.

Clyde Realty   **476-8200**

This ad was inspired by an ad written by Gordon Wearing-Smith for Barry Plant Real Estate, Pty., Ltd., Doncaster, Australia.

808

George Washington Could Have Slept Here

and would have felt totally at home in this extraordinary 9-room, 3BR Mt. Vernon Colonial set on 3 of the most beautiful acres in Southport. The beauty of this fine residence is enhanced by leaded windows, solid maple floors, a flowing staircase and rooms of Herculean dimensions. In an area known for its fine homes, this is a masterpiece at $389,500.

Clyde Realty   **476-8200**

This ad was inspired by an ad written by Gordon Wearing-Smith for Barry Plant Real Estate, Pty., Ltd., Doncaster, Australia.

809

The Roaring Twenties

Rumor has it that the 2 bathtubs of this Gatsby-era, 3-bedroom brick home were once used to manufacture gin. If true, it's the last exciting thing that happened here. Now the home is a very comfortable, but proper, residence. It is so staid, you might say it's boring. Of course, it has all of the goodies of its era: rich, solid walnut paneling; crystal-cut, leaded glass; high ceilings; and magnificently proportioned rooms. Definitely more the home of a successful banker than a rock star, it is respectfully priced at $179,500.

Clyde Realty   **476-8200**

This ad conveys the image of a proper, solid, quality home that doesn't have a great deal of flash. This is the kind of home many buyers desire.

810

Brownstone Magic

A New York-style brownstone that would sell for at least $2 million in Manhattan can be yours for pennies on the dollar. Besides woodwork that puts a newer home to shame, this 3-bedroom residence offers hardwood floors, a private patio and garden, a garage and a price of only $69,500.

Clyde Realty   **476-8200**

This ad reflects the fact that old brownstone residences are very popular in some cities. This increases the home's desirability and makes its price appear a fantastic bargain.

811

A Cocked Hat

was worn by the first owner of this 3-bedroom Carolina Colonial built with timber hewn from giant trees in this prestigious Oakmont setting. Craftsmanship can be seen in every detail. The high ceilings, bright rooms and polished woodwork echo years of gracious living. There's an exquisite carriage house, currently used as a workshop, and a garage that will make a charming studio for an artist or writer. Carefully preserved and updated with every modern convenience, this glorious home can be yours at far less than you would imagine—$179,500.

Clyde Realty   **476-8200**

This ad has an unusual, attention-getting heading.

812

Like a Fine Wine

This 3-bedroom Colonial has improved every year since it was lovingly built in 1858. You'll be entranced with the magnificent detailing, high ceilings, pine floors, and the ambiance of quality living that pervades this fine residence. Every modern expectancy has been skillfully integrated so as not to detract from its basic beauty. The huge lot has several sugar maple trees ready for tapping and an ancient hickory, home to at least 1 family of squirrels. A very special offering at $298,000.

Clyde Realty   **476-8200**

813

Ante Bellum

Carriages and parasols are just part of the history of this magnificent, 9-room, 3BR masterpiece preserved from the past and skillfully updated for your future. You'll marvel at the woodwork that has been lovingly polished for 150 years, the intricate moldings, high ceilings and gracious ambiance this fine home projects. Set on over 1 acre in the finest estate section of Newberry, it is incomparable at $250,000.

Clyde Realty   **476-8200**

"Ante Bellum" means this home was built before the Civil War.

814

San Francisco Victorian

You can live in a 9-room, 3BR, 2-bath masterpiece with a curved glass turret; wraparound front porch; gingerbread trim; high ceilings; spacious, bright rooms; woodwork that belongs in a museum; plus all modern conveniences skillfully integrated so as not to detract from its charm. In San Francisco, this home would sell for well over $1 million, but it's yours in Westhaven for $89,500.

Clyde Realty   **476-8200**

By pointing out how desirable a house would be in another community, you add to its attractiveness.

815

Dixie

Young men sang as they marched down a tree-canopied lane past this then-new 3BR, white-clapboard home. The owners waved the flag with the stars and bars from their rocking-chair front porch. While there have been many changes since that time, the home still stands amidst flowering shrubs and magnolia trees as lovely as long ago. It has been skillfully updated to provide all modern conveniences without sacrificing any of its charm. Available for your family at $79,500.

Clyde Realty   **476-8200**

When advertising a northern home, consider "Battle Hymn of the Republic" as the heading.

816

Benjamin Harrison

was President when this 9-room, 3BR American Traditional was built in what was then a rural setting. What we now call the "garage" held horses, a surrey and a sleigh. The small maple tree planted in the front yard now stands like a sentinel guarding the house. You'll love the rocking-chair front porch, high ceilings, intricate moldings and the many nooks and crannies. This family home, which appears to be right out of a Norman Rockwell painting, can be yours for $89,500, a fraction of what it would take for duplication.

Clyde Realty   **476-8200**

The name of the President who was in office at the time a house was built can be effectively used as the heading for an older home.

817

14 Rooms
Bed and Breakfast
Possibilities

This is an Italian Renaissance home with 4 baths, high ceilings, exquisite detailing inside and out, and it's located in a parklike setting on a well-traveled road. It would make a truly handsome inn and can be purchased for only $179,500.

Clyde Realty   **476-8200**

Large, older homes are in demand for bed and breakfast inns, which are attractive to professionals who want to drop out of high-stress jobs.

818

A Country Inn?

This Colonial masterpiece offers 16 large, bright rooms and the zoning to permit a bed and breakfast inn. It's ideally suited for 7 guest rooms on the second and third floors with a 2-bedroom owner's suite on the first floor. On a huge lot adjoining a well-traveled, scenic route, this can be an investment in a new lifestyle at $118,500.

Clyde Realty   **476-8200**

819

Greek Revival
Masterpiece

Built around 1830 by a prominent physician, this 11-room residence has been home to judges and industrialists. It has been carefully updated to provide the most modern conveniences with the charm of a bygone era. Set on over an acre of impeccably landscaped grounds on the most prestigious street, this home must be seen to be fully appreciated. Offered to the discriminating buyer at $285,000.

Clyde Realty   **476-8200**

The architectural style of a home, if particularly appealing, makes an excellent heading. Prominent former residents make a property seem more desirable.

820

Restored Colonial

This 1763, 9-room, 3BR, center-entrance New England Colonial has been painstakingly restored to all its former glory. From polished maple floors to authentic wall coverings, you'll marvel at its better-than-new condition. Modern systems were skillfully integrated to provide the utmost comfort and convenience without detracting from its gracious charm. Set on a wooded estate site in Westhaven, it will please even the most discriminating buyer at $349,500.

Clyde Realty   **476-8200**

821

Restorable Colonial?

With 11 rooms, this home was built in 1730. George Washington might even have slept here, but it isn't much now. While you'll love the ancient chestnut trees and colorful flowers, you can't spend your entire life outside. Inside, it just looks old. While most of the original moldings and woodwork remain, it's covered with paint. Someone laid ugly linoleum over the solid pine floors and paneled the great room with plywood. They even boarded up one of the fireplaces. Mrs. Thompson of our office, who lives in a Garrison Colonial, cried when she saw what had been done to this place. A local builder told us restoration is possible, but unless the purchaser does the work, it will cost more than the selling price of $69,500.

Clyde Realty   **476-8200**

This ad will have the effect of waving a red flag in front of a bull, for Colonial buffs regard desecration of a fine home as a capital offense. Such a reader will want to rescue the home.

822

Restorable Colonial—4BR

This classic Federal Colonial, with 2 staircases and end fireplaces, appears to be structurally sound with a solid fieldstone foundation and level floors. You'll probably want to erase the attempts at modernization to restore the home to its former glory. Under the vinyl and carpeting are solid heart-of-pine floors to delight any lover of Americana. On a quiet street shaded by huge maples, this is indeed a masterpiece awaiting your unveiling at $189,500.

Clyde Realty   **476-8200**

Be precise as to the architectural style of Colonial homes. This will add prestige to any ad. Structural soundness and classic lines are very important to people interested in restoration.

823

Born Again

Completely restored to its original grandeur, this 3BR, 2½-bath, brownstone residence within walking distance of Madison Avenue reflects all that is gracious in life. The marble foyer; high ceilings; bright, spacious rooms; gleaming hardwood floors; and intricate woodwork make this 10-room showplace the ultimate residence for fine living and entertaining. Proudly offered at $2,600,000.

Clyde Realty   **476-8200**

824

Forget about Restoration

For over 200 years, this 9-room, 3-bedroom family home has been lovingly maintained. It is rare when we are able to offer a

Pennsylvania Colonial

in such immaculate condition. This home reflects the craftsmanship and caring that made America great with its dramatic floating staircase, solid cherry balustrades, high ceilings, pegged maple floors and solid-walnut mantle over the stone fireplace. Modern amenities have been lovingly integrated so as not to detract from its charm. This heirloom, in a storybook setting, can be yours at $319,500.

Clyde Realty   **476-8200**

825

The Old Schoolhouse

has been skillfully converted to a warm and friendly 2BR, 1½-bath home. There's room for a studio corner in the enormous light, bright living room with its soaring ceilings. Modern systems have been skillfully integrated so as not to detract from the building's basic charm. In a villagelike setting with tall trees, you can have a home as individual as yourself at a very affordable $67,500.

Clyde Realty   **476-8200**

This ad can be easily modified for any nonresidential property converted to a home with headings such as "The Old General Store," "The Old Barn," or "The Bicycle Repair Shop." This kind of property has a strong appeal to artistic buyers.

22

Open Houses

While open houses sell many homes, they serve other purposes as well. For example, they bring in prospective buyers who can often be switched to property more suitable to their needs. Prospects are often better listing prospects than sale prospects because they must sell an existing home before they can buy.

Open house ads must indicate the days and hours a particular house is open. Directions to the house and/or its address are essential. Like other ads, the price should be included as well as just enough information to make readers want to find out more about the property.

Besides the adds presented here, ads in other chapters of this book can be readily modified for open houses.

826

Open To Sell
Sat.–Sun., 1–4 P.M.
3822 West 17th Street

This is a like-new, 3BR, 2-bath American Colonial in a premier location. The home includes an attached, double garage; full basement; and every amenity you dream of.

$99,500–
$10,000 Down

Clyde Realty   476-8200

Other headings are "Open for Appreciation," "First Opening," or simply "Open House."

827

First Opening
Sat.–Sun., 1–4 p.m.
4218 Edgewater Circle
(Follow the signs
from the corner of 1st
and Ocean View Drive.)

This 3BR, 2-bath, cedar and stone beach home has an ocean view and is just steps from the sand with off-street parking for 3 cars. This definitely won't last at $249,500.

Clyde Realty   476-8200

Be sure to draw attention to the fact that a home is being offered or opened for the first time. This is important to many buyers who feel something must be wrong with any house that has been on the market for several months. Where parking is in critical supply, your ad should point out any extra parking.

828

Open House
1:00–4:00 p.m.
768 N. Chester
(1 block
west of Main St.)

There's still time to choose the colors, tile and carpet in this brand-new 3BR, 2-bath New Mexico Traditional with an attached 2+-car garage on one of the finest residential streets on the prestigious West Side. With simply great financing, the price is unbelievable.

$164,500

Clyde Realty   476-8200

This ad tells very little about the house. It is intended as a teaser to bring traffic to the house.

829

Open House
1:00 p.m. 'Till Sold

Own this 3BR, 2-bath Colonial at 2947 Claridge Road for only $179,500. We don't expect it to last 'till 2:00 p.m. If you're interested, better make this your first stop and bring your checkbook.

Clyde Realty   476-8200

Note that there is nothing said about the house except the basics and its address. This approach can be used when the price seems low for an area. This ad uses an urgent approach.

830

Open Today
1–4 p.m.—$97,500
Will Be Sold
by Tomorrow
1212 W. Burnham
(1 block
west of Kilbourn)

The owner of this 3BR, 2-bath, Tennessee stone ranch has priced this fine residence for immediate sale. Set on an estate-sized lot in a much sought-after community of fine homes, special features include a massive fireplace in the huge living area, a separate formal dining room, a cozy den and a full basement completely finished with recreation room and workroom. There is even a perfect spot for a photographer's darkroom. Better be the first in line.

Clyde Realty   476-8200

The directions given in an ad must be clear.

831

832

An ad such as this will bring in many curious as well as potential buyers. By qualifying these visitors, you will obtain prospects for less-expensive homes.

23

Pet Owner Ads

Since many buyers regard their pets as full-fledged family members, it is extremely important to them that a home environment be suitable for a pet. The following ads are written for pet owners as well as for those desiring to own pets.

833

A Dog

would love this 3BR, 2-bath, double-garage Carolina Colonial embraced by a pillared portico. There's a fire-plug by the curb and a dog door opening onto a large, fenced backyard with lots of trees for sniffing and squirrels for chasing. The home has an open floor plan, a huge country kitchen with room for a dozen kids and their puppies, a family room ideal for rainy-day romping and luxurious carpeting Fido can't stain. For the best in a dog's life at $149,500, call

Clyde Realty   **476-8200**

834

Lucky Dog

would love the huge fenced yard with its 7 large shade trees. This 3-bedroom Cape Cod even has a dog door for Rover or Fifi to go out all by themselves. Located in a quiet family neighborhood with a fire hydrant on the corner, what more can any dog ask for? All yours for $89,500.

Clyde Realty   **476-8200**

835

Gone to the Dogs

A chain-link dog run comes with this 3BR, 2-bath Cape Cod set on a wooded hillside acre in Bayberry Heights. This fine home offers a 2½-car garage, a full basement, a Great Dane–sized family room and a kitchen to delight any chef. Bring Rover along to check out the accommodations. Definitely not a dog, this home is priced to sell at $179,500.

Clyde Realty   **476-8200**

836

It's a Dog's Life

There are over 60 trees for sniffing on this estate-sized lot in desirable Westhaven plus a 3BR, 2-bath, double-garage Colonial with central air, a family room, closets you can get lost in and a special door just for Rover. A Bow Wowser at $189,500.

Clyde Realty   **476-8200**

837

A Dog's Life

There's a poodle next door, a dalmatian just across the street, a basset on the corner and a fire hydrant right in front of this 3BR, 2-bath California ranch on a large, wooded lot in Clearview Estates. The home features a fireplace to curl up by, a large family room for romping plus a lot of special features to delight your master. A home for the lucky dog at $179,500.

Clyde Realty   **476-8200**

838

K-9 Heaven

Fido will love the huge fenced-in yard with places to explore and room to run. There are 7 large trees just awaiting your dog. A dog door will give instant access to this 3BR, 2-bath New England Contemporary with its large, bright family room. Imagine your dog curled up by your side on those cold nights with a gentle glow from the embers of the fireplace. When you go for walks, Fido will enjoy the quiet, tree-lined streets in this almost rural setting. Ready for you and your dog at $169,500.

Clyde Realty   **476-8200**

839

Dog House

is included with this almost-new 3BR, 2-bath provocative Mediterranean on an estate-sized lot in Westwood. The home features 2 fireplaces, a music room and a family room of exceptional proportions. This is truly a spectacular residence that is family-priced at only $298,500.

Clyde Realty   **476-8200**

Note: The heading "Dog House" can be changed to "Tree House" to make this ad appealing to a family.

840

Go to the Dogs

This 3BR, 2-bath Cape Cod, set on 3 wooded acres, includes a kennel with 6 chain-link runs. The previous owner raised weimaraners. With hundreds of trees and the abundance of squirrels and chipmunks to bark at, what more can your dogs want? You'll be pleasantly surprised by the spacious rooms; the oversized garage; and the finished, full basement. A great place for a dog's life at $179,500.

Clyde Realty   **476-8200**

841

The Collie Next Door

hopes the new owners of this 3BR, 1½-bath, split-level in Washington Heights have a friendly dog to share her trees with and to gossip through the back fence. By the way, besides a fully fenced yard the home offers several large trees of its own, a lovely flower garden (perfect for burying bones), a double garage, a fireplace to cuddle up by, a large family room for romping and a country kitchen with the biggest refrigerator you ever saw (perfect for storing bones). The friendly owner priced it at $87,500, so pick up the phone and give a "whoof" to

Clyde Realty   **476-8200**

842

Comes with a Poodle

The owners of this 3BR, 2-bath ranch home in Westwood are being transferred overseas and can't take their 3-year-old, miniature apricot poodle "Brandy" with them. They hope the new buyers can take Brandy. Incidentally, this home has a large fenced yard. Brandy is well behaved and sleeps in a corner of the family room, although if you let her, she prefers the middle of your bed. The home and Brandy are available at $139,500 with generous seller financing. Call today for a private showing (the house and Brandy).

Clyde Realty   **476-8200**

Often sellers can't take pets with them when they leave because they're moving to an apartment, a mobile home park or they're moving in with children. You can effectively use this when advertising, but do so with the owner's permission.

843

Cat People Special

Your felines will love this 2-bedroom and den Cape Cod on a wooded lot in Albany Hills. There are plenty of cat friends in the neighborhood and a great woods to explore, with trees waiting to be climbed. At $139,500, we'll throw in a ball of yarn and a scratching post.

Clyde Realty   **476-8200**

844

A Friendly Tortoise

comes with the fenced backyard of this 3BR, 2-bath West Side Colonial. He or she (we're not really certain) is named Alfred. We think Alfred eats grass and things that hop, but the owner gives Alfred a little lettuce to munch on. This home has a delightful family room, a double garage, a marble-sheathed fireplace, warm wood paneling and Berber carpets. It is decorated in the neutral tones of the Southwest. Offered to turtle people at an easy $139,500.

Clyde Realty   **476-8200**

This ad can be easily modified for other animals with headings such as "A White Rabbit" or "A Friendly Chipmunk." For rural property, you can advertise that the property comes with a white goose or even a friendly cow.

24

Residential Rental Property

Buyers of residential rental property buy property because they're interested in the income and tax advantages of ownership. Buyers who intend to live in one unit also have the same concerns as any other home buyers.

The most common residential income property is the duplex home, although a single property can contain hundreds of units. The following ads are written specifically for residential income property.

845

Home + Rental

You can own a 3BR, brick split-level with a family room plus a 1-BR rental unit with separate utilities. A large corner lot in Truesdale, a double garage and magnificent landscaping make this a fantastic bargain with your tenant paying about one third of your mortgage payment. This costs no more than an ordinary house at $129,500.

Clyde Realty   476-8200

Homes with a small rental unit often sell at prices similar to comparable homes without the rental unit.

846

2 for 1

You can have 2 homes for the price of 1. This 3BR, 2-bath main house has a separate 1BR guest house that's perfect for your parents; or if rented, it will make your payments very, very reasonable. Both homes are in move-in condition and are priced for immediate sale at $97,500.

Clyde Realty   476-8200

Before you advertise that a second home on one lot can be rented, be certain zoning and/or restrictive covenants don't prohibit rentals.

If a home has desirable features, they should, of course, be mentioned in the ad.

847

Two Homes—One Lot

for one low price. Live in the 3-bedroom American Bungalow and use the 2-bedroom home for your parents or Aunt Suzie. You'll love the classic design of both homes and marvel at getting so much for only $79,500.

Clyde Realty   **476-8200**

This ad is for two separate homes on one lot.

848

Dynamic Duo

This is a 2-bedroom duplex that has everything—fireplaces, garages, built-ins, generous-sized rooms, prime location and a vacancy factor close to zero. Best of all, it's priced less than many small homes at $97,500, but you better hurry.

Clyde Realty   **476-8200**

849

Doubles

You can own 2 spacious, bright 2BR units with all the built-ins, garages and even basement storage rooms. In better-than-new condition on the finest West Side street offered at a price that makes dollars and sense, $97,500.

Clyde Realty   **476-8200**

850

Brick Duplex $79,500

Both 3-bedroom spacious units have separate basements, laundry areas, separate entries and gleaming woodwork that cannot be duplicated today. In a family neighborhood and only a short walk from shopping, schools and public transportation, the location couldn't be better. This is your opportunity to live practically rent-free.

Clyde Realty   **476-8200**

Three facts were included in the above ad heading: duplex, brick and the price. The fact that the home is brick adds desirability because brick homes mean lower maintenance. Include price in a heading when price is comparatively low.

238   Simplified Classifieds

851

Two Families—
One Home?

Each can live alone in this 3BR, 1½-bath brick duplex in Westport. Each will love their light, bright unit with spacious rooms, modern built-ins and separate basement laundry areas. Only one family? Then live in one unit and rent the other. Either way, it's an exceptional opportunity at $97,800.

Clyde Realty   **476-8200**

852

Don't
Throw Mother Out

You'll hardly know she's there in the entirely separate, 1BR English apartment with its own entrance that comes with this 3BR, 1½-bath Cape Cod in delightful Westport Village. There's a 2-car garage plus room for an RV, a great garden spot, and the house is in move-in condition with large, bright rooms. Check this one out quickly at $119,500.

Clyde Realty   **476-8200**

An English apartment is a basement unit. This ad heading is an attention getter that can be used when a house has a small rental unit.

853

Rent-Free—Almost

With this lovely brick North Side duplex, you can live in one 3BR unit and rent the other. Your net monthly payment will be less than half of what would be required for a single-family home. If you're a retiree or are just getting started, this is your opportunity for a home and an investment for only $124,500. FHA low-down financing is available. First come, first served.

Clyde Realty   **476-8200**

854

Be the Landlord

as the owner of this 3-bedroom duplex in a choice family location. Let your tenant make most of your payments for you. With only $8,000 down, this is an opportunity demanding your immediate investigation.

Clyde Realty   **476-8200**

It is not necessary to include the price in the above ad, as the ad is selling down payment and reduced housing costs.

855

No Rent Control

in Westwood. These 8 1BR units show close to a zero vacancy factor, and tenants pay all their own utilities. The brick, 2-story building has exceptional landscaping, is well maintained and has long-term tenants. This property will show a positive cash flow with 30 percent down, at $320,000.

Clyde Realty   476-8200

If other local areas have rent control, "No Rent Control" is an excellent heading.

856

Benevolent Landlord

is offering these 9, 2BR apartments in Southport. They should break even with 20 percent down, but current rents are significantly below market, offering an exceptional opportunity at $395,000.

Clyde Realty   476-8200

Apartments with rents that can be raised are very attractive to purchasers.

857

Ugly Money Maker

These 32 units are of nondescript design. Several have a view (of McDonald's). There's definitely no pride of ownership here, but it's a solid brick building with a waiting list for tenants and an operating statement your accountant will love. At $640,000, it will make dollars and sense.

Clyde Realty   476-8200

858

Beat the IRS

This 38-unit apartment complex will show a totally sheltered, positive cash flow with $150,000 down. If you want to please your accountant, call.

Clyde Realty   476-8200

The price is not given in the above ad, and it need not be given. The down payment and tax-sheltered income are the important elements to potential buyers.

859

24 Units at $30,000/Unit

The owner hasn't raised the rent in 4 years on these 1BR units in Westwood—and they're free of rent control. With 10 percent down and 10 percent owner financing, you'll show a break-even cash flow with only a 10 percent rent increase. Not much pride of ownership here, but great profit potential.

Clyde Realty   476-8200

The total price of the above 24 units is $720,000.

The fact that rents haven't been raised in 4 years will excite many buyers, as they will consider a rent increase of far more than 10 percent.

860

24 Units—Westwood

These are well-maintained 2BR units that have no rent control. There is a tenant waiting list, and this property will show a positive cash flow after a 25 percent down payment with current raisable rents. Full price $720,000.

Clyde Realty   476-8200

The above heading gives the number of units and their location. Raisable rents and positive cash flow are strong plus points.

861

Accountant Pleaser—24 Units

Bring your accountant to check the books on these 8-year-old, brick and cedar, 2-bedroom units. Meticulously maintained and with a close to zero vacancy factor, these units will show an impressive cash-on-cash return. Full price: $720,000.

Clyde Realty   476-8200

The fact that the agent is willing to open the books shows that the property is a reasonable investment.

25

Small Homes

Most homes have 3 bedrooms. Those with more than 3 bedrooms are generally considered large, and those with fewer bedrooms are regarded as small.

Smaller homes usually sell for significantly less than comparable homes having 3 bedrooms. They therefore are economical for buyers who don't need the extra space.

Small homes offer special appeal to singles and couples unlikely to have children. You can tailor ads specifically for these groups. While some ads for small homes are found under condominiums, vacation homes and other categories, the ads in this chapter specifically were written for small homes.

Since the word "small" has a negative connotation, it should generally not be used. Better words to use are "cottage," "studio/home," and so forth.

862

Put Mother in a Home

Imagine a 2-bedroom American brick bungalow on a quiet, friendly street just 1 short block from shopping and public transportation. Think of the rich woodwork and the built-in dining room china cabinets for those special plates and glassware. Think of the warm glow from the fireplace in this solid home, built to endure. There is even an attic in which to store all those memories of the past. Priced for mother at $79,500.

Clyde Realty   476-8200

The ad takes a turn from the attention-getting heading.

863

Why Pay for 3

bedrooms when 2 will do. You'll save big on this enchanting Westwood cottage with its large garage, native stone fireplace and full dry basement. Special features include a very private patio, a delightful garden spot, landscaping you'll love, hardwood floors and a feeling of bright spaciousness. The best part: it can be yours for only $79,500.

Clyde Realty   476-8200

This ad sells the economic advantage of 2 bedrooms.

864

Hermit?

Well, here is your house. This is a 1-bedroom cottage that has a huge living room with fireplace set at the end of a tree-canopied lane with no neighbors in sight. There's no room for a guest, and even if one wants to come, he or she will probably never find the place. This home is ideal for the people hater, writer or anyone on the lam. Its price will please any hermit: $69,500.

Clyde Realty   476-8200

The above heading will attract readers.

865

Lover Come Home

This is an intimate, 2-bedroom home nestled on a large, wooded lot featuring cuddle-up stone fireplace, king-sized master bedroom, and secluded patio ideal for dining. Priced for a couple in love at $89,500.

Clyde Realty   476-8200

866

Masculine

The massive fireplace, built-in bookshelves and leaded French doors leading to the delightful patio add an aura of refined masculinity to this huge 1-bedroom town house just minutes from the civic center. All that is desired in a sophisticated adult lifestyle can be yours for $79,500.

Clyde Realty   476-8200

This ad is specifically aimed at a single male. See the next ad for a different approach.

867

Feminine

A fireplace for cuddling up, an old-fashioned bay window with a window box for those special things, a sun-drenched kitchen and a patio ablaze with colorful plantings add the aura of gentle femininity to this spacious 1-bedroom town house just minutes from the civic center. Everything you desire for an independent lifestyle can be yours for $79,500.

Clyde Realty   476-8200

868

There's No Room for In-Laws

in this 1-bedroom American bungalow set amidst towering trees and flowering shrubs in a delightful West Side neighborhood where owners take pride in their homes and respect each other's privacy. With the generous-sized rooms and large garage, there's plenty of room for a single or a couple. There's even the ideal spot for a garden. Personally priced for you at $69,500.

Clyde Realty   476-8200

This ad turns small into a virtue.

869

Only 1 Bedroom

That's right. The only guests you'll have better be mighty good friends. Designed for a couple, this miniature estate offers an expansive living area that looks out upon a private garden patio. There's also a dream kitchen with an illuminated ceiling and a large double garage. All the space you need at an affordable $79,500.

Clyde Realty   476-8200

This ad is for a single-family home, but it could also be used for a condominium.

870

Writer's Studio

This is the perfect spot for a writer or artist. There is a massive living room/dining area with room for bookcases, easels or even a grand piano. The bedroom is large enough for a king-sized bed as well as a desk. You'll love the orchard stone fireplace, delightful dining patio and colorful garden. The garage can be converted to a separate studio or guest suite. This is a home created for your very special needs at an amazingly affordable $69,500.

Clyde Realty   476-8200

This ad gives a 1-bedroom home desirability. It is aimed at single people who regard themselves as artistic.

871

Studio/Home

Located in a villagelike, wooded setting, this very special home features a huge sun-drenched living area offering a myriad of possibilities for the artist or writer, a king-sized master bedroom and an efficient galley kitchen with every conceivable built-in. There's an attached garage with expansion possibilities. The starving artist will appreciate the garden. All at an affordable $59,500.

Clyde Realty   476-8200

This home has 1 bedroom, 1 bath and a 1-car, attached garage.

872

Goose Bumps All Over

said Mrs. Callahan of our office after viewing this 2-bedroom, ivy-covered cottage secluded in its woodland setting. Snuggle up to watch the flames and hear the crackle of burning wood in the stone fireplace. With its rich wood paneling, leaded-glass entry and ambiance of comfort and quality, this home will seem a fulfillment of all your fantasies at a price bound to excite—$97,500.

Clyde Realty   476-8200

873

Attention Hedonists

If you believe personal pleasure is the chief goal of life, we have found the perfect residence. This baroque masterpiece has 2 huge master suites with closets you can get lost in and baths sheathed in marble that would be the envy of a Roman emperor. You'll love relaxing in the soothing hot spa or redwood sauna. The living areas were designed for entertaining both small intimate groups and large formal affairs. This is your opportunity to pamper yourself at $249,500.

Clyde Realty   476-8200

The home described above would appeal most strongly to singles; however, it is a 2-bedroom home. This type of ad can be used for a home or condominium.

874

Think Small

As the owner of this 2-bedroom American Craftsman bungalow on its garden-sized lot on a quiet, tree-lined street in Westport. You'll have hardwood floors; built-in cabinetry; a separate dining room plus a sun-drenched, eat-in kitchen; and your own garage at a little bitty price, $49,500.

Clyde Realty   476-8200

875

This ad was tailored for a gate-guarded community catering to retirees. It can also be used for a condominium.

26

Swimming Pools

While swimming pool "language" is included in the ads in other chapters of this book, the following ads were written specifically to sell the virtues of pools and spas.

876

Attention
Skinny-Dippers

The French doors of the master suite open onto a secluded, sparkling pool and spa, making keeping fit fun. You'll love the lush plantings and colorful flowers in the picture-book yard. Incidentally, this all comes with a 3BR, 2½-bath California Colonial in the choicest Holiday Hills location you could possibly want. This fine residence is model-home perfect and comes with every amenity in the book for only $219,000, and unbelievable financing is available. Call today for a refreshing tomorrow.

Clyde Realty   476-8200

877

Skinny-Dipping
Allowed

in the very private pool and hot spa that come with this 3BR, 2-bath Monterey Colonial with its double tile roof, sparkling white walls, bubbling fountain courtyard, heavy Mexican floor tile, huge carved beams and gentle arches. A studio overlooks the 2-story living area. There is a formal dining room as well as a dining patio and an eat-in kitchen. This is a very comfortable place just to be yourself. Available now at $287,000.

Clyde Realty   476-8200

878
Splish! Splash!

through the sliding-glass doors of the master suite of this 3BR, 2-bath Westhaven ranch home, and you are just 6 steps from the sparkling pool or tantalizing hot spa. The backyard has a privacy wall, so you can swim in nature's garment. You'll love the myriad of flowers and shrubs, the stately chestnut tree and the delightfully covered dining patio overlooking the pool. There's a 2-car garage, a paneled family room and a dream kitchen. At $132,500, it's time to grab your towel and call.

Clyde Realty   **476-8200**

879
Swim at Home

with this 3BR, 2½-bath, Holiday Hills California Colonial with its shimmering pool and tantalizing hot spa. One problem, though, is that with this house not only will your children never leave home, but you can expect all of their friends as well; then again, it's a lot better than some of the alternatives. Let us explain the exceptional financing. Family-priced at $169,500.

Clyde Realty   **476-8200**

This ad sells the idea that the swimming pool will add to family cohesiveness.

880
Iron Man Special

Swim in your own sparkling pool, jog over miles of wooded trails and bike on quiet streets as the owner of this 3BR, 2-bath, Frank Lloyd Wright-inspired Contemporary in the quiet, family community of Arlington. The unfinished basement is ideal for a home fitness center and sauna. Generously proportioned rooms, a private study and a garage with room for 2 cars and a dozen bikes make this the home of your dreams. The only problem—you won't want to run away. We won't have to twist your arm to buy this beauty at $179,500.

Clyde Realty   **476-8200**

This ad is targeted at people interested or involved in fitness training.

881
Free Pool

An in-ground, heated pool with all the extras is included free with this 3BR, 2-bath New England Colonial on an estate-sized lot in exclusive Country Club Estates. The home includes a 30-foot family room that looks out over the pool, a double garage and a full basement. The price compares with similar homes not offering a pool. This is your chance to get in the swim at $169,500.

Clyde Realty   **476-8200**

In many areas of the country, a pool won't increase the sales price of a home. This ad capitalizes on that fact.

27

Terms

When a property can be purchased with exceptional terms such as no or low down payment, a below-market interest rate or a no-qualifying loan assumption, this information should be mentioned in the classified ad for the property. Terms can be the focal point of an ad since for many buyers, they are as important or more important than any other feature of a property. The ads provided in this chapter use terms as the primary attention-getting feature.

882

> ## Seller
> ## Wants $5,000
>
> and buyer assumes the low 9-per-cent loan on this 3-bedroom ranch with full basement and 2+++-car garage in a prime West Side neighborhood. With a full price of only $79,500, we strongly recommend you call immediately.
>
> **Clyde Realty**   **476-8200**

The approach in the above heading forces a house hunter to read the entire ad. The price is ridiculous for a home, but after reading, it becomes clear $5,000 is the down payment and the balance is the loan assumption.

883

$1 Down

That's right. We have the financing if you qualify. A 3-bedroom home with full basement and garage can be yours with payments easy as rent. We only have one home at these terms, so call now.

Clyde Realty   **476-8200**

The price could have been included in the above ad, but it wasn't necessary as the ad is selling terms. The people it is designed to attract are primarily interested in terms, not price. This approach can be used for a home suitable for a no-down-payment, VA loan or in cases where owner financing exists. Possible variations on this heading are "$100 Down," "$1,000 Down," "0 Down," or "No Down Payment."

884

Move In Free

Sure it sounds like a come-on, but call us and we'll show you that this 2BR, 1¾-bath, expandable Cape Cod in the most desirable neighborhood in Southport can be available to qualified buyers without a down payment. The large, dormered walk-up attic can be readily converted to 2 additional bedrooms. This is a not-to-be-repeated opportunity at $98,500.

Clyde Realty   **476-8200**

885

Zilch Down

That's right. There's no down payment if you qualify for this

4BR, 2-Bath Colonial

in a highly desirable West Side neighborhood. Call now, as it won't last long at $89,500.

Clyde Realty   **476-8200**

The important facts—no down payment and 4BR—come across well with this split-heading ad.

886

Nothing Down

That's right. If you qualify, you can assume the existing loan, and the seller will carry the balance of the purchase price on this 3BR, 2-bath Dutch Village Colonial set on a quiet cul-de-sac in highly desired Westview Acres. This home features pegged, hardwood floors; a St. Charles dream kitchen with microwave and ice-dispensing refrigerator; and a huge dry basement ready for finishing. There's even an apple tree right by the back door. The problem is at $149,000, it won't last long.

Clyde Realty   **476-8200**

This ad does much more than sell terms. It describes the house in a very positive manner, and readers will fall in love with the house before seeing it.

887

Your Money Tied Up in Groceries?

No Down Payment?

Not to worry. We have a 3BR brick Traditional on a quiet, tree-lined street in a friendly West Side neighborhood that can be purchased by qualified buyers with no down payment. The home offers a large garage; full basement; huge, bright rooms; hardwood floors; lovely landscaping; a perfect garden spot and payments that will probably work out to less than you're paying in rent. Call quickly to see if you qualify as the owner.

Clyde Realty   476-8200

The price is not included above, although it could be. It is really not needed, as this ad focuses on terms (i.e., no down payment).

888

Got the "Shorts"?

Like to own a home but can't come up with the down stroke? Well, fret no more. Let us show you how it might be possible to move into a 3BR, 1½-bath Cape Cod with full basement and double garage in a friendly family neighborhood without opening your wallet. The payments will seem like rent with the $58,000 price.

Clyde Realty   476-8200

An alternative heading is "Short on the Green?"

889

Short on Money?

Then you'll appreciate the low- and no-down financing alternatives we can offer for this 3BR, 2-bath ranch in the Hillside School District. There's even a 2+-car garage, full basement, fireplace, delightful patio, an ancient oak tree and a perfect garden spot at only $87,500.

Clyde Realty   476-8200

890

Almost Nothing Down

You'll love this 3BR, 2-bath Colonial ranch with an assumable FHA loan at

9½ Percent Interest

and the owner will carry the balance after your modest down payment. This is definitely an opportunity you'll want to investigate. Full price only $89,500.

Clyde Realty   476-8200

This split-heading ad is designed to pique the interest of readers, as the amount of the down payment isn't given.

The area should be indicated if the home is in a desirable location.

891

As in some of the previous ads, the price is not included. This ad sells the virtues of low down payment and low monthly payments.

892

893

894

The price is not stated, nor is price important. What is important are the terms. The payments are left out in this ad to encourage telephone traffic. Readers will be interested enough to call for additional information.

895

Herman Didn't Know

that he could buy a 3-bedroom, brick home with garage on a large, landscaped lot in a choice West Side location for

$2,000 Down

and a full price of $56,000. That's why Herman is still renting.

Clyde Realty   **476-8200**

This unusual heading will attract the reader's attention.

896

Illegal

A deal this good can't be legal. A 3BR, 2-bath, double-garage Colonial in Westport Heights for

$5,000 Down

with a kitchen any chef would envy, central air, a family room with fireplace and lush landscaping. At a full price of only $98,500, it has to be a steal.

Clyde Realty   **476-8200**

Split headings can be very effective. The heading "Illegal" is an excellent attention getter.

897

Let's Make a Deal— 4BR

The owners indicate that they will carry the mortgage after a low down payment with a trustworthy buyer. If you qualify, you can be the owner of this brick Traditional in a friendly, family neighborhood with an oversized garage, full basement and delightful landscaping. Best of all, it's priced at only $89,500.

Clyde Realty   **476-8200**

If a home has only 3 bedrooms, it should be included in the ad body rather than in the heading.
While the above heading arouses curiosity, it isn't as strong as "$5,000 Down."

898

Let's Swap

We'll give you this 3BR, 2-bath, American Traditional on an oversized lot in the friendliest West Side neighborhood if you'll come up with $5,000 cash and 3 bubble-gum cards. The balance of the purchase is an assumable FHA loan at below-market interest. We're being more than fair at a total price of only $89,500.

Clyde Realty   **476-8200**

Both the above heading and ad body are attention getters designed to elicit calls.

899

An Enormous Mortgage

can be assumed when you purchase this 3BR, 2½-bath, rather-imposing Spanish Colonial in Southport. Besides the usual, this home features a hacienda-style adult playroom with wet bar, gigantic beams, graceful arches, tons of tile and a bubbling fountain. A king's ransom was spent by the owner on the lush landscaping. If you want to go into debt in real style, at $349,500 this is it.

Clyde Realty   **476-8200**

The negative approach in the above ad is used with humor, and it will encourage readers to call.

900

Can't Qualify?

Don't worry. The low-interest, FHA loan is assumable by anyone on this 3BR Traditional in desirable Westlake. A $5,000 initial investment should make you a home owner. First come, first served.

Clyde Realty   **476-8200**

This ad will attract buyers who have credit problems or have yet to establish credit.

"First come, first served" is used to create a sense of urgency.

901

Question

With only $5,000 in savings, is it possible to find a 3BR, 2-bath home with a large fenced yard in the Elmdale School District at a total price under $120,000?

Answer

Such a house does exist, and it comes with a finished basement recreation room, 2-car garage and even space to park an RV. Interested? Then hurry and call.

Clyde Realty   **476-8200**

Question and answer formats almost force potential buyers to read the entire ad. It is an extremely effective approach and can be readily modified for any property.

This type of ad was developed by Gordon Wearing-Smith, the advertising manager for Barry Plant Real Estate Pty., Ltd., in Doncaster, Victoria, Australia.

902

Assume VA Loan

A low-interest, VA loan can be yours even if you aren't a veteran. With a low down payment, you can be the owner of this 3-bedroom, brick ranch in a great West Side neighborhood. With a full price of only $79,500, call *now!*

Clyde Realty   **476-8200**

If the interest rate is considerably less than the current rate, an effective heading is "Assume 8-percent VA Loan."

903

Rejected
for a Loan?
No Qualifying—
Assume FHA

This 3-bedroom West Side ranch with attached, double garage can be yours with

$7,000 Down

A very special home, it's bound to sell fast at $93,500.

Clyde Realty   **476-8200**

This ad appeals to people who are afraid they may not qualify for a loan, as well as to those who have been turned down.

If there is an attractive interest rate on the assumable loan, it should be stated.

904

Name Your Terms

The owner is flexible with the financing of this 3BR, 2-bath, West Side Colonial on an estate-sized, wooded lot. This impressive home has a fireplace, a 2+++-car garage, a family room and a full basement. Interested? Then you better be the first to call because at $129,500, it's an opportunity that won't last.

Clyde Realty   **476-8200**

This ad has an attention-getting heading followed by a positive description. The end of the ad communicates a sense of urgency.

905

Fixed Rate—9%

assumable loan available for this 3BR, 1¾-bath American Traditional in one of the most desirable West Side locations. This home features a 2-car garage, hardwood floors, a country-sized kitchen, delightful landscaping, a perfect garden spot and central air. The best part is the price—only $79,500.

Clyde Realty   **476-8200**

This ad is most effective when local lenders are resisting fixed-rate loans in favor of adjustable rate mortgages.

906

Only 7% Interest

for the first 2 years on this like-new, 3BR, 2-bath Nantucket Colonial on the nicest block of the nicest street in Westport. The home features a double garage, central air and every conceivable built-in. Because of unusual circumstances, it is available at only $149,500.

Clyde Realty   **476-8200**

Adjustable rate mortgages often have teaser rates for a period of time. In some cases, sellers or builders actually buy down the interest rate.

The reason for the sale is not given in the above ad, but "unusual circumstances" leads readers to believe that the price is advantageous.

907
9%
Qualifying Interest

is available on this 3BR, 2½-bath French Regency town house in a delightful West Side location. With hardwood floors, central air, a double garage, a very private patio and garden and every conceivable built-in, it's a rare offering at $149,500.

Clyde Realty   476-8200

Adjustable rate loans often use below-market interest rates (initial teaser rates) as the loan rates for qualifying buyers. This allows buyers to qualify when they otherwise might not.

908
Worthless

That's what rent receipts are. You can't deduct them from taxes, they provide no equity and they certainly don't appreciate in value. You don't have to remain a renter because with only

$3,000 Down

we can make you the owner of your own 3BR, 2-bath home in the sought-after family community of Washburn. Sorry, we only have 1 home available, so it's first come, first served.

Clyde Realty   476-8200

This ad doesn't mention price, but it isn't necessary. The ad sells the low down payment and is aimed at first-time buyers who are presently renting.

909
In a Renter's Trap?

Is your rent so high you can't save the down payment? Bid farewell to your landlord. This 3-bedroom West Side Cape Cod is available with

No Down Payment

to approved applicants. A large, wooded lot with room for a garden; a separate garage; a full basement; and hardwood floors are just a few of the features to delight you, but you must act fast and call.

Clyde Realty   476-8200

Like the previous ad, this ad is aimed at first-time home buyers who are renting. Again, it sells the down payment.

910
Adios Landlord!

You'll wave goodbye when you find you can own this 3-bedroom, brick charmer for only $2,000 down and payments of less than $500 per month. Call today and forget rent forever.

Clyde Realty   476-8200

The price is not given, and it isn't needed. This ad sells low down payment and low monthly mortgage payments.

911

Don't Rent

If you can pay rent of $600 per month, then you can

Be the Owner

of this 3BR, 2-bath home that is only a short walk from schools and shopping. Let's talk now.

Clyde Realty   **476-8200**

This ad is selling terms, not price. Keep in mind that because of income tax advantages, a buyer can make payments of $800 to $900 per month as owner and have the same net costs as $600 in rent.

912

Bye-Bye Landlord

With almost no down payment and monthly payments less than $500, this 3BR, 2-bath home in highly desirable Westhaven will end your rent-paying days for good. If you want equity, not rent receipts, call now.

Clyde Realty   **476-8200**

Again, the price isn't given. This ad is similar to the last ad and simply sells terms.

913

Renter to Owner with $1,000 Down

You can have a 3BR, brick rambler with a 2-car garage on a lovely garden lot in the Hillsdale School District, and the price is only $67,500.

Clyde Realty   **476-8200**

This is a short but effective ad.

914

Renter's Revolt

Kiss your landlord goodbye and become the owner of this 2-bedroom expandable Cape Cod with a full basement and attached garage set among giant maples in a delightful neighborhood.

Only $3,000 Down

and payments that will probably prove less than your present rent make this your chance for independence at $69,500.

Clyde Realty   **476-8200**

Keep in mind that the deductibility of interest and taxes allows people to pay considerably more for house payments than for rent and still have lower net housing costs.

915

Low Down Payment

West Side 3BR	$79,500
West Side 2BR	$83,700
Northview 3BR	$92,800
Northview 4BR	$112,700
Hilton Estates 3BR	$137,500
Clyde Realty	**476-8200**

A simple listing of homes under a heading that emphasizes terms will show readers that there is a choice available, and this will increase calls.

28

Time Shares

As more time shares are sold, resales will increase, and more brokers will begin to handle resales. Because of lower dollar costs of time shares, commission structures are generally higher than other types of property to allow brokers to advertise.

Because a time share is a type of vacation property, a buyer will be interested in the amenities of a development and its location (e.g., Is it close to ski lifts?) as well as the particulars of a unit and its price. Some time shares are for a specific lease period rather than a fee ownership forever. If this is the case, an ad should spell this out with language such as "until 2020."

If a newspaper has a separate category for time shares, they should appear under that category, although they can appear under vacation property categories (providing a time share is clearly presented as such). The following time share ads are for new time share developments as well as for resales.

916

A Sample of Paradise

For only $100, we offer qualified adults the opportunity to enjoy 3 days and 2 nights at Bass Lake Highlands. This includes use of a fully furnished, 2-bedroom villa; fishing and ski boats; the health club; tennis; and unlimited golf. Two weeks each and every year forever start at $19,500 under our unique shared ownership plan. Best of all, your initial investment will only be $1,000. Call today to arrange to sample what paradise is like.

Clyde Realty   **476-8200**

This ad is a promotion that offers a visit to the resort. This type of approach is for original sales, not resales. It should appear under the time share heading "Vacation Homes" and/or "Vacation Rentals."

Most time shares are sold with low down payments.

917

Lake Louise

You'll love the sunsets over the water from the private patio of your very own 2-bedroom lakeside chalet. Your own boat will be available for fishing or water skiing. You can spend 2 weeks in this water wonderland each and every year with our remarkable shared ownership plan offering full price purchases as low as $17,500. Don't make any investment until you are absolutely certain this is what you want. Call today for an opportunity to sample life in this special water paradise.

Clyde Realty   **476-8200**

While this ad is similar to the previous ad, no details are given as to the particulars of the "sample."

918

Buy the Beach

Live like a millionaire for 2 weeks each and every year as one of the owners of this luxuriously appointed, 2BR, 2½-bath, beach-front unit that includes full use of health club, tennis courts, pools, spas and clubhouse. You'll have 2 choice weeks forever at only $24,500 with only $2,500 down.

Clyde Realty   **476-8200**

Other possible headings are "A Place on the Beach," "The Sound of the Surf," or "Stroll on the Beach."

919

Your Passport to Fun

You can have 2 of the best weeks of sheer luxury in a world-class, beach-front resort on fabulous Hilton Head. There are 2 master suites, each with its own fireplace; a state-of-the-art kitchen; wet bar; furnishings your friends will envy; and use of all the great resort facilities at no charge. You can be the owner forever for only $27,500.

Clyde Realty   **476-8200**

This ad uses a slightly different approach than the previous ad, even though it is for a similar property. Note that both ads make it clear that this is a time share.

920

Why Pay

for a whole year when you only use your vacation home for 1 month? With our shared ownership plan, you can own this 3-bedroom lakeside villa in prestigious Lake Geneva Estates that includes use of boats, golf, tennis and pools at a fraction of its real cost. One month a year forever in this paradise of millionaires is available with unbelievable financing at a full price as low as $17,500 with a low-low down payment.

Clyde Realty   **476-8200**

The price quoted here is the lowest new price. For a resale, use the listed price.

921

Guarantee
Your Future

Would you like a 2-bedroom vacation home for your family on a quiet, fish-filled lake in Berkshire Hills that is yours forever? The perfect spot for your family now and for future family reunions? How about a home taken care of by others and all you have to do is relax and enjoy the resort lifestyle? Through shared ownership, you can own this magnificent villa for 1 full week each and every year for as little as $9,700 and only 10 percent down. Call today for tomorrow's fun.

Clyde Realty   **476-8200**

This ad is not for a resale. It quotes the lowest price for the least-desirable period. For a resale, you should quote the listed price for the property.

922

Time Share—
Tree House Ranch

The price has been squeezed dry on this 2 weeks each year in July that goes on forever. Originally, this 2-bedroom water-view villa, with all the amenities one expects in a world-class resort, sold for $24,500. It can be yours today for only $16,000, but you better call now.

Clyde Realty   **476-8200**

Time share resales are often deeply discounted from their original selling prices.

If an area or development is well known, use it in the heading. Otherwise, you can feature the time period or price reduction (e.g., "Time Share—40 Percent Discount").

923

Wisconsin or Hawaii?

Spend 2 weeks each year in your own 2BR, 2-bath chalet on the shores of Lake Geneva. Of course it includes all the luxury resort facilities such as boats and golf. Or, for a change of pace, trade your time for 2 weeks in Kona Bay on the Island of Oahu or any of 87 different resorts. Best of all, you own your 2 weeks forever, and it's yours for $24,500 with only $2,500 down.

Clyde Realty   **476-8200**

Many time shares have exchange privileges with other units.

29

Trees, Gardens and Landscaping

Ads can be written with language that describes a particular tree, garden or landscaping. Gardening, in some form or other, is America's No. 1 outdoor activity. Even people who have never worked in a garden have the image of a pleasant, mentally relaxing activity. Ads focusing on these three areas will strike a chord of interest among many readers.

924

A Sea of Grass

A riding mower goes with this 3BR, 2-bath, California Monterey villa set on a green, velvet lawn covering most of the half-acre site. You'll love the ancient oak tree in the front yard, the separate workroom in the 2½-car garage, and the huge family room opening to a delightful patio. This is a home that will grow on you for $175,000.

Clyde Realty   **476-8200**

925

Splendor in the Grass

Surrounded by verdant, luxuriously manicured lawns studded with stately trees and flowering shrubs, you'll love this 3BR, 2-bath, traditional Colonial with its white-clapboard siding, massive cut-stone fireplace, screened breezeway and workshop in the double garage. The high, dry basement is ideal for hobbies, a recreation room or a home fitness center. You can have charm and dignity at a very affordable $139,500.

Clyde Realty   **476-8200**

926

Yard Sale

A charming white picket fence embraces the parklike lawn, and the roses are ablaze with color. There's even the perfect spot for a vegetable garden or greenhouse. The yard comes complete with a 3BR, 2-bath, double-garage Colonial that will delight the most meticulous buyer. Everything is impressive except the price, $159,500.

Clyde Realty   **476-8200**

927

Stop— Smell the Flowers

The roses are in bloom at this picturesque 2-bedroom Cape Cod home in Hillsdale Estates. Actually, at least 15 varieties of flowers make this yard ablaze with color. Gardeners will love the potting shed and glass seedling frames. This home offers a full dry basement that can be finished for living space and a 2-car garage. The 24-foot living room opens to a delightful patio. This is the perfect spot to lower your blood pressure for only $89,500.

Clyde Realty   **476-8200**

928

Orchids and Daisies

will flourish in the solar-heated greenhouse sitting amidst your private botanical gardens on this estate in Westchester. The main house shows a Mediterranean influence with 3 bedrooms, a den and a family room. The marble entry and Roman baths typify the quality features found throughout this fine residence. It's definitely your place to grow at $349,500.

Clyde Realty   **476-8200**

929

A Botanical Wonderland

surrounds this 3BR, 2-bath, double-garage New England Traditional in Westwood. The garden lover will want to spend every waking moment in a labor of love tending specimen plantings gathered from around the world as well as the more traditional roses. There's an ideal spot for a greenhouse. Priced for the green thumb at $189,500.

Clyde Realty   **476-8200**

Very little is mentioned about the house. The ad is designed to appeal specifically to gardeners.

930

An Organic Garden

to please anyone concerned about their health goes with this 3-bedroom American Traditional in Westport. Bid farewell to preservative-loaded foods, insecticides, chemical fertilizers and additives. There's plenty of room for your tools in the oversized garage. If you manage to get inside the house, you'll find gleaming hardwood floors, a tribe-sized kitchen, a dining room large enough to hold a family reunion and an almost indescribable feeling of comfort. At $137,000, this is an investment in yourself.

Clyde Realty   **476-8200**

This is an ad for an older home with a garden.

931

Garden Therapy

A vegetable garden that is a farmer's envy and a myriad of flowers provide an opportunity to forget the cares of the world and unwind while doing what you love. The gardens come with a garden shed as well as a 3BR, 2-bath American Traditional on an estate-sized lot in Westwood. There's plenty of room in the oversized double garage for your potting bench. This home offers a classic fireplace and every modern convenience in an atmosphere of warmth and comfort. This is truly a must-see-now opportunity at $98,500.

Clyde Realty   **476-8200**

932

Gardener's Paradise

This 3-bedroom Traditional, set on almost an acre of rich loam soil, has the finest rose garden in the neighborhood. There also are specimen plantings from around the world, a family-sized vegetable garden and your own greenhouse. There's plenty of room in the garden shed for all your tools. There's also a full, dry basement perfect for potting and winter storage of bulbs. Priced for the green thumb, this can be all yours at $93,500.

Clyde Realty   **476-8200**

933

Vegetarian's Delight

The organic garden included with this 3BR, 2-bath Cape Cod in one of the nicest West Side neighborhoods produces enough vegetables to fill half a dozen large freezers. There is much more: 2 apple trees and a pear tree produce abundant fruit and an oak tree in the front yard is home to at least 1 family of very friendly squirrels. The oversized double garage has plenty of room for bikes and trikes, and there's even a garden shed. The home itself is delightful and bright. Come and see what home really looks like. Proudly offered at $119,500 with flexible financing.

Clyde Realty   **476-8200**

934

A Strawberry Patch

comes with this 3BR, 1½-bath ranch home. There's also an apple tree, bearing grape vines and a lovely garden. A delight for green thumbs at $89,500.

Clyde Realty   476-8200

Other potential headings are "A Watermelon Patch," "A Grape Arbor," "A Cornfield," or "Carrots and Radishes."

935

Little Jack Horner

would have loved this 3BR, 2½-bath Contemporary designed in the spirit of the Southwest. There are 6 plum trees in the picturesque backyard to keep Jack in plum pies and pudding. The house has a 3-car garage; a postcard view of Mount Shasta; and a soaring, 30-foot stone fireplace. You'll love the feeling of comfort in such an impressive residence. Priced for immediate sale at $249,500.

Clyde Realty   476-8200

936

Johnny Appleseed

must have come this way. There are 6 mature apple trees ideal for cider, sauce, pies or just munching that come with this 3-bedroom Garrison Colonial set on a half-acre of deep loam soil. There is a perfect spot for a vegetable garden, and the home features an old-fashioned root cellar; gleaming maple woodwork; a screened and glassed porch; a red barn; a bright, family-sized kitchen; and updated systems for modern living. This is your home for a very happy future at $89,500.

Clyde Realty   476-8200

If the above ad were for a newer home, the reference to "updated systems" would be eliminated and "newer" could be inserted before "3-bedroom."

937

Apple Pie on Sunday

You'll have bushels of apples from the 3 apple trees in the yard of this 3BR, white-clapboard Traditional set on an oversized lot in the friendly community of Middleton. The large "Welcome Home" front porch will probably be one of your favorite spots. Besides the generous size of the rooms, you'll delight in the fine maple woodwork and abundance of storage space. There's room for everything you have ever owned. A home for a beautiful tomorrow at an affordable $79,500.

Clyde Realty   476-8200

938

Raw Apple Pie

There are 2 Jonathan apple trees in the backyard of this 3BR, 1½-bath Gloucester Cape Cod. We'll pick the apples if you'll bake the pie. The huge kitchen will give you plenty of working space. There is also a full basement, garage, storage attic and a yard with more flowers than you have ever seen. The price is "appleing" at $79,950.

Clyde Realty   **476-8200**

Mentioning the specific variety of fruit tree on the property tends to enhance desirability.

939

Apple Blossoms

bloom in the spring, and there's apple pie in the fall. This 3-bedroom American Craftsman bungalow has 6 bearing trees, also great for climbing, plus a garden area and a large garage. You'll love the gleaming oak floors, bright gallery dining room, tribe-sized kitchen and old-fashioned front porch. With only a short walk to grade schools and playgrounds, it's a home to be cherished at $89,500.

Clyde Realty   **476-8200**

Note the use of adjectives such as "gallery," "tribe-sized," and "gleaming."
Plum or peach can be substituted for apple.

940

Apple Trees

Six of them come with this 3BR, white-clapboard Traditional set on a huge West Side lot. A 2-car garage, a beautiful garden and a separate storage shed with cider press are included at $129,500.

Clyde Realty   **476-8200**

941

Birds, Bees and Apple Trees

You'll fall in love with this delightful 3BR, 1½-bath authentic Cape Cod on a full half-acre in a suburban area of fine homes and good schools. The oversized double garage has room for bikes, trikes and family cars. The home comes complete with an apple orchard and a friendly family of squirrels at $149,500.

Clyde Realty   **476-8200**

942

Nuts

and fruit trees as well go with this 3BR, 2½-bath Monterey Colonial in prestigious Eagle Point. Set on almost a full acre, there are pecan and walnut as well as apple, pear and peach trees. This home has a feeling of understated elegance with its large bright rooms and delicate crystal-cut windows. There is a 2½-car garage as well as a separate storage shed that will make an ideal artist studio. For $179,500, you can start picking.

Clyde Realty   476-8200

943

Apple—Pear—Plum

This 2-bedroom expandable Cape Cod has it all, including a double garage, full basement, central air, fireplace, patio and a sunny garden spot among the fruit trees. Available for the first time at $87,500.

Clyde Realty   476-8200

944

Maple Syrup

will be available from your own maple trees as the owner of this 3BR and garage Cape Cod on a wooded acre in Southport with 7 maple trees. There's also a sunny spot for a garden and a large storage shed great for a hobbiest's or artist's studio. The price is sweet at $87,500.

Clyde Realty   476-8200

945

Beneath a Majestic Oak

in a quiet family neighborhood stands the home of your dreams. This 3BR, white-clapboard, expandable Cape Cod with its 2-car garage and delightful dining patio offers comfort, beauty and all the conveniences you can want at a price you can afford—$89,500.

Clyde Realty   476-8200

946

Guarded
by a Giant Oak

The gently rolling hills of Westwood create a haven for this 3BR, 2-bath, double-garage Arizona Contemporary set on a majestic half-acre site. This home has all the amenities you can ask for plus a view that must be experienced. Priced below replacement value at $249,500.

Clyde Realty   **476-8200**

947

A Cathedral

of tall trees shelters this 2-bedroom American bungalow on its estate-sized lot in desirable Westwood. You'll love the extensive use of gleaming hardwoods, the native stone fireplace, the old-fashioned front porch and family-sized garden. There is a garage and separate work shed that will make an ideal studio. Just about the perfect home at $69,900.

Clyde Realty   **476-8200**

This ad paints a very attractive picture. In this case, the home is an older bungalow on a wooded lot.

948

In the Wild

Lost in an acre of ancient oaks and towering beech is this 3BR, 1¾-bath Pennsylvania Colonial. You'll love the wide terrace that is perfect for entertaining or simply relaxing and watching the birds and squirrels. This is a very private world that is closer than you would believe, and it's family-priced at $149,500.

Clyde Realty   **476-8200**

949

I Never
Touched a Drop

said Mr. Casey of our office, who swears he met the little people in the woods bordering this 3BR, 2-bath Nantucket Colonial in Foresthaven. Besides very genial neighbors, the home boasts a full basement; a lion-sized, paneled den or music room; 2 fireplaces; a kitchen that would make even Mr. Casey take up cooking; a 3-car garage; and a paved circle drive. All this plus the little guys and gals in green for $269,500.

Clyde Realty   **476-8200**

This light ad has an attention-getting heading that almost guarantees it will be read.

950

Orchids and Rubber Trees

The conservatory of this 3BR, 4½-bath French Provincial is the perfect spot to raise orchids or other exotic flowers. Outside there are abundant flower beds, impressive plantings and the perfect spot for a vegetable garden or tennis court. The home has an ambiance of quiet elegance with details such as crystal leaded glass, French doors leading to the dining patio, impeccably matched woodwork and a massive den with its own fireplace. The master suite includes a sitting room, dual baths sheathed in Carrara marble and his and her walk-in closets. Impressive, but not ostentatious at $689,000.

Clyde Realty   **476-8200**

This ad appeals to the people interested in flowers or to those with the desire to take up gardening as a hobby.

30

Vacation Homes

Ads for vacation homes differ from other ads in that they primarily sell a lifestyle rather than dirt and mortar. In this way, they are similar to ads for retirement homes. In fact, many of the properties advertised as vacation homes are purchased as primary residences by retirees.

Vacation homes are more apt to be fully or partially furnished than are other homes. They are often sold along with boats, vehicles, tools and/or furnishings.

951

Where the Trees Grow Tall and the Sun Meets the Sea

You'll find that this 3-bedroom, cedar-shake Cape Cod was built to last for the ages. The river-rock fireplace, massive beams and hardwood floors give this home an ambiance of permanence seldom found today. This is your opportunity for a place on the beach at a price within your reach. $369,500.

Clyde Realty   476-8200

If a house has water frontage, it should be included in the heading. This home is beach-oriented but does not have water frontage. If a home has a view of the ocean, it should also be mentioned.

952
Sand
Between Your Toes

the constant sound of the surf, skimpy bathing suits and a laid-back attitude are aspects of the beach you'll have to endure as the owner of this 2BR, cedar-shake cottage just steps from the sand. There's a large screened porch perfect for summer sleeping and a wood-burning fireplace for those brisk mornings. Much more than a home, it's a whole new lifestyle at $218,000.

Clyde Realty   476-8200

953
Blue Water—
White Sand

You waited a long time, but at last we have an authentic 3BR, 2-bath Nantucket Colonial only steps from the sand. With its massive fieldstone fireplace; random-planked, pegged maple floors; mullioned windows; and private patio for dining or sunning, this is definitely the finest beach house in our inventory. If you're ready, so are we at $269,500.

Clyde Realty   476-8200

954
On the Sand

Kick off your shoes and walk the white beaches! Enjoy the morning mist and the haunting cry of seagulls. Pick up exotic shells and watch the waves. This 2-bedroom Cape Cod with its huge, beamed living room; toe-warming fireplace; large screened porch; and attached garage can turn your dreams into reality. Make every day a vacation at $239,500.

Clyde Realty   476-8200

If there is water frontage, consider headings such as "Your Own Beach" or "On the Water."

955
100 Footsteps
to the Sand

You can take morning walks with your dog along hard-packed sand enjoying the sights, sounds and smells of the sea. Watch the fog roll in on wintry days, enjoy the sunset over the water. You'll want to take off your shoes and run barefoot through the sand. Beach living turns back the clock as you enjoy the simple pleasures of yesterday and every nuance of nature. This 3-bedroom beach cottage was built with you in mind. The ocean can be yours for $319,000.

Clyde Realty   476-8200

If a cottage has strong features (such as a view), this should be covered in the ad.

956

The Sound of the Surf

will lull you into a sound sleep, and the morning call of gulls will invite you to walk barefoot in the sand. The beach lifestyle of this 2-bedroom beach bungalow will relieve your stress far more effectively than medication or a psychiatrist's couch. It's investment in yourself at $389,000.

Clyde Realty   **476-8200**

This ad presents a rational health reason for buying into this type of lifestyle.

957

Reach Out
Touch the Surf

There's nothing quite like the smell of sea air at your doorstep or the gentle sound of the waves to lull you to sleep. An ambiance of quiet contentment encompasses this large 1-bedroom, oceanfront cabana unit. At night you can swim unnoticed in nature's garment or simply sit and watch the variegated lights of paradise. This is truly the end of the rainbow and the address of your future. Unexcelled at $385,000.

Clyde Realty   **476-8200**

This award-winning ad, written by Ian Price of Surfer's Paradise, Queensland, Australia, drew 217 calls.

958

Buy the Sea

The cry of gulls will be your morning call. You'll breakfast on the terrace to the sound of waves caressing the shore. You'll walk barefoot along the sand in the solitude of your thoughts. This 2-bedroom cottage is just steps from the sand. Tranquility can be yours at $269,500.

Clyde Realty   **476-8200**

Note: The property is not on the waterfront, nor is an ocean view implied. If there's a view, change the words to ". . . on the terrace entranced by the sight and sound of waves gently carressing the shore."

If the property is on the water, change the ad heading to "Ocean Front," "Water Front," "River Front," "Lake Front" or "On Lake Charles."

959

Sailor's Dream

You can own a superb, fully furnished, waterfront, 2BR and den, year-round home with a deep-water dock in the boating capital of the nation. Whether it's sail or power or just watching from dry land, every day is going to seem like a vacation. The home includes a window wall offering a glorious view, a screened gazebo, a waterfront patio and a 2+++-car garage. Bring along your toothbrush because once you see it, you'll never want to leave. Your future at $249,500.

Clyde Realty   **476-8200**

960

Watch the Ships

from the deck of this 2-bedroom New England Colonial. Bike to the beach and walk the sand. Enjoy the lifestyle the rest of the world can only dream of for only $239,500.

Clyde Realty   **476-8200**

If a property is closer to the beach, you can use the words "just steps to the sand."

961

One-Legged Alligator Hunter

has decided to sell this 3BR, 2-bath waterfront home on beautiful Lake Louise. There's a gentle sand beach where fishing from the dock is reported to be great! You'll love the fully screened Florida room, where you can sit and enjoy the sunset. For weekends, weeks on end or a lifetime, this can be your very special place. Specially priced for you at $119,500.

Clyde Realty   **476-8200**

The heading is, of course, a spoof to get the reader's attention.

962

Bass Lake—3BR Home

We sent Mr. Higgins of our office to check on this new listing last week, and he hasn't returned. He did call to say, "Bring more bait." Apparently, the fishing is great right from the dock. There is a large glassed and screened porch for the perfect spot to watch the sunset over the water. You'll love the warmth of solid pine paneling and the native stone fireplace. Priced at $89,500, it's your opportunity for the good life. If you see Mr. Higgins, tell him his wife and children have been asking about him.

Clyde Realty   **476-8200**

963

Log Home— Lake Owens

This near-new, 2BR and loft, whole-log home with 100 feet of sandy beach offers the utmost in today's comfort with the warmth of the material of yesterday. You'll love the native stone fireplace and dream kitchen loaded with built-ins. It's the ideal vacation or year-round home at a very affordable $112,500.

Clyde Realty   **476-8200**

The two strong points in the above ad, "Log Home" and "Lake Owens", are combined in the heading.

964

Chalet by the Lake

Own a 2-bedroom, glass and cedar home on the shore of a large fish-filled lake less than 2 hours from the city. Tall trees, clean air and a sandy beach with over 5 acres make this a very special opportunity at $79,500.

Clyde Realty   **476-8200**

If the name of the lake is a strong feature, it should be included in the ad. (See the following ad.)

965

Lake Charles— $49,900

With only a short walk to the beach and public landing, this 2-bedroom + screened sleeping porch can be your cottage on the sand. You'll love the cast-iron Franklin fireplace for those cool nights and the beautiful, solid pine paneling. Completely furnished, all it needs is your family.

Clyde Realty   **476-8200**

Note: This home does not have water frontage.

966

Lake Charles—100'

Enjoy your own white sand beach; towering pines; and 3BR, year-round lake home with a full basement and attached double garage. Fish from your own 40-foot dock or just relax and enjoy the sunset over the water from your screened and glassed porch. In move-in condition, one look and it will be yours at $89,500.

Clyde Realty   **476-8200**

If the lake is well known, the name of it makes the most effective heading. Shoreline footage is a primary determinant of value for lakefront property.

967

Escape to Wisconsin

Buy your own 3-bedroom vacation home with 100' of sandy beach on beautiful Lake Hilldale, just 4 hours from Chicago. This is a great place for swimming, boating, fishing or just lying back and relaxing in the beauty of nature. The home has all modern conveniences and can be used year-round. For weekends, vacations or the rest of your life, this is an investment in yourself at $98,500.

Clyde Realty   **476-8200**

This ad advertises a Wisconsin property but is aimed at Illinois residents.

274   Simplified Classifieds

968 Escape to Minocqua

The brisk, clean morning air; picture-book sunsets; towering, century-old pines; and 100' of the finest waterfront on a spring-fed, crystal-clear, fish-filled lake go with this 3BR vacation chalet. You'll love the warm wood paneling and the natural rock fireplace for those cool evenings. A place for weekends, weeks on end or a lifetime, this can be yours for $89,500.

Clyde Realty   476-8200

969 Lakeside Living Let It All Hang Out

as the owner of this very private 3-bedroom, beachfront chalet with every modern convenience on a huge, wooded parcel just 4 hours from Chicago. For fishing, hunting, boating, canoeing, water skiing, bird watching or just being lazy, this is the place. Priced to excite at $79,500.

Clyde Realty   476-8200

If the lake is highly desirable, it should be stated in the ad's heading.

970 When Is a Log Cabin Not a Log Cabin?

The answer to this question is when it is a custom-built, 3BR, 2½-bath residence with soaring cathedral ceilings and all the amenities of tomorrow. Set on a full wooded acre with a breathtaking view of Lake Geneva, this can be all yours for $289,500.

Clyde Realty   476-8200

971 Enjoy Sunset over the Water

and fish off your own dock as the owner of this 2-bedroom cottage among the pines set on 100' of pristine shoreline on Lake Louise. There's a large, screened sleeping porch; automatic heat; a modern tile bath; and a separate garage. At $67,500, it's a small price for happiness.

Clyde Realty   476-8200

If the lake is well known and desirable, a more effective heading is simply "Lake Louise—100'."

972

Fish or Cut Bait

Lake access and your own dock on Bass Lake come with this 2BR cottage featuring a screened sleeping porch that holds half a Boy Scout troop. You'll love the fully remodeled kitchen and bath. George Stevens of our office claims the last time he was on the lake he had to use a club to keep the fish from jumping in the boat. There is, however, nothing fishy about the price at $79,500. Act fast or say, "I should have . . ."

Clyde Realty   **476-8200**

Lake access generally means an easement.

973

Lake Owens Estate

Picture a turn-of-the-century brick manor house with 11 large rooms and an emerald-green lawn flowing down to the water's edge. Picture an old-fashioned wet boathouse with a railed porch. Fully modernized to provide the best in comfort yet retaining the warmth of another era, we are proud to offer this fine estate on 7 acres at $549,000.

Clyde Realty   **476-8200**

974

Sh! Don't Tell the Relatives!

that you purchased this 3-bedroom waterfront home on Bass Lake. They'll want to sleep on the large screened porch, use your boats, fish off your dock or even camp on the emerald-green lawn flowing to the water's edge. You'll likely discover cousins you have never heard of. The price at least won't scare you, $89,500.

Clyde Realty   **476-8200**

Since the heading doesn't mention waterfront property, the newspaper category should indicate that it is water-related property. Otherwise, your heading can read "Bass Lake Frontage/Don't Tell the Relatives."

975

A Rowboat for $119,500

comes with this 3BR, lakeshore Cape Cod with double garage and separate workshop on an almost a half-acre lot. You can fish and sun off your own dock or just relax and dangle your feet in the water.

Clyde Realty   **476-8200**

276   Simplified Classifieds

976

Thoreau

would have never wanted to leave the shore of this picturesque pond set amidst the pines behind a newer 3BR, 1½-bath, California-style ranch home in immaculate condition. Mr. Simpson from our office tried fishing in the pond, but it was a disaster. Something kept breaking his line. Don't contemplate too long, as it's priced for the philosopher. Complete with a full pond at $89,500.

Clyde Realty   **476-8200**

977

Don't Worry— Be Happy

and you will be as the owner of this 4-season, 2BR, lakefront condominium with its natural stone fireplace, screened porch and private dock on a 600-acre lake overflowing with fish. Even the price is happy, $67,500.

Clyde Realty   **476-8200**

978

The Loon Calls

and a canoe glides across the tranquil water of Lake Ojibwa. This 2BR, year-round waterfront vacation or retirement home can be yours fully furnished including boat, motor and a canoe. The home features central heat; a modern tiled bath; and a screened and glassed porch ideal for entertaining or just watching the sunset over the water. You can catch fish sitting on the bench at the end of your very own dock. This is a rare opportunity for the family that enjoys being together at $79,500.

Clyde Realty   **476-8200**

979

Paddle-Wheel Steamboat

The Tom Sawyer in you will fall in love with this 3BR, white-clapboard river-front home that could have inspired Mark Twain. The veranda offers a river view that seems to reach back to yesterday. You'll imagine the rafts and canoes of the early traders and the steamboats that followed. It's a quiet place where tensions seem to be washed away by the gently flowing waters. It's the perfect spot for Tom and Becky at $119,500.

Clyde Realty   **476-8200**

980

Small Cabin— Small Price

It only has 1 bedroom and a huge living room/kitchen, but there are expansion possibilities. The cabin has running water, but the bath is 100 feet away, down the path. It's just a getaway fun place on one of the most beautiful wooded acres you'll ever find, and it's only minutes from one of the finest trout streams around. Priced far less than you'd expect at $19,500, and terms are possible.

Clyde Realty   **476-8200**

981

For Play

or carefree year-round living, this 2BR, 2-bath mountain chalet just 2 hours from the city offers you the easy life. It's just minutes from the ski lifts or golf courses, with miles of trails for hiking or jogging, clean invigorating air and views right out of a travel folder. You'll love the Swedish freestanding fireplace, the walls of insulated glass and the soaring ceilings. This is a one-of-a-kind architectural masterpiece at an affordable $149,500.

Clyde Realty   **476-8200**

982

Fish and Paddle

You can own a 2BR, modern cabin on 7 acres, with over 200 feet on the White River. Great canoeing and even greater fishing can be yours for a modest $32,500.

Clyde Realty   **476-8200**

When describing a cabin, the word modern *means it has indoor plumbing.*

983

Sunrise—Sunset

Glorious day will follow glorious day in this newer, 2-bedroom mountain chalet set amidst towering pines. You'll relish walking the paths of nature as the seasons change, watching eagles soar or reading at night by the fireplace with your dog at your side. The joy and tranquility of living where every neighbor knows your name but respects your privacy can be yours forever at $89,500.

Clyde Realty   **476-8200**

This ad is targeted toward retirees. It can be used for most rural or resort areas. If a home has other positive features, expand on them with descriptions such as "the walls of glass make nature your decorator" or "you'll relish the feeling of substance that solid wood paneling brings to one's home."

984

Paradise Found

Own a 3BR, 1½-bath chalet on 2 wooded hillside acres with a forever view from the redwood deck. That's not all. There's a Swedish fireplace, a soaring living room, walls of glass, a Eurostyle kitchen, a double garage and every convenience imaginable in a setting that seems as one with nature yet is only minutes away from golf courses and ski lifts. Priced within your budget at $119,500.

Clyde Realty   **476-8200**

985

Buy the Snow

Set amidst towering pines is this almost-new, 2+BR, 2-bath chalet just minutes from the lifts at Snow Valley. You'll love the massive stone fireplace, luxurious carpeting, solid pine paneling, soaring ceilings and walls of insulated glass that give the feeling of being as one with nature. There's even a 2-car, heated garage plus every conceivable built-in. You can own a fine estate for no more than the price of a condominium. $198,500.

Clyde Realty   **476-8200**

986

Buy the Sun

Enjoy 360 days of Palm Springs sunshine for golf, tennis or simple relaxation as the owner of this 2BR, 2-bath hacienda. This distinctive home has a red-tiled roof, attached double garage and family room overlooking a sparkling pool and bubbling spa. Over a dozen tall palms stand like sentinels over this walled mini-estate with its colorful flowers. Automatic sprinklers and every conceivable luxury make this your place for everlasting summer at $149,500.

Clyde Realty   **476-8200**

987

Good-Time Place

The Palm Springs lifestyle can be yours with this 2-bedroom and den villa with its own pool and spa. Set amidst exotic flowering plantings and soaring palms on a walled estate in a South Side lot, the home features a 2-car garage, family room, fireplace and a delightful covered patio for dining and entertaining. It won't last long at $149,500.

Clyde Realty   **476-8200**

31

View Homes

To many buyers, a beautiful view can be more important than the physical aspects of a property.

Views of the water are particularly popular, and because of their desirability, such property sells at a premium price. (See chapter 30 for examples of ads for water views.) Other desirable views are mountains, farms, forests or views overlooking a city. If a property has an excellent view, it should be mentioned in an ad. While ads in other chapters in this book emphasize view, the following ads use it as their focal point.

988

A View of Nature

and not the neighbors. If you find quiet solitude desirable, consider this 3BR, 2-bath Colonial set in a delightful clearing on a wooded acre. While only 40 minutes from the city, you'll see raccoons, squirrels, and perhaps a wily fox and an occasional deer right in your backyard. This is your chance for a whole new way of life for $149,500.

Clyde Realty   476-8200

This ad sells the setting and gives little information about the house.

989

Ansel Adams

loved these majestic mountains framed through the walls of glass in this Colorado Contemporary. The view comes complete with 3 bedrooms, 2½ baths, a 30-foot family room opening onto a deck with a stone barbecue and just about every convenience known to man. The view goes on forever, but at $249,500 your opportunity is right now.

Clyde Realty   **476-8200**

This ad is targeted at an artistic buyer likely to recognize the name of Ansel Adams, world-renowned photographer known for his mountain vistas.

If you are advertising for other than a mountain view, you can say that Ansel Adams "would have loved . . ."

990

God Was
the Decorator

who created the intoxicating mountain vistas that seem as one with this redwood and stone Contemporary set beneath magnificent pines. The 3BR, 2½-bath home has an open floor plan and glass doors opening to cantilevered decks bringing you even closer to the natural wonders. You'll love the huge stone fireplace and the peaceful ambiance that permeates this fine residence. A home that must be seen to be believed is proudly offered at $298,500.

Clyde Realty   **476-8200**

991

Why Buy a Painting?

when you can see the real thing through the windowed walls of this Thomas Hillman Arizona Contemporary, which blends into the hillside and looks out over a wide valley with practically a forever view? The home features 3 bedrooms, 2½ baths, an oversized double garage, an RV parking area, soaring ceilings and a feeling of being as one with nature. You'll love the cantilevered redwood decks for dining or just watching the setting sun and the city lights below. A special home truly above it all at $385,000.

Clyde Realty   **476-8200**

Since the heading doesn't indicate that the home is a view property, this ad is better for a small paper with relatively few ads. The ad could otherwise be missed by readers looking for view homes.

992

Reached the Top?
Then Live There!

This 3BR, 2½-bath French Provincial sits on the highest point looking down on all the rest. Besides the magnificent view, you'll enjoy the baronial-sized rooms, exquisite detailing, the very special studio and a terrace perfect for relaxation or entertaining. A lifestyle to be envied at $349,500.

Clyde Realty   **476-8200**

This is an effective two-line heading.

993

City Lights

will sparkle at your feet as the owner of this 3BR, 3½-bath, brick and stone English Tudor that looks down upon a million souls. Many steps above the others as to location and quality, you'll be entranced by the intricate woodwork, massive beams, gleaming hardwood floors, leaded glass and French doors opening onto a dream terrace. Other features include an English paneled den with its own fireplace, a 3-car garage and flower beds that are the envy of any garden club. A truly impeccable residence for one of the fortunate few. $795,000.

Clyde Realty   **476-8200**

994

Eagle's Nest

The rest of the world will live in your shadow as the owner of this American Traditional set high above the variegated fairyland of light below. You'll revel in watching the sunset from your very private deck. This home features 3 bedrooms, 2½ baths and a 3-car garage. The huge, dry basement can be used as a hobby room, home gym or ?. This is the chance to have the city at your feet for $219,500.

Clyde Realty   **476-8200**

995

Mansion in the Sky

The unmistakable air of elegance is expressed eloquently in this 3BR, 2½-bath, 8-room estate that looks down on a myriad of city lights. Soaring ceilings, rooms of Herculean proportions and an address reserved for just a few make "magnificent" appear as an understatement. If you promised yourself the best in life, what better time than now to keep that promise. Proudly offered at $2,850,000.

Clyde Realty   **476-8200**

This ad was written for a high-rise condo, although it could apply to a hillside home.

996

Afraid of Heights?

Then don't even consider this 3BR, 2½-bath Colorado Contemporary. It's perched on a mountainside, and the deck seems to be suspended in space offering Ansel Adams quality vistas. The open planning, soaring ceilings and walls of glass make the outdoors seem part of the living area. The home has 3,000+ sq. ft. of luxury living area at far less than reproduction costs. Yours at $349,500.

Clyde Realty   **476-8200**

This ad can easily be tailored for an upper-floor condominium: "The deck on this 32nd floor unit seems to be suspended in space offering city vistas reserved for a very few."

997

Close to Heaven

On just about the highest point for miles, this 3BR, 2½-bath Colorado Contemporary offers fantastic vistas of the city lights and the sparkling stars from its 2 cantilevered decks. Amenities include floor-to-ceiling walls of glass, a 3-car garage, 2 fireplaces and magnificent sheltering pine trees. Offered for those who are reaching for the stars at $415,000.

Clyde Realty   **476-8200**

998

King of the Hill

You'll feel like royalty looking down at your domain. Everything will be at your feet as the owner of this architecturally perfect Colorado Contemporary that boasts a flowing floor plan, magnificently proportioned rooms, 2 separate master suites plus a guest or maid's room and a music loft overlooking the great room. While the view will last forever, your opportunity is now at $379,500.

Clyde Realty   **476-8200**

999

Above It All

is this 3BR, 2½-bath Colorado Contemporary perched on a hillside with views unlikely to be excelled. Offering wide decks, walls of glass, soaring ceilings, 2 massive stone fireplaces and a 2++-car garage, it's indeed a rare opportunity at $289,500.

Clyde Realty   **476-8200**

1000

Own the City

Everything is beneath you as the owner of this 3BR, 2½-bath architectural masterpiece perched on a wooded hillside amidst towering pines. You'll love the cantilevered wraparound decks, soaring ceilings, walls of glass, massive fieldstone fireplace and state-of-the-art kitchen. The 3-car garage is heated, and the home has zone-controlled central air. A home unlikely to be excelled at $596,000.

Clyde Realty   **476-8200**

1001

RSVP

Right Address—Malibu Hills
Size—3BR/2 Baths and Den
View—Mountains and Valley
Price—Only $147,500

Clyde Realty   **476-8200**

This ad is a simple attention getter for a view home.

Index

A

Absentee owner, 34, *#121*

Acreage
 undeveloped, 1–9, *#1–33*
 with home, 10, 138–49, 279,
  #35, 510–53, 988

Adult housing, 54, 59, *#196, 215*

Air conditioning, 27, 82, 131, *#95,
 294–96,486*

Animals, wild, 3, 4, 5, 7, 138, 140,
 142, 224, 267, 279, *#9–10, 13–
 14, 16–17, 511, 518, 519, 527,
 812, 949, 988*

Apple trees, 143, 264–65, *#531,
 936–41*

Appliances, 132, 133, 134, *#487,
 493, 497*

Appreciation, 96, 98, 99, 170,
 #350, 359, 364, 623

Architect, named, 15, 16, 17, 23,
 101, 105, 280, *#52, 55, 57, 58,
 61, 63, 80, 371, 389, 991*

Architecture, 10–18, *#34–64*
 Colonial, 10–12, 18, *#34–41,
  64*
 Contemporary, 16–17, *#56–62*
 English, 12–14, *#42–49*
 French, 14–15, *#51, 52*
 Irish, 14, *#50*
 Spanish, 15, *#53–55*
 Town house, 13, *#47*

Arches, 15, *#53, 54*

Astrological signs, 19–29, *#65–103*
 Aries, 19–20, *#65–67*

Aquarius, 28, *#98–100*
Cancer, 22, 23, *#75–78*
Capricorn, 27, *#95–97*
Gemini, 21–22, *#71–74*
Leo, 22, 23, *#79–81*
Libra, 25, *#86–88*
Pisces, 28–29, *#101–3*
Sagittarius, 26–27, *#92–94*
Scorpio, 25–26, *#89–92*
Taurus, 20–21, *#68–70*
Virgo, 24, *#82–85*

Attic, 29, 223, 249, *#102, 805, 884*

Auction, 37, *#130–32*

B

Balcony, 15, 47, *#55, 170*

Bargain homes, 30–44, 53, 55,
 196, 197, 212, *#104–61, 194,
 200, 201, 713, 718, 766, 767*
 absentee owner, 34, *#121*
 auction, 37, *#130–32*
 below cost, 31, *#109*
 corporate sales, 41, *#148, 149*
 court ordered sale, 42, *#150,
  151*
 divorce, 35, *#123*
 estate sale, 34, *#120*
 fixer-upper, 44, *#159*
 foreclosure, 36, 37, 38, 39,
  #129, 131, 137–41
 motivated seller, 31, 33, 34,
  35, 36, 37, 38, 39, *#108,*

 *115–19, 122, 123, 131, 133,
 136–41*
 new homes, 33, 35, 38, *#116,
  124, 136*
 price reduced, 42–43, *#153–56*
 repossession, 39–40, *#141–45*
 sale failed, 114–15, *#425–29*
 terms, 44, *#161*
 vacant, 127, *#474*

Barns, 3, 143, 144, 146–49, 151–
 52, *#7, 531–34, 539, 541, 543,
 545, 548, 549, 552, 555–58, 561,
 562*

Basement, 22, 24, 28, 29, 34, 61,
 86, 97, 113, 121, 157, 182, 247,
 261, 263, *#76, 84, 101, 103,
 118, 221, 309, 354, 421, 452,
 576, 667, 880, 925, 932*

Bath, 18, 136, 185, 268, 276, *#64,
 505, 673, 950, 978*

Beach property, 270–71, 273,
 #952–58, 965, 966

Beams, 15, 17, *#54, 55, 60*

Bed and breakfast, 226, *#817, 818*

Bedroom, 63, 107, 112, *#227, 229,
 388, 417*

Birds, 122, 123, 141, 143, *#457–
 59, 520, 529*

Bungalow, 17, *#63*

Note: Reference numbers in italic
refer to ad numbers.

C

Camping, 7, 8, *#25, 27*
Cats, 235, *#843*
Ceilings, 15, 16, 117, *#55, 59, 435, 436*
Christmas, 136–37, *#505–8*
Closets, 166, 185, 193, *#612, 673, 705*
Colonial, 10–12, 89, 102, *#34–41, 322, 375*
Colors, 28, 235, *#101, 844*
Columbus Day, 135, *#501*
Columns, 10–11, *#35–36*
Condominium, 45–59, 135, 242, 243, 244, 245, 281, *#162–217, 500, 866, 867, 873, 875, 995, 996*
    balcony, 47, *#170*
    bargain, 53, 55, *#194, 200, 201*
    furnished, 45, *#162*
    golf, 46–47, *#166, 167*
    highrise, 47–48, *#168–72*
    large, 49, *#175, 177*
    loft, 50–51, *#182–84*
    lifestyle, 49, 52, 53, 54, 55, 58, 59, *#176, 188–91, 195, 200, 202, 214, 216, 217*
    new, 51, *#185, 186*
    privacy, 49, 57, *#178, 200*
    recreational, 46–47, 49, *#163–67, 176, 178*
    retirement, 52, 54, *#187, 195*
    security, 48, 57, *#173, 210*
    tennis, 52–53, *#190, 191*
    view, 47, *#168*
Conservatory, 11, 268, *#36, 950*
Contemporary style, 16–17, 99, 117, 141, *#56–62, 362, 435, 520*
Corporate sale, 41, *#148, 149*
Court ordered sale, 42, *#150, 151*
Courtyard, 15, *#55*
Crown molding, 11, 12, *#38, 40*
Cul-de-sac, 61, *#222*

D

Darkroom, 89, 114, *#321, 323, 424*
Deck, 17, 139, *#62, 514*
Decorating, 50, 69, 85, 86, 93, 130, *#179, 248, 306, 309, 338, 481*
Decorator, 87, 88, *#313, 315, 317*
Den, 134, 214, *#495, 770*
Desert homes, 278, *#986, 987*
Development-ready, 1–2, *#2, 3*

Dining room, 154, 241, *#565, 862*
Dogs, 82, 232–34, *#297, 833–42*
Driveway, 90, *#326*
Duplex, 237–38, *#848–54*

E

Easter, 133, *#492*
English architecture, 12–14, 163, 185, 190, *#42–49, 598, 676, 693*
Equal Housing Opportunity, 131, *#485*
Escapist, 142, 143, *#524, 530*
Estate sale, 34, *#120*

F

Family home, 61–65, 131, 153–56, 163, 165, 247, 251, 265, *#218–38, 486, 563–72, 599, 607–8, 879, 892, 939, 941*
Family room, 134, 150, *#495, 554*
Farmhouse, 144–45, 146, 147–48, 149, *#532–37, 539, 541, 544, 550–53*
Father's Day, 133–34, *#494, 495*
Fence, 150, 151, 152, 262, *#554, 557, 561, 926*
Financing. *See* Terms
Fire damage, 78, *#281*
Fireplace, 11, 12, 17, 20, 23, 25, 63, 102, 137, 139, 244, 270, 277, *#39–41, 62, 69, 81, 89, 228, 376, 508, 514, 872, 952, 983*
Fishing, 4–5, 9, 272, 273, 275, 276, *#14, 15, 32, 961, 962, 964, 966, 967, 972, 974, 976–78*
Fixer-upper, 44, 67–78, 143, 149, 177, 220, 221, *#159, 240–82, 528, 549, 646, 797, 801*
Floor plan, 16, 17, 122, *#56, 62, 456*
Flooring, 11, *#37*
Flowers, 15, 109, 112, 262, 263, 265, 268, 281, *#53, 403, 414, 927, 931, 932, 938, 950, 993*
Foreclosure, 36, 37, 38, 39–40, *#129, 131, 137, 139, 141–45*
Forest, 3, *#9–10*
Fountain, 15, 192, *#55, 702*
Frank Lloyd Wright, 16, *#57, 58*
Fruit trees, 143, 263, 264–66, *#531, 933, 935–43*
Fuel bills, 79, *#284. See also* Utility costs

Furnished, 45, 184, 271, 273, 276, *#162, 676, 959, 965, 978*

G

Garage, 11, 21, 63, 91, 97, 137, 148, 244, 263, *#38, 72, 228, 332, 354, 508, 550, 871, 931*
Garden, 13, 14, 80, 82, 121, 156, 262, 263–64, *#46–48, 286, 295, 450, 926, 930–34, 936*
Geodesic dome, 107, *#895*
George Washington's Birthday, 132, *#489, 490*
Glass, 16, *#56, 58*
Golf, 46–47, 128–30, 199, *#166, 167, 475–81, 724*
Golf and tennis homes, 128–30, *#475–84*
Granny flat, 155, *#570, 571*
Greenhouse, 262, *#928, 929*
Ground Hog Day, 131, *#486*
Guest apartment, 12, *#42*
Guest house, 13, *#46*

H

Halloween, 135–36, 217, *#502, 503, 784*
Highrise, condo, 47–48, 281, *#168–72, 995*
Historical event, 8, 9, *#28, 29, 31, 32*
Holidays, 131–37, *#485–509*
    Christmas, 136–37, *#505–8*
    Columbus Day, 135, *#501*
    Easter, 133, *#492*
    Father's Day, 133–34, *#494, 495*
    George Washington's Birthday, 132, *#489, 490*
    Ground Hog Day, 131, *#486*
    Halloween, 135–36, *#502, 503*
    Independence Day, 134–35, *#496–99*
    Labor Day, 135, *#500*
    Lincoln's Birthday, 132, *#487*
    Martin Luther King, Jr. Day, 131, *#485*
    Mother's Day, 133, *#493*
    New Year's, 137, *#509*
    Saint Patrick's Day, 133, *#491*

Note: Reference numbers in italic refer to ad numbers.

Thanksgiving, 136, *#504*
Valentines Day, 132, *#488*
Homes, general, 79–127, *#283–474*
Horse property, 1, 3, 150–52, *#1, 7, 554–62*

I–K

Independence Day, 134–35, *#496–99*
Indian artifacts, 2, 3, *#6, 10*
Inflation, 96, 98, *#350, 359. See also* Appreciation
Insulation, 157, *#578*
Investment property, land, 2, 5, *#4, 5, 18*
July 4th. *See* Independence Day
Kitchen, 11, 16, 17, 19, 22, 23, 25, 27, 85, 109, 144, 150, 154, 156, 185, 188, 244, 249, *#38, 56, 62, 65, 77, 80, 86, 95, 305, 402, 532, 554, 564, 565, 575, 673, 687, 871, 886*

L

Labor Day, 135, *#500*
Land. *See* Acreage and Lots
Landscaping, 14, 20, 80, 81, 92, 93, 99, 113, 119, 121, 130, 133, 134, 162, 220, 262–68, *#48, 66, 288, 292, 333, 339, 361, 419, 444, 451, 494, 497, 593, 796, 924–50*
Large homes, 49, 71, 72, 73, 74, 153–59, 185, 186–87, 189, 190, 191, 202, 226, 231, *#175, 177, 226, 256, 257, 264, 265, 563–86, 675, 676, 678–81, 690, 691, 695, 697–99, 734, 817–19, 832*
Large rooms, 13, 15, 16, 49, 53, *#45, 52, 55, 58, 175, 193*
Lawn, 23, 261, 275, *#78, 924, 925, 974. See also* Landscaping
Library, 12, *#42*
Lifestyle, 49, 54, 55, 58, 59, *#176, 195, 200, 202, 214, 216, 217*
Lincoln's Birthday, 132, *#487*
Living room, 137, 186, *#508, 679*
Location, 66, 160–66, *#239, 587–612*
Loft, 17, 50–51, *#62, 182–84*
Log home, 141, 272, 274, *#521, 963, 970*

Lots, 167–74, *#613–40*
Low-priced homes, 175–82, 196–97, *#639–67, 712–17*

M

Maintenance, 56, *#203, 206*
Maple trees, 3, 145, 149, 266, *#8, 538, 552, 944*
Martin Luther King, Jr. Day, 131, *#485*
Meadow, 6, 8, *#19, 29*
Mobile homes, 194–99, *#707–25*
Mother's Day, 133, *#493*
Motivated seller, 31, 33, 34, 35, 36, 37, 38–39, *#108, 115–19, 122, 123, 128, 131, 133, 136–41*
Mountain site, 6, 277, 278, 280, 281, *#21, 981, 983, 985, 989, 990, 996*
Music room, 119, *#443*

N

Negative approach, 53, 94, 105, 106, 159, 200–207, 239, 253, *#192, 194, 341, 388, 393, 586, 726–52, 857, 899. See also* Fixer-upper
Neighborhood, 20, 23, 25, 61, 62, 64, 65, 94, 100, 101, 104, 108, 111, 113, 123, 135, 213, 216, 217, 220, 222, 238, 243, *#67, 79, 87, 220, 223–25, 231, 233, 237, 342, 368, 370, 382, 383, 399, 413, 420, 459, 499, 501, 768, 779, 785, 794, 803, 868*
New home, 33, 35, 38, 51, 208–12, 230, 231, *#116, 124, 136, 185, 186, 753–67, 828, 831*
New on market, 83, *#299–301*
New Year's, 137, *#509*
Nursery, 63, *#227*

O

Office, home, 13, *#46*
Older homes, 11, 80, 81, 166, 213–28, *#38, 287, 292, 609, 768–825. See also* Farmhouse
Open house, 229–31, *#826–32*

Orchard, 148, *#550. See also* Fruit trees
Owner, prestige; celebrity, 85–87, *#306–14*

P–Q

Patio, 11, 25, 97, 102, 109, 116, 129, 133, *#39, 87, 354, 374, 403, 405, 430, 479, 494. See also* Veranda
Pets, 232–35, *#833–44*
Porch, 10, 21, 37, 97, 106, 131, 136, 213, 214, 215, 264, 270, 273, 276, *#34, 72, 133, 356, 392, 486, 506, 507, 768, 769, 771, 777, 937, 952, 966, 978*
Portico, 10, *#35*
Price reduction, 42–43, 132, *#153–56, 489*
Privacy, 4, 7, 20, 48, 49, 52, 57, 89, 118, 138, 139, 140, 141, 143, 148, 155, 187, 190, 192, 242, 246, 247, 279, *#12, 23, 26, 68, 174, 178, 188, 208, 324, 441, 511, 513, 514, 517, 518, 523, 530, 547, 548, 567–70, 683, 695, 701, 864, 877, 878, 988*
Privy, 143, *#528, 530*
Question and answer ads, 1, 168, 253, *#1, 616, 901*

R

Recreational homes, 46–47, 49, *#163–67, 176, 178. See also* Vacation homes
RV parking, 20, 120, *#66, 448*
Recreation room, 137, *#509*
Rental property, 236–40, *#845–61*
Repossession. *See* Foreclosure
Restorable homes, 227, *#821, 822*
Restored homes, 227, *#823*
Retirement homes, 52, 54, 199, *#187, 195, 724, 725. See also* Vacation homes
River property, 6, 7, 9, 142, 146, *#20, 26, 32, 524, 539*
Roof, 14, 15, *#51, 52*
Rose bushes, 13, 14, 23, *#46, 48, 79*

Note: Reference numbers in italic refer to ad numbers.

Note: Reference numbers in italic refer to ad numbers.